Kenya: the struggle for a new constitutional order

edited by Godwin R. Murunga, Duncan Okello
and Anders Sjögren

Nordiska Afrikainstitutet
The Nordic Africa Institute

Zed Books
LONDON

Kenya: the struggle for a new constitutional order was first published in 2014 in association with the Nordic Africa Institute, PO Box 1703, SE-751 47 Uppsala, Sweden by Zed Books Ltd, 7 Cynthia Street, London N1 9JF, UK.

www.zedbooks.co.uk
www.nai.uu.se

Set in OurType Arnhem, Monotype Gill Sans Heavy by Ewan Smith
Index: ed.emery@thefreeuniversity.net
Cover designed by www.roguefour.co.uk

A catalogue record for this book is available from the British Library

ISBN 978-1-78032-366-4 hardback
ISBN 978-1-78032-365-7 paperback
ISBN 978-1-78032-367-1 pdf
ISBN 978-1-78032-368-8 epub
ISBN 978-1-78032-369-5 mobi

Africa Now

Africa Now is published by Zed Books in association with the internationally respected Nordic Africa Institute. Featuring high-quality, cutting-edge research from leading academics, the series addresses the big issues confronting Africa today. Accessible but in-depth, and wide-ranging in its scope, Africa Now engages with the critical political, economic, sociological and development debates affecting the continent, shedding new light on pressing concerns.

Nordic Africa Institute

The Nordic Africa Institute (Nordiska Afrikainstitutet) is a centre for research, documentation and information on modern Africa. Based in Uppsala, Sweden, the Institute is dedicated to providing timely, critical and alternative research and analysis of Africa and to co-operation with African researchers. As a hub and a meeting place for a growing field of research and analysis, the Institute strives to put knowledge of African issues within reach of scholars, policy makers, politicians, media, students and the general public. The Institute is financed jointly by the Nordic countries (Denmark, Finland, Iceland, Norway and Sweden).

www.nai.uu.se

Forthcoming titles

Lisa Åkesson and Maria Eriksson Baaz (eds), *Africa's Return Migrants*
Thiven Reddy, *South Africa: Beyond Apartheid and Liberal Democracy*
Anders Themner (ed.), *Warlord Democrats in Africa*

Titles already published

Fantu Cheru and Cyril Obi (eds), *The Rise of China and India in Africa*
Ilda Lindell (ed.), *Africa's Informal Workers*
Iman Hashim and Dorte Thorsen, *Child Migration in Africa*
Prosper B. Matondi, Kjell Havnevik and Atakilte Beyene (eds), *Biofuels, Land Grabbing and Food Security in Africa*
Cyril Obi and Siri Aas Rustad (eds), *Oil and Insurgency in the Niger Delta*
Mats Utas (ed.), *African Conflicts and Informal Power*
Prosper B. Matondi, *Zimbabwe's Fast Track Land Reform*
Maria Eriksson Baaz and Maria Stern, *Sexual Violence as a Weapon of War?*
Fantu Cheru and Renu Modi (eds), *Agricultural Development and Food Security in Africa*
Amanda Hammar (ed.), *Displacement Economies in Africa*
Mary Njeri Kinyanjui, *Women and the Informal Economy in Urban Africa*
Liisa Laakso and Petri Hautaniemi (eds), *Diasporas, Development and Peace-making in the Horn of Africa*
Margaret C. Lee, *Africa's World Trade*

About the editors

Godwin R. Murunga is a senior research fellow in the Institute of Development Studies, University of Nairobi, and director of the African Leadership Centre. He is also a visiting professor in the Global Institutes at King's College London. He is a trained historian with a PhD from Northwestern University in Illinois, specialising in urban history but with research interests in democratisation processes in Africa, politics of knowledge production and masculinities in Africa. His current research project focuses on the role of settlements in peace-building and state-building in Kenya.

Duncan Okello is currently the Chief of Staff in the Office of the Chief Justice, Republic of Kenya. He holds a BA degree in political science and history as well as a law degree, both from the University of Nairobi. He also holds an MA in international relations from the University of Kent at Canterbury, UK. His policy and research interests revolve around questions of democratisation and institution-building for societies in transition, constitutionalism and the rule of law, and how development outcomes mediate and influence state and citizen relations in Africa. He previously worked as director of programmes at the Institute of Economic Affairs in Kenya, and as the Regional Director for Eastern Africa for the Society for International Development.

Anders Sjögren is a senior researcher with the Nordic Africa Institute in Uppsala. He holds a PhD in political science from Stockholm University. Working in the field of the comparative political economy of development and state–society relations in Africa, his current research is on land conflicts, state formation and citizenship in Kenya and Uganda.

Contents

Acronyms and abbreviations

4Cs	Citizens' Coalition for Constitutional Change
AU	African Union
CCP	Concerned Citizens for Peace
CCRC	Comprehensive Constitution Reform Coalition
CIC	Commission for the Implementation of the Constitution
CIPEV	Commission of Inquiry into Post-Election Violence
CKRC	Constitution of Kenya Review Commission
CMD-K	Centre for Multiparty Democracy-Kenya
CNC	Coalition for a National Convention
CoE	Committee of Experts
CORD	Coalition for Reforms and Democracy
COTU	Central Organisation of Trade Unions
CPJC	Catholic Peace and Justice Commission
CRECO	Constitution and Reform Education Consortium
CSO	civil society organisation
DP	Democratic Party
ECK	Electoral Commission of Kenya
ELOG	Kenyan Elections Observation Group
EU	European Union
FORD	Forum for the Restoration of Democracy
FORD-A	Forum for the Restoration of Democracy-Asili
FORD-K	Forum for the Restoration of Democracy-Kenya
GEMA	Gikuyu, Embu and Meru Association
ICC	International Criminal Court
IEBC	Independent Electoral and Boundaries Commission
IPOA	Independent Policing Oversight Authority
IPPG	Inter-Party Parliamentary Group
JDF	Joint Dialogue Forum
JSC	Judicial Service Commission
KADU	Kenya African Democratic Union
KANU	Kenya African National Union
KHRC	Kenya Human Rights Commission
KI	Katiba Institute
KNCHR	Kenya National Commission on Human Rights
KNDR	Kenya National Dialogue and Reconciliation
KPTJ	Kenyans for Peace, Truth and Justice
KPU	Kenya People's Union
KYFM	Kenya Youth Foundation Movement

LDP	Liberal Democratic Party
LSK	Law Society of Kenya
MoU	memorandum of understanding
MP	member of parliament
MSRF	Multi-Sectoral Review Forum
NAK	National Alliance Party of Kenya
NARC	National Alliance Rainbow Coalition
NCCK	National Council of the Churches of Kenya
NCEC	National Convention Executive Council
NCPC	National Convention Preparatory Committee
NDC	National Dialogue Conference
NDP	National Democratic Party
NGO	non-governmental organisation
NIS	National Intelligence Service
NSIS	National Security Intelligence Service
NUKS	National Union of Kenya Students
ODM	Orange Democratic Movement
ODM-K	Orange Democratic Movement-Kenya
PAF	Policy Advisory Foundation
PCK	People's Commission of Kenya
PNU	Party of National Unity
PSC	parliamentary select committee
RPP	Release Political Prisoners
SAP	structural adjustment programme
SCOK	Supreme Court of Kenya
SODNET	Social Development Network
SONU	Students Organization of Nairobi University
TI	Transparency International
TNA	The National Alliance
UN	United Nations
UNDP	United Nations Development Programme
URP	United Republican Party

Preface

This study of Kenya's constitution-making process is a joint initiative between the Nordic Africa Institute and the Institute for Development Studies, University of Nairobi. It was motivated by several concerns, foremost among these the need to document a remarkable and historic people-driven process of constitution-making in Kenya. Second, the study aimed to go beyond a mere celebration of the promulgation of the constitution in August 2010 in order to highlight the challenges that most attempts at implementing a new constitution often confront. There was no shortfall of examples of such challenges in Africa. For too long, the experience in Africa since the attainment of the second *uhuru* has been that new constitutions are promulgated in euphoric moments, as happened in Benin, Nigeria and Uganda, followed by attempts by the political elite to torpedo moves towards entrenching the culture of constitutionalism. This has turned several potentially innovative, people-centred constitutional dispensations into moments of utter frustration and despair.

We felt that thinking about and envisioning constitutionalism would be an indispensable contribution to a better understanding and implementation of the Kenyan constitution, but also hoped that such thinking would inform a policy advocacy position in relation to the gains of the new constitution. The Kenyan constitutional story has not received academic treatment commensurate with its importance, and comprehensive studies of the constitution are few and far between. This is the case even though Kenyan intellectuals, such as the late Professor Hastings W. Okoth-Ogendo and Professor Yash Pal Ghai, are trailblazers in the theoretical study of constitutionalism and are world-renowned figures in constitution-making. Among the few notable studies of constitution-making in Kenya are the late Peter Habenga Okondo's *A Commentary on the Constitution of Kenya* (Nairobi: Phoenix Publishers, 1995) and Willy Mutunga's *Constitution-making from the Middle: Civil society and transition politics in Kenya, 1992–1997* (Nairobi: SAREAT, 1999). Although these studies offer an important analysis of the challenges of constitution-making and constitutionalism, they could not provide the kind of updated and in-depth study of the content of the constitution over a longer-term historical period.

The challenges to the establishment of a culture of constitutionalism are many. Indeed, Kenyans were under no illusion about whether the implementation of the new constitution would be smooth. However, the expectations put on a new constitution have long been enormous and the hype during the 2010 referendum campaigns only raised them. Since the promulgation, the process of implementing the constitution has faced several anticipated and unanticipated challenges, some of which are simply the work of those who opposed it and continue to manipulate every opportunity to derail its implementation. Soon after the constitution was passed, for instance, the then President of Kenya, Emilio Mwai Kibaki, tested the resolve of Kenyans by seeking unilaterally to appoint the chief justice, the director of public prosecutions and the attorney general. In doing this, he ignored the provisions of the law that set up a transparent mechanism for appointing these officers. This first salvo against the new constitution was met with vigorous resistance from Kenyans, resistance that confirmed that the many years spent negotiating the new constitution had introduced into the Kenyan body politic a fresh civic sensitivity against rule by presidential fiat. The president withdrew the appointments and a constitutionally compliant process was initiated soon afterwards; this led, for example, to the appointment of Dr Willy Mutunga as chief justice. The story of the implementation of the constitution since then has included periodic gains and instant reversals.

The reversals, however, have been alarmingly many and consistent, confirming Yash Pal Ghai's argument that 'the internal logic and dynamics of the constitution will have to compete with the larger social forces, the most powerful of which may have little commitment to its values' (see page 127). The 2013 elections did not help matters. Not only did the pre-election period witness many instances in which the Kibaki government either ignored or abused aspects of the new constitution, but the contentious declaration of Uhuru Kenyatta and William Ruto as president and vice president and the confirmation of this by the supreme court of Kenya raised many questions about the capacity of institutions charged with protecting the constitution to actually do so fairly, vigorously and consistently. In particular, these institutions skirted around the provisions of Chapter 6 of the constitution on leadership and integrity and managed somehow to 'allow' persons indicted before the International Criminal Court to run for the presidency. Not only did this failure to fully address the leadership and integrity issue test the viability of the provisions, it also opened the way to more attempts to evade constitutional provisions through political manoeuvres that in themselves position politics as more important than constitutionalism.

Since assuming power, the Jubilee Alliance, with its majority in the National Assembly, has continued with attempts to sidestep, mutilate or ignore certain provisions of the constitution. The Jubilee Alliance has been selectively strategic about how to accomplish these goals, including occasionally co-opting Coalition for Reforms and Democracy (CORD) members into this agenda. Key members of the Alliance have on occasion publicly acknowledged the importance of some provisions while working behind the scenes to undermine other provisions they do not like. For example, the provisions on devolution have been the subject of occasional advances, with generous amounts of funds devolved to counties but with oversight retained at the centre in ways that reveal the Jubilee Alliance's uneasiness with the complete overhaul of the centralised presidential system. More recently, and through careful deployment of constitutional provisions, the presidency has entrenched powers in county commissioners, who appear more as competitors to governors than as complementary officers in the counties.

The fear of constitutionalism has also been expressed with respect to the security sector, where the executive, working closely with its majority in the National Assembly, has submitted a bill that would undermine civilian oversight of the sector by increasing executive control and entrenching the power of the inspector general of the police to a level never previously attained in Kenya, not even under the authoritarian rule of President Daniel arap Moi. Further, the relationship of the executive to the judiciary has revealed presidential suspicion of the latter. Not only have Jubilee Alliance-aligned politicians threatened the independence of the judiciary through the National Assembly – often threatening to use their power to reduce funding to the judiciary or summoning the Judicial Service Commission (JSC) on issues where parliament has no such mandate – the presidency also showed its complicity in this when the president appointed activists with links to the Jubilee Alliance to lead a tribunal to inquire into the conduct of some members of the JSC. The extent of the challenge to constitutionalism is illustrated by the fact that this has been done with the occasional complicity of CORD members such as Ababu Namwamba (MP for Budalangi Constituency) and Agostinho Neto (MP for Ndhiwa Constituency), both of whom made acerbic contributions during one of the motions against the judiciary.

These examples, by no means exhaustive, paint a picture of the challenges facing the constitutional implementation process in Kenya. Perhaps we should not be surprised. After all, the Jubilee Alliance onslaught on the constitution is consistent: its bedrock in Rift Valley voted overwhelmingly against the constitution. This provides a historical context for understanding the current experiences with implementation. This is the reason why a study of this kind is not only necessary but urgent. In publishing this book, we hope to highlight the contexts for the constitution-making process, and the cumulative gains resulting from the redrawing of the political map and power bases of Kenyan politics. The study delves into diverse aspects of Kenya's constitution, its making and the resulting content, its promises and how their realisation has been tested over time. We hope that the study provides inspiration for more studies on Kenya's political development in recent times and helps educate those seeking local perspectives on the struggle for a new constitutional order.

A study like this one would not have been possible without the direct and indirect assistance of many. We would therefore like to conclude by thanking those many institutions and people whose input has enabled the publication of this book: the Nordic Africa Institute, the Institute for Development Studies, University of Nairobi, the African Leadership Centre in Nairobi and the Society for International Development, where Duncan Okello worked when the idea of this manuscript was initiated. We would also like to thank our respective families for cheering us on even when we played less of the roles we would want to. Colleagues who have provided different kinds of assistance deserve a special mention. At the African Leadership Centre, we thank Mr Sylvanus Wekesa for stepping in for Godwin R. Murunga whenever he was called upon. Many heartfelt thanks are due to Ken Barlow at Zed Books for his patience and confidence. Finally, a very special *asante sana* goes to the members of *The Panel*. Its collective insights into Kenyan politics are reflected on and between the lines of our contribution.

Godwin R. Murunga, Duncan Okello, Nairobi, Kenya
and Anders Sjögren, Stockholm, Sweden

Towards a new constitutional order in Kenya: an introduction

Godwin R. Murunga, Duncan Okello and
Anders Sjögren

The decision by the Kenyan electorate in the 2010 referendum to support the proposed new constitution was the culmination of political work carried out over a generation. At least since the reintroduction of multiparty politics in 1991, struggles for democracy had centred on the twin aims of removing from power the Kenya African National Union (KANU) government under President Daniel arap Moi and effecting constitutional change. The latter demand intensified as it became evident, following repeated manipulated general elections in 1992 and 1997, that the mere tweaking of the constitution to reintroduce multiparty politics was insufficient to entrench and safeguard democracy. The architecture of power created by the pre-2010 constitution made the effective practice of plural politics impossible and prevented the country's transition from an imperial presidency to a constitutional democracy (Kramon and Posner 2011; Mati 2013; Mutua 2008; Mutunga 1999). Moi and KANU left power following the 2002 elections, but constitutional reforms remained elusive for almost another decade after Mwai Kibaki, who came to power riding on the wave of democratisation, assumed the presidency.

This book explores the struggles around democratising the Kenyan state, and does so by taking as its point of departure the passing of the new constitution. The contributions to this book place the constitution within its historical and political context. Together, they interrogate its roots and implications. They explain why struggles for reforms were blocked in the past but were successful this time around, and they explore the scope for implementation of the constitution and associated reforms in the face of continued resistance by powerful groups. The contributors set out from the observation that the making and implementation of any constitution is about the organisation and exercise of power. The scope for institutional transformation is constituted by relations of domination, and these relations are partly structurally conditioned, partly politically negotiated. The promulgation of the constitution was, of course, only the starting point for new efforts to transform the Kenyan state: the new constitution created the possibilities for change but in no way did it guarantee that change. Just as the making of the constitution

I

was a struggle between political forces resulting in mixed outcomes, so too will be the implementation. Once in place, however, the constitution reshapes the conditions for future political struggles. In this introductory chapter, we review the major issues in the debates on constitutional reform in Kenya as a way of framing the subsequent chapters in this study.

Struggles for constitutional reform in Kenya: comparative and historical perspectives

The Kenyan experience is of significance well past its borders. It informs debates on fundamental issues of the organisation and exercise of political power, and the scope for democracy, social justice and national cohesion all around the African continent and beyond. Kenya was not alone among African countries in transitioning to multiparty politics in the early 1990s: a great number of countries introduced political pluralism at the time. However, the expectations that first met these changes gradually faded away. Some countries fell back into military or one-party rule. In other cases, formal democratic institutions were established but came to be epitomised by their shallow character and limited reach (Diamond and Plattner 2010; Sandbrook 2000). Such setbacks suggest deeply rooted patterns of political authoritarianism enforced by the structural characteristics of many African social orders, including social and political inequalities; fragile and incapacitated state institutions controlled by elite coalitions; factional political parties without a solid social base; and weak civil societies, often typified by ethno-regional fragmentation and disrupted links between the urban and rural populations (Joseph 1997; Sandbrook 2000). Much of this applies to Kenya too.

The scope for citizens to make effective use of democratic institutions and rights differs markedly between societies; for a long time this has been captured by distinctions between electoral, liberal and social democracy. Over the last decade, however, academic debates relating to political regimes have shifted to conceptualising and theorising those regimes that are neither democratic nor fully authoritarian, a phenomenon discussed in terms of authoritarianism – either competitive (Levitsky and Way 2010) or electoral (Schedler 2006) – referring broadly to polities where elections are competitive but not free and fair, and where these elections are conducted in a broader context of authoritarianism.

Kenya during the 1990s fits the latter description. The elections in both 1992 (Barkan 1993) and 1997 (Barkan and Ng'ethe 1998) were seriously flawed as a result of the machinations by an authoritarian executive. It was against this background that demands for constitutional reforms were raised as a way of safeguarding and effectuating formal institutions and processes. Over the decade following the 1997 elections, such demands would continue to be voiced, albeit in dramatically shifting circumstances. While the victory of the opposition in the 2002 elections reignited Kenyans' belief in change through the formal political process, the 2007 elections fiasco (Gibson and Long 2009) almost wiped out such convictions. However, and turning the tables again, the negotiated settlement after the 2007–08 elections and violence was crucial in promoting constitutional change in 2010 (see Chapter 3 in this book).

Why has constitutional reform been regarded as so important for democratisation in Kenya and in many other places in Africa? During the early years after independence, a gap developed between the content of the constitutions and the actual practice of constitutionalism, or the lack of it (see Chapter 6). This gap was a consequence of and central to the logic of the struggles for democracy, as it illuminated the need for open and legitimate modes of governance.

The African experience of diluted constitutionalism was anchored in statism, an ideology that sprung directly from discredited notions of colonial developmentalism and was justified and practised by postcolonial African leadership as a trade-off between democracy and development. Consequently, and as the late Joseph Ki-Zerbo quipped, all across the continent the mantra of developmentalism became 'silence, development in progress'. In this trade-off, Kwame Nkrumah's admonition to 'seek ye first the political kingdom' easily translated into a suspension of the constitution in some countries and the mutilation of some of its provisions in others. The cumulative effect of this was that the culture of constitutionalism was undermined in most countries. Three decades later, there was silence in Africa, but also no development. Authoritarianism had flourished while development floundered. As discussed by Zeleza in Chapter 1, overall, neither statist nor neoliberal authoritarianism has succeeded in creating transformative development in Africa.

In Kenya, discomfort with this record initially expressed itself through the demand for plural politics and eventually for constitutional reforms. There were both immediate tactical reasons and long-term general explanations for the latter demand. In the short term, in a country where elections had become a high-stakes zero-sum game, the old constitution made possible their manipulation. In the absence of constitutional reforms guaranteeing fair competition, the opposition feared that it would be very difficult, if not impossible, to remove the ruling party from power through the ballot. The underlying reason why the constitution allowed for electoral rigging was that, over time, it had been changed from a document for democratic governance into an instrument of highly concentrated and authoritarian executive power (Nyong'o 1989). With the provision of a president who was effectively above the law, the constitution could be overridden through presidential fiat, something that was experienced repeatedly under President Kenyatta and President Moi.

According to the government's critics, the problems that plagued Kenya – poverty, inequality and exclusion along lines of region, ethnicity, class and gender – were rooted in the social order but vouchsafed and promoted by

3

the constitution and by state power in general. Thus, the problems, as well as the perceived solutions to them, pointed to the importance of transforming the exercise of state power – and, by extension, political control more broadly – from impunity and exclusion to accountability and inclusion. To grasp the feasibility of this transformation requires an understanding of the history of control and resistance in Kenya since independence as this has been entrenched, constitutionally or otherwise, in the nature of the state.

The postcolonial state in Kenya was transformed from a relatively open multiparty system whose structures were devolved to the regions in 1963 to a de facto single party state in 1978, when Kenya's first president, Mzee Jomo Kenyatta, died. During this time, the basis of an authoritarian state was created, largely following the outlines of similar developments in many other African countries, such as Ghana, Tanzania and Uganda. This pattern was based on the centralisation of power in the presidency and the elimination of any potential foci of organised opposition (Tamarkin 1978). This centralisation was initially a constitutional act, involving changes to the constitution to entrench powers in the presidency, as well as a concomitant process of building an authoritarian structure through the provincial administration that radiated from the presidency outwards into the regions (see Chapter 7). Together with development of this network of provincial administration, there was a concentration of the security powers – the military, paramilitary and police – within the office of the president and their transformation into a key lever of power through repeated public displays to intimidate, silence and instil fear, as Ruteere shows in his contribution to this volume (Chapter 8). The preferred means of securing the loyalty of security agencies was to ethnicise their leadership by appointing into their command structures trusted people from the president's own ethnic group. The enforced disbanding of the Kenya African Democratic Union and, a few years later, the Kenya People's Union (Mueller 1984) meant that KANU emerged as the sole political party and the presidency became the core of any political activity. When the presidency encountered resistance to its centralising agenda in parliament, not only were the dissenting voices hounded out of parliament, others were detained, assassinated or fled into exile, leaving behind a system of politics that reproduced exclusion and impunity (Odhiambo 1987).

When President Moi assumed power in 1978, the stage was set for further constitutional amendments and extrajudicial repression. He transformed the political system into a de jure one-party state controlled by the presidency through a constitutional amendment moved by Mwai Kibaki. Moi channelled this control via the party, KANU, which he used to control or sidestep parliament and to embed a network of provincial administrators whose unquestioning loyalty spread fear, despondency and exclusion in the countryside. The security agencies backed up this system; the spying agencies acquired notoriety not only for conducting surveillance in the interest of state security but in using the excuse of state security to harass, apprehend, detain and torture real or perceived enemies of the Moi state. The levels of suspicion grew to alarming heights, with special branch officers spreading across all spaces of civic engagement in Kenya, spying in every nook and cranny. The greatest effect of this network of spies was felt in the few remaining sites of resistance, especially the universities (Amutabi 2002). The prominent place that the Nyayo House torture chambers and Nyati House, the headquarters of the special branch, acquired in the 1980s is a reflection of how often extrajudicial means were adopted to asphyxiate civil society discourse.

It did not help matters that judicial means of addressing the situation were undermined or closed. The Moi regime removed the security of tenure of judges in 1988, operated an opaque system of appointments of judges that engendered loyalty, and began a pattern of intimidating judges who displayed any streak of independence. But, where this did not happen, 'judicial subservience', as Makau Mutua (2001) describes it, peppered the growing authoritarianism, with judges taking openly partisan positions that undermined the democratic struggle and often referring to the constitution to back up their claims. Institutionally, the judiciary was emasculated by the executive. In the structure and organisation of government, the judiciary was listed as a mere department under the office of the attorney general, grossly underfunded and understaffed. The bench itself was feeble at best and hostile at worst in the validation of rights. In one prominent case, Justice Dugdale declared Kenya's bill of rights inoperative and unenforceable, setting the stage for what has been described as the rise of delinquent jurisprudence on rights in the Kenyan courts.

Like Kenyatta, Moi developed a network of trusted leaders whom he appointed into positions of authority, both in government and within the party. Their key function was to protect the presidency and they usually unleashed a chorus of condemnation of any leaders whose loyalty they perceived to be below the desired level. By 1988, the Moi regime was at its authoritarian worst and felt confident enough to mercilessly rig the 1988 elections through a *mlolongo* (queuing) system of voting. This ensured that KANU got rid of most of the unwanted politicians in a way that left no means for appeals through the court. This direct assault on parliament, together with the fact that all spaces for civic engagement had been constricted completely, generated a new logic of struggle, one that had to operate outside the constitution and away from formal spaces of civic engagement to achieve its goals. It is precisely because of this logic that the focus on democratic struggle moved quickly, especially in the run-up to the 1997 elections, emphasising constitutional reform as the only way in which the political interests of those outside KANU could be liberated and exercised. Clearly, the old constitution, inherited from colonial times and repeatedly amended to further concentrate power in the presidency, had served Kenya poorly. By 1992, all key institutions – the judiciary, public services, security forces, provincial administration and parliament – had been reduced to instruments of authoritarian domination. Thus, when the struggle for the reintroduction of political pluralism peaked in the early 1990s, all of the fundamental issues that shaped the Kenyan state and society – struggles over accountability in the exercise of power and respect for human rights; the distribution of resources; and the politics of ethnic relations and the national question, to name but a few – had, in one way or another, a constitutional dimension. If the struggle for democracy were to succeed, it had to insist on restructuring the state and the political system and to place a premium on sharing and checking power, both at the centre and between the centre and the regions.

The push for constitutional reform that began in earnest in the mid-1990s was beset by a series of subversions and manipulations. The National Rainbow Coalition (NARC) government came to power in 2002 after campaigning on a platform for a new constitution. This promise was to be betrayed too. After a popular-driven draft was torpedoed, the diluted proposal of the conservative wing of the divided government was rejected resoundingly in a referendum in 2005 (Cottrell and Ghai 2006). The resistance of this conservative wing was all the more frustrating as it had previously supported the same provisions of de-concentrating powers from the presidency that they now rejected. The popular frustration with the failed promises of the NARC government, the re-emergence of political privilege organised around what came to be popularly called the Mount Kenya Mafia and the corresponding exclusion of key constituencies that constituted NARC (Murunga and Nasong'o 2006) fed into, as Gachigua argues (Chapter 2), the hardened positions that characterised the 2007 campaigns, reinforced by key institutions including the media. The urge to remove from power the conservative wing of NARC – led by Mwai Kibaki and which reconstituted itself in the run-up to the 2007 general elections as the Party of National Unity – was as strong among the Orange Democratic Movement opponents led by Raila Odinga as was the desire on the part of this conservative wing to retain power at all costs. The result was the 2007 bungled elections and the post-election violence (Berman et al. 2011; Githinji and Holmquist 2008; Mueller 2011; Murunga 2011).

The making of the 2010 constitution

One outstanding trait about the 2010 constitution is the widely recognised progressive character of some of its content, such as the bill of rights and the checks on power. Given the strong resistance by large sections of the Kenyan ruling elite to political demands seeking to improve and secure freedom and justice, through the constitution or otherwise, this begs the question of how such a constitution was possible.

The contributions to this book bring out the range of factors and actors involved in the process, from the long-term struggles discussed by Zeleza (Chapter 1) to the immediate shock of 2007–08 highlighted by Wamai (Chapter 3); from people-driven processes spearheaded by civil society that Nasong'o expounds (Chapter 5) to the elite pacts emphasised by Muhula and Ndegwa (Chapter 4). The referendum and the constitution would not have come about without longstanding demands for democracy. But they were also the outcome of the National Accord of 2008, negotiated in the wake of the bungled 2007 elections and their violent aftermath. The crisis brought into focus enduring and deep-running problems of the Kenyan state and society. The agreement, and the mandate for the Grand Coalition Government that it entailed, included a wide range of accompanying reform processes (such as land policy, electoral and security sector reforms) and set off a number of commissions (the Independent Review Commission; the Commission of Investigation of Post-Election Violence; the Truth, Justice and Reconciliation Commission, to mention just some of the most significant). These reform processes and commissions are more or less closely connected to the constitution, being affected by it as well as shaping its implementation (Kanyinga and Long 2012).

How important will the constitution prove to be? How strong will it be, in view of the hostile and powerful forces operating within and outside the political system and the weak individuals and weakened institutions that were meant to strengthen the practice of constitutionalism? The history of Kenya has been marked by false dawns. Conservative forces hijacked earlier achievements, such as independence in 1963, the transition to multiparty politics in 1991 and the ousting of KANU from power in 2002. The vested interests opposing a democratised state and policies for social justice remain extremely powerful. Constant and sustained vigilance by democratic forces in political parties and civil society will be needed to prevent a repetition of that pattern, by blocking attempts to subvert the intentions of the constitution and by realising its potential through giving effect to its words. While longstanding popular struggles laid the foundations for a progressive document, and the immediate post-2008 circumstances triggered the reactivation of the process in a context that conspired against elite manipulation, at least in its crudest sense, one must not be naïve regarding either the document itself or the scope for realising its potential. The tensions revealed by the uncharacteristically strong popular influence on the document are evident and significant, and there are clear signs that powerful interests are busy trying to undercut the democratic advances of the constitution. The 2013 general elections illustrate this with fine clarity.

The 2013 general elections have been the biggest test ever for operationalising the provisions of the constitution. Unlike previous elections, there was a new elite consensus around the new rules of the game and their ability to guarantee a fair electoral process. Not only was there a new electoral management board in place – the Independent Electoral and Boundaries Commission (IEBC), headed by a commissioner who had been publicly and competitively vetted – there were also public institutions designed to oversee elements of politics considered critical for free and fair elections. These institutions included constitutional commissions and a reformed judiciary with the mandate to adjudicate on election disputes. In fact, the IEBC took the initiative early on to determine independently the date for the general elections almost one year in advance.

As elections approached, the show of fairness and transparency crumbled, however, amid the failure of the IEBC to conduct a transparent process of selecting a company to supply the electronic voting machines, with rumours of infighting within the commission. This soon gave way to the Grand Coalition Government's single-supplier sourcing of electronic voting equipment in a way that illustrated the IEBC's inability to operate independently from government. The electronic equipment was eventually sourced through government, but the process of configuring it to secure efficient balloting, counting and tallying remains one of the major scandals of the 2013 general elections. In some cases, the equipment was never fully configured on time to be used for voting. In others, the laptops either malfunctioned or their batteries were not properly charged to ensure a smooth voting process. The result was that the expected electronic record of the results, against which the paper versions would be confirmed, was abandoned midway as the IEBC reverted to manual methods of tallying, the very method that was widely condemned by the Kriegler-led Independent Review Commission that investigated the 2007 election.

A few weeks before voting, the company contracted to facilitate the transmission of voting data warned that the IEBC was unprepared and unresponsive to key concerns relating to the electronic system. A review of the vote tallies has consequently shown many cases of impropriety, including a significant number of missing balloting forms that should have formed the basis of a proper count and consistent data issued by the IEBC. Worse, by the day voting took place, the IEBC did not have a single register against which vote tallies would be gauged. On the contrary, it had four separate registers, including the Provisional Register, the Gazetted Register, the March Register and the Green Book, each with a slightly different tally of voters. Detailed examinations of the problems that marred the 2013 elections have been undertaken by Barkan (2013), Long et al. (2013) and Ferree at el. (2014). The fact that the supreme court of Kenya legitimised the existence of many voter registers remains one of the key dilemmas facing the future of electoral politics. These election-related problems carried immense consequences. The constitution provides that, in order to avoid a run-off, the winner in the first round must get 50 per cent plus one vote. In other words, any slight gaps in the voter data are

8

of great significance. Uhuru Kenyatta surpassed this requirement by fewer than 10,000 votes.

The legitimacy of any election results in a liberal democratic setting rests with the assumption that there is certainty in the process leading up to balloting and uncertainty with regard to the eventual winner (Mozaffar and Schedler 2002: 11). The overall question for Kenya is whether the challenges affecting the process exceeded the threshold of acceptable error, thereby compromising the possibility of a free and fair process and outcome. For many Kenyan voters, the process leading to the March elections was carefully choreographed to achieve a predetermined outcome, an outcome that left more questions than answers as the media retreated into a mode of operation that silenced voices critical of the conduct of officials and politicians and foregrounded those of peace activists. When Raila Odinga and sections of civil society led by the Africa Centre for Open Governance petitioned the supreme court against the result, the expectation was therefore very high that the court would provide a better means of resolving the silenced and outstanding issues surrounding the elections.

If, in 2007, few thought the judiciary had sufficient credibility for handling the disputes, in 2013 most people easily submitted to the court's discretion. However, the ruling was appalling in its standard of jurisprudence as well as in its public presentation. Reviewing the ruling of the court with respect to its key finding, Wachira Maina described the judgment as 'both detailed and important, but the parts that are detailed are not important and those that are important are not detailed' (Maina 2013). For instance, the court rejected on a technicality voluminous evidence that might have illustrated that the threshold of error was significant enough as to close the 10,000-vote gap between the winner and the constitutional threshold of 50 per cent plus one vote. Further, the court made the aforementioned problematic ruling regarding the voter registers, thereby allowing the IEBC to continue with diverse numbers of registers and total voter tallies. Also significant was the decision of the court to dismiss 'spoilt votes' in calculating the overall percentage. As Maina argues, in dismissing the spoilt votes, the court elevated 'the right to vote' to being 'equal to the right to choose one of the candidates on [the] ballot'. He contends that the right to vote has three elements:

> The right to make a choice from among the candidates on the ballot; the right to refuse to participate in the election by abstaining and the right to cast a protest vote by rejecting all the candidates on the ballot. The right to cast a protest vote can be expressed by deliberately spoiling a ballot.

The eventual result of all this is that the supreme court, like the IEBC before it, bungled its constitutional mandate to ensure free and fair elections by ensuring that the level of error did not exceed the threshold of acceptable error.

The management of the 2013 elections casts serious doubts on the independence and capacity of these important institutional bodies created by electoral and judicial reform. Furthermore, as demonstrated by Ruteere and Ghai in their chapters in this book (Chapters 8 and 6 respectively), there are serious concerns regarding the pace and direction of security sector reforms and devolution – and, one might add, land reforms. Together, this reaffirms the apprehensions about the possibilities of upholding the letter and spirit of the progressive constitution in a society and a political order characterised by inequality and the concentration of power and resources.

The contributions to this volume

The first part of the book discusses how the process of constitution-making has been shaped both by longstanding struggles and by the dramatic rupture caused by the violence in 2008 that followed the 2007 elections. It examines the role of actors in political parties and civil society as they operate in the contexts conditioned by political institutions and socio-economic structures.

Chapter 1, by Paul Tiyambe Zeleza, is a broad-ranging chapter locating the constitutional changes in Kenya within the context of Kenya's history. He examines the different epochs in Kenya's constitutional struggle, from independence to the constitutional reform moments from 1992 to 2010. The struggle for constitutional reform in Kenya has been a long one. The first government of independent Kenya emasculated the provisions of the independence constitution and set the stage for the emergence of an imperial presidency. This generated the struggle for the 'Second Liberation', of which the enactment of a new and democratic constitution was a large part. Whereas a number of post-independence struggles did not openly bear the tag of 'constitutional reforms', they were, in substance and essence, of a constitutional nature. The chapter examines the bases for these struggles, their consistency and divergences, and to what extent the new constitution upholds or betrays them.

Chapter 2, by Sammy Gakero Gachigua, discusses a particular dimension of the 2007 post-election violence – the role of the print media. This aspect is important for understanding how key actors in Kenya's struggle for democracy, in this case the media, misjudged the tenor of the electoral debates going into the 2007 elections. In failing to fulfil their mandate of informing the citizenry, the media played into the divisive and ultimately catastrophic manipulation both of the content of news and in the manner in which the news presented the election as a do-or-die struggle. Gachigua analyses the media's role in the public sphere, illustrating how a retreat into the hard news genre not only compromised the media's ability to be objective interlocutors in the range of electoral debates but also presented the media as partisans in the unfolding drama that ended in violence. Although the chapter does not draw a direct link between this model of reporting and the constitutional moment, one can easily infer the connection when thinking about the opportunities to inform and critically engage when news is presented in the hard news genre.

Chapter 3, by E. Njoki Wamai, examines how the post-election violence and the subsequent negotiated settlement created a 'constitutional moment'. In other words, the chapter illustrates how the deep crisis was turned into a possibility for substantive change in a way that previous attempts had failed to realise. Focusing its attention on the pre-negotiation and negotiation efforts led by Kofi Annan, the chapter discusses how the mediation approach was built around a strategy that removed all possible competing avenues for the protagonists to sidestep the Annan process, thereby ensuring that items on the agenda were given their undivided attention. The chapter then explores the numerous agenda items, and in particular how the agenda of long-term reforms ensured that constitutional review remained the priority. From the mediation process, Wamai draws three important lessons. One is the need to keep mediation separate from constitution-making; the second is about understanding when the time is ripe for a constitutional moment; and the third is about the relationship between the composition of the mediation team and the outcomes of the process, including, of course, the constitutional review itself.

The last two chapters of the first part of the book address the role of actors at elite and popular levels of politics. Chapter 4, by Raymond Muhula and Stephen Ndegwa, analyses the role of pact-making by political elites. The authors examine the interplay between elite manoeuvring and the context in which these actors operate, and demonstrate that, while instrumentalist pacts blocked constitutional reforms for many years, they nevertheless, under different circumstances following the post-election violence and the National Accord in 2008, made possible the new constitution. This contextual analysis of the content of pacts calls into question the routine critique of political elites as being inherently hostile to democratic reform.

Chapter 5, by Wanjala Nasong'o, interrogates the role of civil society in the making of the new constitution. Organisations in civil society have played a significant part in the push for democratisation in general and constitutional reforms in particular. Civil society has been credited with being the instrument of intellectual and political mobilisation for the successful clamour for a new constitutional dispensation. However, civil society is encumbered by the social, economic and political cleavages that characterise Kenyan society at large. Viewing civil society as a diverse group, the chapter analyses the ways in which the balance of forces for and against constitutional reform played out on the level of society.

Read together, the chapters by Muhula and Ndegwa and by Nasong'o point to more general theoretical reflections about political projects. Political rule is exercised through institutional arrangements of political systems and state structures, but in ways that are rooted in economy and society. Democracy, authoritarianism or hybrid variants of political regimes are promoted and resisted by competing coalitions of political forces, with their bases in both civil society and political parties, as well as in the state itself. Very rarely are lines of conflict drawn between civil society as a whole and the state or the political elite as a unified entity. One factor that needs to be underlined is that, compared with other countries in the region, Kenya has always had a relatively significant number of influential political leaders pushing for political reforms in a forceful way. During critical moments, these leaders have been indispensable in translating popular demands into organised politics, policy and law.

The second part turns to the document itself, and is devoted to an interrogation of the content of the constitution from legal, political and ideological points of view. The chapters in this part also examine the opportunities and challenges of the new constitutional order.

Chapter 6, by Yash Pal Ghai, analyses to what extent the structure and demarcation of power in the new constitution may engender a culture of accountability that will give meaning to the constitution. A major governance problem in Africa is the phenomenon of constitutions without constitutionalism. The difficulty is not so much the absence of good rules as the existence of bad habits: the disinclination to obey rules. Governments routinely ignore constitutional provisions and act capriciously whenever a constitutional provision becomes inconvenient in their exercise of power. This is why a number of constitutional amendments are undertaken with the intention of shifting power from the people to the state. A new constitution, however robust, will not cure the problem if the cultural deficit of obedience persists. Ghai poses the difficult questions of whether Kenya's political economy is inherently antithetical to a constitutional architecture of power, and if the constitution can have a sufficiently restraining effect in the exercise of power.

Chapter 7, by Godwin R. Murunga, interrogates ideological divergences in the struggle surrounding the constitution and the implications they hold for its implementation. Kenya's new constitution is a compromise document; the struggle for constitutional change has been fought against strong proponents of the status quo, organised mainly as competing groups of elites. The eventual victory by the progressives was, however, not achieved without compromises. Through vague phrasing, compounded drafting and deferred legislation, the two sides found ways of dealing with issues on which they could not agree; on others, the pre-eminence of one side or the other is clearly visible. The power relations between the two groups are reflected in different chapters of the constitution. The liberals' greatest imprint can be seen in the bill of rights, while the conservatives are strongest in the system of government and security clauses. Further, cultural wars also emerged in the constitutional process, particularly with respect to women's reproductive rights.

Chapter 8, by Mutuma Ruteere, examines the extent to which the new constitution has inverted the state-centric logic of security in Kenya. Security forces have been the leading abusers of human rights; civilian control of the security forces has been weak and accountability mechanisms absent. The training, culture and general orientation of the security apparatus has been decidedly pro-state and hostile to human rights. Whereas the conflict between security and human rights is a universal and old one, two developments have accentuated this problem: first, the 'war on terror', which many countries, including Kenya, have conveniently appropriated as a pretext for clamping down on human rights; and second, the upsurge of militia crimes, through which security forces have tapped into public fears to undermine human rights objectives. Ruteere examines whether the human rights regime adopted in the constitution provides a sufficient check to state excesses; and interrogates the future interplay between security, human rights and global politics within the context of such a liberal constitution.

References

Amutabi, M. N. (2002) 'Crisis and student protest in universities in Kenya'. *African Studies Review* 45(2): 157–78.

Barkan, J. D. (1993) 'Kenya: lessons from a flawed election'. *Journal of Democracy* 4(3): 85–99.

— (2013) 'Technology is not democracy'. *Journal of Democracy* 24(3): 156–65.

— and N. Ng'ethe (1998) 'Kenya tries again'. *Journal of Democracy* 9(2): 32–48.

Berman, B. J., J. Cottrell and Y. Ghai (2011) 'Patrons, clients, and constitutions: ethnic politics and political reform in Kenya'. *Canadian Journal of African Studies* 43(3): 462–506.

Cottrell, J. and Y. Ghai (2006) 'Constitution making and democratization in Kenya (2000–2005)'. *Democratization* 14(1): 1–25.

Diamond, L. and M. F. Plattner (eds) (2010) *Democratization in Africa: Progress and retreat*. Baltimore, MD: Johns Hopkins University Press.

Ferree, K. E., C. C. Gibson and J. D. Long (2014) 'Voting behaviour and electoral irregularities in Kenya's 2013 election'. *Journal of Eastern African Studies* 8(1): 153–72.

Gibson, C. C. and J. D. Long (2009) 'The presidential and parliamentary elections in Kenya, December, 2007'. *Electoral Studies* 28(3): 492–517.

Githinji, M. and F. Holmquist (2008) 'Anatomy of a crisis of exclusion'. *Journal of Eastern African Studies* 2(2): 344–58.

Joseph, R. (1997) 'Democratisation in Africa after 1989: comparative and theoretical perspectives'. *Comparative Politics* 29(3): 363–82.

Kanyinga, K. and J. D. Long (2012) 'The political economy of reforms in Kenya: the post-2007 election violence and a new constitution'. *African Studies Review* 55(1): 31–51.

Kramon, E. and D. N. Posner (2011) 'Kenya's new constitution'. *Journal of Democracy* 22(2): 89–103.

Levitsky, S. and L. A. Way (2010) *Competitive Authoritarianism: Hybrid regimes after the Cold War*. Cambridge: Cambridge University Press.

Long, J. D., K. Kanyinga, K. E. Ferree and C. C. Gibson (2013) 'Choosing peace over democracy'. *Journal of Democracy* 24(3): 140–55.

Maina, W. (2013) 'Verdict on Kenya's presidential election petition: five reasons the judgement fails the legal test'. *The East African*, 20 April.

Mati, J. M. (2013) 'Antinomies in the

struggle for the transformation of the Kenyan constitution (1990–2010)'. *Journal of Contemporary African Studies* 31(2): 235–54.

Mozaffar, S. and A. Schedler (2002) 'The comparative study of electoral governance – introduction'. *International Political Science Review* 23(1): 5–27.

Mueller, S. D. (1984) 'Government and opposition in Kenya, 1966–1969'. *Journal of Modern African Studies* 22(3): 399–427.

— (2011) 'Dying to win: elections, political violence and institutional decay in Kenya'. *Journal of Contemporary African Studies* 29(1): 99–117.

Murunga, G. R. (2011) *Spontaneous or Premeditated? Post-election violence in Kenya*. Discussion Paper No. 57. Uppsala: Nordic Africa Institute.

— and S. W. Nasong'o (2006) 'Bent on self-destruction: the Kibaki regime in Kenya'. *Journal of Contemporary African Studies* 24(1): 1–28.

Mutua, M. W. (2001) 'Justice under siege: the rule of law and judicial subservience in Kenya'. *Human Rights Quarterly* 23: 96–118.

— (2008) *Kenya's Quest for Democracy: Taming leviathan*. Boulder, CO: Lynne Rienner Publishers.

Mutunga, W. (1999) *Constitution-making from the Middle: Civil society and transition politics in Kenya 1992–1997*. Nairobi and Harare: SAREAT and MWENGO.

Nyong'o, P. A. (1989) 'State and society in Kenya: the disintegration of the nationalist coalitions and the rise of presidential authoritarianism 1963–78'. *African Affairs* 88(351): 229–51.

Odhiambo, E. S. A. (1987) 'Democracy and the ideology of order in Kenya'. In M. G. Schatzberg (ed.) *The Political Economy of Kenya*. New York, NY: Praeger, pp. 177–201.

Sandbrook, R. (2000) *Closing the Circle: Democratisation and development in Africa*. London: Zed Books.

Schedler, A. (ed.) (2006) *Electoral Authoritarianism: The dynamics of unfree competition*. Boulder, CO: Lynne Rienner Publishers.

Tamarkin, M. (1978) 'The roots of political stability in Kenya'. *African Affairs* 77(308): 297–320.

PART ONE

Contexts and actors in the making of a new constitution

1 | The protracted transition to the Second Republic in Kenya

Paul Tiyambe Zeleza

In 2007 and 2010, two crucial events took place with profound implications for Kenyan history and society. The first event was the tragedy that followed the disputed general elections of 27 December 2007. The violence that convulsed the country left 1,100 people dead and 600,000 displaced, and threatened the very survival of Kenya.

The second event marked a rare moment of triumph. Kenyans, chastened by the ghosts of 2007 and anxious for new beginnings, voted for change. The voter turnout was high for a traumatised demos that seemed to understand that the referendum offered a historic opportunity for the country to remake itself in the wake of its battered past. If 2007 marked the nadir of the 'First Republic', 2010 represented the possible birth of a 'Second Republic' based on inclusive citizenship, good governance, devolution of power and more equitable development.

The first moment gave rise to profound despair about Kenya's future, while the second has been greeted with exaggerated hopes. Having stared into the abyss in December 2007 and January 2008, the country pulled back, and the political class made tepid compromises to save their nation through the formation of a coalition government, which delivered a new constitution in August 2010. Clearly, the crisis begat the constitution; in short, the possibilities of democracy and development promised by the new constitutional dispensation were incubated in the violent maelstrom two and a half years earlier, a development few could have predicted.

From the moment the implosion started, there was a continuous stream of commentaries and analyses all over the old and new media in Kenya itself, among the Kenyan diaspora, and from the country's friends and foes around the world. The Kenyan observers and intelligentsia were bitterly divided as the crisis unleashed intolerant ideological, political and ethnic chauvinisms. Some were quite apocalyptic about Kenya's future. Introducing a special issue of the *Journal of Contemporary African Studies*, Peter Kagwanja and Roger Southall wrote: 'The post-election crisis of January 2008 brought Kenya close to collapse and the status of a failed state.' They located 'the origin of the crisis in, variously, a background of population growth and extensive poverty; and ethnic disputes relating to land going back to colonial times (notably between Kalenjin and Kikuyu in the Rift Valley). More immediately, what stoked the conflict is the construction of political coalitions around Kenya's 42 ethnic groups.' And they were not too hopeful about the future, suggesting that 'a reluctance by the Grand Coalition partners to undertake fundamental reform of the constitution means that Kenya remains a "democracy at risk", and faces a real possibility of slipping into state failure' (Kagwanja and Southall 2009: 259). Several articles in this issue and another special issue of the *Journal of Eastern African Studies* variously attributed the crisis to elite fragmentation and the existence of non-programmatic clientelist parties, political liberalisation and institutional fragility, the informalisation and criminalisation of the state, and the decentralisation and privatisation of violence (Branch and Cheeseman 2009; Lafargue 2009; Mueller 2008).

Often thick with political details, many of the existing analyses tend to be thin on the economic dynamics of the crisis, even those that purport to advance a political economy perspective. Also, their nods to the historical context – that this crisis is rooted in Kenya's complex past – tend to be perfunctory in so far as their primary focus centres on the contemporary dynamics of the crisis. In this chapter, I seek to provide a much longer-term mapping of the historical trajectory of Kenya's political economy, which culminated in both the tragic and the triumphant events of 2007 and 2010 respectively. My argument is that both events are rooted in, and reflect, Kenya's contradictory colonial and postcolonial histories; they mirror the intertwined challenges of development and democracy; and they represent simultaneously the failures of, the struggles for, and the possibilities of constructing a developmental democratic state from the debilitating burdens of colonial underdevelopment and despotism and postcolonial developmentalism and dictatorship. The contrasting, yet connected, developments between 2007 and 2009 underscore the challenges of historical analysis and prediction.

I begin with a brief outline of the legacies of British colonialism in Kenya, the structural underpinnings and ideological parameters of which were inherited by the postcolonial state. Then I examine, again sketchily, the modes of governance and development during what I would call the period of authoritarian developmentalism between independence and 1980, which was followed by the era of neoliberal authoritarianism that lasted until 2002. Finally, I focus on the changes and contradictions ushered in by democratisation, out of which erupted both the failed elections of 2007 and the successful referendum of 2010. Throughout, I try to put Kenya in the context of wider trends in African and global histories for the obvious reason that the country is an integral part of both, and its constitutional story is part of this long and still unfolding historical process.

The political economy of colonialism and its legacies

Colonialism was, fundamentally, an economic enterprise that required political execution and ideological justification. Thus, any meaningful analysis of colonialism and its legacies in Kenya or elsewhere has to examine the nature and dynamics of colonial capitalism, the colonial state and colonial ideology. The construction of these elements entailed the coercive imposition, countervailing resistance and subsequent articulation of European and African systems and structures. The colonisation of Africa was broadly driven by the needs of the industrial capitalist countries to find markets for manufactured goods, outlets for investment and sources of raw materials. It was conditioned in different African regions by more specific dynamics, what I have called elsewhere the imperatives of finance capital in North Africa, merchant capital in West Africa, mining capital in Southern Africa, and speculative capital in Central and Eastern Africa (Zeleza 1993). Typically, colonial economies were extraverted (export-oriented), monocultural (reliant on a narrow range of commodities), disarticulated (their sectors were disconnected and suffered from uneven productivity) and dependent (dominated from outside in terms of markets, technology and capital). They were not designed for the sustainable development of colonial societies. Of course, this does not mean that they did not transform the economic systems of these societies: new modes of production and social relations were established that were to have a profound effect on subsequent African history.

The colonial state was the midwife of colonial capitalism. It was a conquest state, established through physical violence and maintained through political violence. Created as an appendage of the imperial state, the colonial state was peculiar in that it enjoyed only some of the crucial attributes of the modern state and could not exercise many of its imperatives. As a conquest state, its hegemony was excessively coercive, so it enjoyed little legitimacy. Also, its territoriality was ambiguous, its sovereignty disputed, its institutions of rule, legal order and ideological representation were all extraverted and embedded in metropolitan practices and traditions, and its revenue base was weak. Charged with the onerous tasks of creating or promoting colonial capitalism, linking the colony to the metropolis and consolidating colonial rule, it is not surprising that the colonial state was both very interventionist and fragile, authoritarian and weak, and it exercised domination without hegemony, all of which ensured its eventual downfall much sooner than the colonisers had anticipated (Young 1994).

Unsurprisingly, to its architects, colonialism was justified in the noble names of civilisation and pacification, and later, when such patently racist discourses were discarded in the barbarities of the Nazi holocaust and the Second World War, it was recast in the seductive terms of development and modernisation. Colonial rule gave rise to the racialisation and ethnicisation of colonial society, and to divisions between the colonisers and colonised and among the colonised. The colonised were denied the rights of citizenship because of race and were subjected to traditions of so-called 'tribal' custom often invented by colonialism itself. Thus, colonial despotism sought to create ethnic identities or to give fluid social and spatial identities ethnographic purity that did not exist previously as instruments of divide and rule. As Mahmood Mamdani (1996) noted, the colonial state ordained and enforced so-called customary traditions, which had the least historical depth and were monarchical, authoritarian and patriarchal.

Colonial economies, states and ideologies were, of course, diverse because of the differences between the European imperial powers and the African societies they colonised. The dynamics of colonialism were determined by each region's precolonial economic, political, social, cultural, religious and gender systems, the length and extent of its contact with Europe, the dynamics of resistance against colonisation, and the presence or absence of European settlers. This has led several scholars to place African colonies into different categories. First, there is the tripartite division of Africa developed by Samir Amin: the Africa of the labour reserves where Africans were primarily expected to provide labour for European colonial enterprises; the Africa of trade where Africa produced the bulk of the commodities traded by colonial companies; and the Africa of concession companies where chartered companies enjoyed economic and administrative control over African labour and produce (Amin 1972). Second, there is Thandika Mkandawire's typology distinguishing between rentier and merchant economies, in which surpluses were extracted from rents from mining and taxes from agriculture (Mkandawire 1995). Third, there is the distinction often drawn between settler and peasant economies, in which production was dominated by either peasants or European settlers. Under these typologies, colonial Kenya could be considered a labour reserve economy, a merchant economy, or a settler economy (Denoon 1983; Elkins 2005b).

Using the latter categorisation explains much about colonialism in Kenya and its legacies. Settler colonialism was characterised by several features: the exclusion of competition because of settler control of key economic resources, including land, the allocation of infrastructure, banking and marketing at the expense of the indigenous people; the predominance of the migrant labour system, which allowed the costs of reproducing labour power to be borne by the rural reserves; generalised repression, whereby direct and brutal force was used regularly; and the close intersection of race and class, in which, as Frantz Fanon stated, 'you're rich because you're white, you're white because you're rich' (Fanon 1967).

In most settler societies, the violence of the conquest state and the bifurcations of colonial society were particularly acute. In such societies, the colonised people faced onerous exclusions from economic and social opportunities including cash crop agriculture, stabilised wage labour, access to education and political representation. Consequently, they were forced to wage protracted liberation wars, and after independence they faced the challenges of how to democratise the state – particularly customary power – de-racialise civil society, promote African accumulation, and restructure unequal external relations of dependency.

Kenya's history as a settler colony is too long and complex to be fully covered in this chapter (see Berman 1999; Berman and Lonsdale 1992a: 1992b; Ochieng' 1988; Shaw 1995). However, the colonial political economy can be divided into three phases: first, from the 1890s to the First World War, when colonial infrastructures, institutions and ideologies were laid in the face of what historians call primary resistance against colonisation. The period was characterised by the development of settler agrarian capital built on the back of massive land alienation, coercive proletarianisation, varied patterns of peasantisation (despite efforts at marginalising peasant production), the growth of Asian and European merchant capital, the construction of new spaces and structures of colonial socialisation – the segregated colonial towns and schools – the creation of racialised social hierarchies, and the reconstruction of class, gender, ethnic and national identities.

This was followed by the interwar period during which these processes intensified. The colonial order became consolidated at the same time as new challenges against it rose from the landless squatters, impoverished workers and restless indigenous elites that were reinforced by the disasters of the Great Depression and the Second World War, which fatally undermined the promises of colonial capitalism and the supremacy of the colonial powers respectively. From these disruptions emerged a changed colonial capitalism in which the settlers who had expanded their production and power were pitted against the swelling armies of squatters desperate for land, and peasants clamouring for access to lucrative cash crops and marketing opportunities. The expanded and increasingly militant labour force became more differentiated with the introduction of import substitution industrialisation and the growth of trade unionism, and elite protest found political muscle in mass nationalism. Kenya, like much of colonial Africa, had entered the final phase of colonial rule – decolonisation.

African nationalism had a dual face: it was a struggle *against* European rule and hegemony and a struggle *for* African autonomy and reconstruction, a drive to recapture Africa's historical agency. It was woven out of many strands. Ignited and refuelled by the specific grievances of different classes, genders and generations against colonial oppression and exploitation, it also drew ideological inspiration from diverse sources – local and transnational, traditional and contemporary. If the nationalist movement constituted the primary institutional vehicle for nationalist expression and struggle, decolonisation was the immediate objective. It cannot be overemphasised that the nature and dynamics of African nationalism were exceedingly complex. To begin with, the spatial and social locus of the 'nation' imagined by the nationalists was fluid. It could entail the expansive visions of pan-African liberation and integration, territorial nation-building, or the invocation of ethnic identities. Secular and religious visions also competed for ascendancy (Zeleza 2008).

Articulated and fought on many fronts, nationalism varied from colony to colony, even in colonies under the same imperial power. Nationalist movements encompassed political parties and civic organisations, trade unions, peasant movements, women's movements, religious and cultural movements, and youth movements, each of which waged its struggles using methods, tactics and spaces that were both separate and interconnected. It was the very plurality of nationalist movements that often sowed the seeds of postcolonial discord, as independence removed the lid of unity for the disparate elements struggling for *uhuru*.

In Kenya, the nationalist struggle was dominated by the liberation war, popularly known as Mau Mau, waged from 1952 to the end of the decade by the Land and Freedom Army, although the military phase had peaked by 1955. The war was triggered by colonial state intransigence and refusal to address demands for reform. After failing to stem the rising flames of nationalist rage, as manifested in the Mombasa and Nairobi general strikes of 1947 and 1950, and the growing signs of rural revolt, the colonial state declared a state of emergency in October 1952. Concentrated in central Kenya, where the oppressive and exploitative effects of settler colonialism were most evident, the Mau Mau struggle found support among radical urban trade unionists and attracted the active participation of many women and youths, although it was dominated by dispossessed squatters and poor peasants (Anderson 2005; Atieno-Odhiambo 2003; Branch 2009).

A state of emergency was declared in order to preserve colonialism in Kenya, but, ironically, the settlers, the custodians of that very regime, were the first to be sacrificed. Soon, the Mau Mau fighters also found themselves left in the lurch, denied the right to inherit the political kingdom. In other words, the emergency generated new social and political processes that destroyed the basis of settler power, restructured the class and institutional bases of the colonial state, and altered the balance of class forces, so that both the settlers and the armed freedom fighters, the protagonists in the political crisis of 1952, had become marginalised by the time of Kenya's independence in 1963.

The war was brutal and left behind deep scars that were to haunt postcolonial Kenya. Tens of thousands of workers and squatters were deported en masse from Nairobi and European farms to concentration camps and compulsory villages, where a horrific regime of torture and forced labour led to castration, maiming, insanity and many deaths. Caroline Elkins (2005a) claims that tens or even hundreds of thousands died, far more than the 11,000 admitted in official records, and the British sought victory by trying to detain almost the entire Kikuyu population of 1.5 million. At the height of the war, it became clear to the British government, which deployed more than 50,000 troops, that reform was imperative.

A watershed year in Kenya's tortuous road to independence was 1954. Not only was it the year of the draconian repatriations, it also saw the birth of several programmes that, in their various ways, embodied the new state policies; in turn, these reflected, and further shaped, the underlying structural changes in Kenya's political economy that would set its postcolonial path. The Swynnerton Plan, for example, provided the funding and rationale for a programme of capitalist land reform and removed the remaining restrictions against African production of lucrative cash crops. The beneficiaries were the 'loyalists' who became targets of the Mau Mau fighters. The long-term effect was to entrench capitalist agriculture, intensify rural differentiation, and increase landlessness among the poor peasants. Under the Lyttelton Constitution, the process began towards greater African political representation, which only whetted the appetites of the nationalists to demand more power.

In 1960, the principle of African independence was finally accepted, although the next three years were marked by intense political struggles and negotiations over Kenya's political future. It was during this period that political factionalism began to rear its head, something that would haunt postcolonial Kenya. At the root of this factionalism, which became less ideological and more ethnic and regional as time went on, lay the conjuncture of approaching independence in a society suffering from acutely uneven development, corresponding to regional, ethnic and class factors. In spite of the emergency – in fact, because of it – the Central Province, populated mostly by the Kikuyu, had continued its relatively fast rate of development. This ensured that the Kikuyu petty bourgeoisie, numerically the largest in the country, would be central to any postcolonial dispensation. But during the emergency, political leadership of the nationalist movement had passed on to a leadership that was predominantly Luo, the second largest ethnic group in Kenya at the time, who inhabited a region that was also significantly penetrated by colonial capitalism, albeit in different forms. By the time the emergency was lifted and Kikuyu leaders were allowed to re-enter politics, Luo leaders such as Tom Mboya and Oginga Odinga were sufficiently entrenched not to fear for their positions and influence, although the overall scope of leadership conflict was broadened, thus making it more intense and open.

In contrast, in the Rift Valley and the coastal regions, where colonial capitalism was less developed, their petty bourgeois classes were much smaller and more vulnerable at the national level. The Kalenjin peoples of the Rift Valley lived in close geographic proximity to the so-called White Highlands bordering their areas. They feared not only the possibility that the Kikuyu would over-ride their territorial claims, but also that they might 'colonise' their areas, especially now that there were tens of thousands of landless Kikuyu agitating for land. The official anti-Kikuyu propaganda of the emergency merely served to inflate these fears. The Kalenjin and other smaller ethnic groups sought to protect their interests by campaigning for regionalism, for federated rather than centralised government.

Underlying the broader regional cleavages, there were local social, economic and political divisions that provided the basis for local factional and leadership rivalries and future inter-ethnic and inter-regional political realignments. In fact, both the Kenya African National Union (KANU) and the Kenya African Democratic Union (KADU), formed following the Lancaster House Constitutional Conference in 1960, were basically loose coalitions with weak central party machinery, so that almost from the beginning they were given to internal political splits and realignments. The fact that these parties were formed in the midst of the transition to independence meant that there was not enough time to consolidate the party structures and therefore to institutionalise inter-party competition, hence the relative ease with which KADU dissolved into KANU in November 1964 (Ochieng' and Ogot 1996; Percox 2004; Rothchild 1973; Wasserman 1976).

The era of authoritarian developmentalism

Decolonisation was undoubtedly a great achievement for colonised peoples, one of the monumental events of the twentieth century. As in much of Africa, at independence euphoric Kenyans were full of great expectations. They had achieved one of the five historic and humanistic tasks of African nationalism – decolonisation – the other four being nation-building, development, democracy and regional integration. The pursuit of the nationalist agendas of develop-ment, democracy and self-determination were motivated, but simultaneously constrained, by the legacies of colonialism. Economically, colonialism left behind underdeveloped economies characterised by high levels of uneven development and external dependency, which fostered regional and ethnic tensions and made them extremely vulnerable to external pressures. Politi-cally, the newly independent countries faced the challenges of nation-building – how to turn the divided multi-ethnic, multi-cultural, multi-religious and multi-racial cartographic contraptions of colonialism into coherent nation states; the democratisation of state power and politics – how to wean the state from its deeply entrenched colonial authoritarian propensities; and national development – how to build national economies without colonial despotism.

It is possible to identify three broad trends in Africa's development paradigms and processes since independence. First, the era of authoritar-ian developmentalism from 1960 to 1980; second, the period of neoliberal authoritarianism from 1980 to 2000; and third, the current phase of possible democratic developmentalism (Kayizzi-Mugerwa 1999; Paulson 1996; van de Walle 2001; Zeleza 1997). In the 1960s, the new independent countries were characterised by statism – the growth of state power – and, driven by developmentalism, the pursuit of development at all costs. The intensification of statism after independence was accentuated by the underdeveloped nature of the indigenous capitalist class and the weak material base of the new rulers. The state became their instrument of accumulation. It is also important to remember that the legitimacy of the postcolonial state lay in meeting the huge developmental backlog of colonialism, and in providing more schools, hospitals, jobs and other services and opportunities to the expectant masses. So, after independence, the postcolonial state was under enormous pressure to mediate between national capital, foreign capital and the increasingly differentiated populace.

State intervention in the organisation of the economic, social, cultural and political process intensified as the contradictions deepened and became more open. The monopolisation of politics by the state was justified in the name of development. Developmentalism and development planning attained the sanctity of religious rituals. But, like many such rituals, the plans increasingly lost touch with reality. As the crisis of growth and accumulation intensified globally from the 1970s onwards, the postcolonial state assumed a progressively more precarious and openly repressive character.

Kenya escaped the fate of many of its neighbours – such as Uganda, Ethiopia and Somalia – that underwent coups, civil wars and, in the case of Somalia, the complete implosion of the state. Living in such a dangerous neighbourhood, its star appeared to shine more brightly than it really did, for Kenya became increasingly authoritarian from the late 1960s until the early 1990s.

The KANU government moved quickly to centralise the state apparatus: regionalism was abolished in 1964, a republican constitution was promulgated, and the senate was abolished two years later. The new ruling class gradually consolidated immense power in the hands of the executive. The civil service bureaucracy, on whom the post-independence administration depended, was dominated by personnel drawn from the loyalist elements first recruited into government during the emergency. Besides the civil service, many other colonial institutions, such as the army, police and judiciary, were left intact, some with Europeans holding key positions.

Clearly, the struggle over state power intensified as the centrifugal forces of nationalism jostled for a share of the fruits of *uhuru*. KADU's dissolution and absorption into KANU marked the beginning of the slide to the one-party state, a slide that was accelerated by the bitter disputes between radicals and conservatives over the direction of the country's political economy. The radicals, organised around Vice President Odinga, pushed for an aggressive programme of distribution of settler lands to the landless; nationalisation of the major means of production, especially foreign-owned enterprises; provision of free social services, including education and health; and adoption of a more progressive, non-aligned foreign policy – all measures that the conservatives surrounding President Kenyatta found anathema. Matters came to a head when Odinga resigned as vice president in April 1966 and formed a new party, the Kenya People's Union (KPU). In the 'Little General Election' of May 1966, the KPU was trounced. Only nine of its twenty-nine members of parliament managed to retain their seats. The government used the state machinery to harass the KPU leaders, who were portrayed as unpatriotic, subversive and 'tribalistic'. The fact that seven of the nine were Luo certainly did not help matters, nor did the August 1969 defection of the Mau Mau hero Bildad Kaggia from the KPU, together with virtually the whole of the rest of the KPU's Kikuyu leadership. Two months later, Odinga and all the KPU leaders were arrested. Three days later, at the end of October 1969, the KPU was banned.

The banning of the KPU not only turned Kenya into a de facto one-party state, it also silenced the radicals, and ruptured the Kikuyu–Luo alliance forged in the heady years of decolonisation in the late 1950s and early 1960s. Broadly speaking, the struggles between the various factions of the political class between 1964 and 1970 were indicative of the disintegrating alliance that had been formed between the restive petty bourgeoisie and disaffected masses in the struggle for independence. New alliances were now emerging, primarily between the landed capitalists, many of whom had been loyalists, the expanding bureaucratic and managerial classes, and those peasants who benefited from the land resettlement schemes – in short, all those who stood to gain if the state used its powers to confirm rights to property acquired during and after the emergency or who wished to break into areas of accumulation formerly reserved for European settlers and Asians (Gertzel 1970; Lamb 1974; Sandbrook 1975).

No wonder the KANU leadership, representing this class alliance, increasingly became conservative or moderate in its political orientation and economic policies. By 1970, the dominance of this new ruling class was firmly established, although that did not mark the end of intense factionalism within the political class. As the parameters of national political discourse and parliamentary debate narrowed and lost their ideological edge, ethnic mobilisation and contestations assumed greater salience. This suggests that authoritarian developmentalism required the suppression of economic and class solidarities and struggles, which could threaten the material interests of the political class seeking to accumulate their way into a hegemonic national bourgeoisie.

Despite the drift to authoritarianism, in the first two decades of independence, Kenya enjoyed the reputation of being a stable country with a rapidly growing economy. The truth was far more complicated. I would argue that since independence, the Kenyan economy has undergone four phases in terms of development policy. In the first decade of independence, official development policy was termed 'African socialism', as outlined in Sessional Paper 10 of 1965 – this term was used more as a sop to the radicals who were then still influential. The policy called for the development of a mixed economy and its 'Kenyanisation', although the framework was undoubtedly capitalist. The state not only encouraged domestic and foreign private enterprise but also created large public sector corporations and invested heavily in the physical and social infrastructure. Growth rates were high, averaging 6.6 per cent between 1963 and 1973. But by the early 1970s it had become clear that growth by itself was not a panacea for the intricate problems of economic development, as evidence mounted that regional and social inequalities, poverty and unemployment persisted and, in fact, were deepening (Kitching 1980; Leys 1975; Swainson 1980).

Meanwhile, a global economic crisis erupted, bringing to an end the long post-war boom. The struggle between the developed and developing countries for a new international economic order intensified. Growth and redistribution on a world scale entered the international political and economic agenda. It was in this context that Kenya adopted the policy of 'redistribution through growth' in the 1970s; this entailed pursuing rapid growth through increased investments to meet the basic needs of the poor, including those in the informal sector. But the basic needs strategy did not survive for long. It was jettisoned in the face of the recessions that hit the world economy and engulfed Kenya in the late 1970s and early 1980s. It once again became fashionable to lay more emphasis on growth than on redistribution.

These two policy regimes coincided with Jomo Kenyatta's presidency. By the time of Kenyatta's death in 1978, a national bourgeoisie had emerged, even if its hegemony was limited by the deepening crises of development and democracy. The Kenya of 1978 was vastly different in its social character from the Kenya of 1963. Settler influence on social life had all but disappeared. The Africanisation of the former White Highlands was unmistakable. The rates of growth and development continued to vary between and within regions along the hierarchies of class, gender and generation. The Central Province maintained its economic dominance, even as it failed to settle the old landless from colonialism and the new landless generated by the postcolonial expansion of commodity production, some of whom found refuge in, or were channelled to, the Rift Valley, thus sowing the seeds of later conflicts. The pastoral regions remained peripheral, and the centrality of the coast to the country's booming tourism and transportation industries did not mitigate the marginalisation of its people.

Thus, the Kenya of 1978 was a capitalist Kenya, more extensively so than the Kenya of 1963. Agriculture, commerce and industry had all expanded, and indigenous capital had become completely dominant in the first sector, was preponderant in the second, and was beginning to raise its stakes in the third. The agrarian bourgeoisie had expanded and consolidated itself, just as the class of poor and landless peasants had grown. Manufacturing production had increased, and so had unemployment. In the meantime, the nationalisation of the Kenyan economy was accompanied by its internationalisation. Thus, the dynamics of internal uneven development and integration into the world capitalist system had strengthened. It was during the reign of President Moi, who succeeded Kenyatta, that the contradictions of authoritarian-dependent capitalist development became more evident and explosive, perhaps providing a good pointer to the eventuality that became the 2007 post-election violence.

The era of neoliberal authoritarianism

Under the Moi presidency, authoritarianism scaled new heights. Following the attempted coup of 1982, a constitutional amendment was passed formally making Kenya a one-party state. The centralisation of power intensified as associational space shrunk; KANU was revitalised, the security apparatuses were strengthened, and a personality cult was enhanced around the president. Civil society organisations with any oppositional potential were banned outright, muzzled by draconian laws, or tamed by being incorporated into KANU, a fate that befell ethnic associations such as the once powerful GEMA (Gikuyu, Embu and Meru Association), the weakened trade union movement, COTU (Central Organisation of Trade Unions), and the women's movement, Maendeleo ya Wanawake. Not even the once vibrant growers' associations escaped as the Moi regime banned or reorganised farmers' unions. Only religious groups and a few professional organisations such as the Law Society of Kenya survived the tightening noose of tyranny (Haugerud 1997; Himbara 1994; Schatzberg 1987).

As social movements were driven underground, KANU was turned into a powerful weapon to discipline members of the political class themselves, and a mechanism for patron–client dispensations of resources. Enforcing the deteriorating political order were emboldened security organs of the state, especially the dreaded police agency (the General Service Unit) and the Directorate of Security Intelligence. The Kenyan state was transformed from what some have called the 'imperial presidency' under Kenyatta to 'personal rule' under Moi, whose often incoherent and paranoid utterances were dignified by his intellectual sycophants as a philosophy – 'Nyayo philosophy'.

The Moi presidency coincided with the bleakest period in postcolonial African history, most notably the era of structural adjustment programmes (SAPs). These programmes created the conditions for the resurgence of struggles for the 'second independence', or for democratisation, although, of course, the architects of these programmes had not intended this, despite their retrospective claims to the contrary. The introduction of SAPs reflected the conjunction of the interests between factions of the national bourgeoisie that had outgrown state

28

patronage with those of global capital that sought to dismantle the post-war fetters of Keynesian capitalist regulation. This argument qualifies conventional analyses of SAPs in Africa as conspiracies against the continent: SAPs were welcomed by sections of the African capitalist class and were applied in the core capitalist countries themselves. The relatively harsher consequences of SAPs for Africa and other countries in the global South reflected the enduring reality that economically weaker countries and the poorer classes always pay the highest prices for capitalist restructuring (Akonor 2006; Mkandawire and Olukoshi 1995; Sahn et al. 1999). The SAPs called for currency devaluation, interest and exchange rate deregulation, liberalisation of trade, privatisation of state enterprises, withdrawal of public subsidies, and retrenchment of public services: in short, for a minimalist state and extension of the market logic to all spheres of economic activity.

The results were disastrous for African economies. Structural adjustment failed to stem the tide of stagnation or even decline, or to stabilise and return these economies to the path of growth and transform their structures. If anything, structural adjustment became part and parcel of the dynamic of decline in African economies. Initially, the International Monetary Fund and the World Bank dismissed the evident difficulties as temporary. As the problems persisted, the blame was shifted to African governments and the behaviour of their supposedly corrupt, rent-seeking elites who were allegedly reluctant to reform and give up their 'illicit' privileges accumulated under the old interventionist model of development that encouraged the flowering of growth-retarding patronage and clientelist systems. By the 1990s, it had become clear that SAPs were deeply flawed in conception and execution, that they had little to show in terms of economic growth, and that it made little sense to apply their lethal medicine in countries with vastly different economic experiences and ailments. Kenya's economic growth rate went from 6 per cent in 1973 to 4 per cent in 1990 and 0 per cent in 2000.

Structural adjustment not only failed to deliver economic development, it bolstered authoritarianism in so far as it was often imposed with little parliamentary, let alone popular, participation. On the one hand, the SAPs reinforced the triple crises of legitimation, regulation and sovereignty in the postcolonial state, and on the other they fuelled struggles for fundamental transformation, culminating in the crusade for the 'second independence'. Structural adjustment did not introduce state monopolies of production and power – in fact, it sought to tame them – but it could be implemented only by authoritarian states. The miseries of the two lost decades of structural adjustment engendered new struggles for democracy and development, as the increasingly pauperised middle classes and the working masses rose in defiance against the tottering leviathan, as re-energised old and new civil society organisations emerged from underground, and as opposition parties resurfaced from the political wilderness.

The birth pangs of democratic developmentalism

The road to democracy in Africa has proved long and arduous. In 1990, all but five of Africa's fifty-four countries were dictatorships, either civilian or military. By 2014, the majority of these countries had introduced political reforms and either had become democratic or were in the process of doing so, although instances of reversal, election-related tensions and relapse into post-election tensions and violence threaten the process of political reforms. African transitions to democracy from the late 1980s onwards were varied and characterised by progress, blockages and reversals. However, the mechanisms and modalities of transition from dictatorship to democracy took three broad paths (Ake 1995; Bratton and van de Walle 1997; Lindberg 2006; Woldemariam 2009).

First, there were countries in which opposition parties were legalised and multiparty elections authorised through amendments to the existing constitutions by the incumbent regime. This pattern was followed mainly in one-party states in which the opposition forces were too weak or fragmented to force national regime capitulation and the regimes still enjoyed considerable repressive resources and hegemonic capacities. Second, there were countries where the transition to democracy was effected through national conferences in which members of the political class and the elites of civil society came together to forge a new political and constitutional order. Finally, there was the path of managed transition pursued by military regimes, which tried to oversee and tightly control the process and pace of political reform. Kenya fell into the first category.

The transition to democracy in Kenya started at the turn of the 1990s with the resurgence of civil society organisations (Kaiser and Okumu 2004; Murunga and Nasong'o 2007; Mutua 2008). These included non-governmental organisations, many supported by Western donors, that had emerged to address the social crises caused by structural adjustment, and religious movements, both old and new, that encompassed the three major religious traditions in Kenya – Christianity, Islam and the traditional religions. They also included the women's movement, which coalesced around new organisations such as the League of Kenya Women Voters and the National Commission on the Status of Women, both formed in 1992, that espoused more radical feminist agendas. And finally, civil society organisations also included the youth movement, which tapped into the frustrations and aspirations of what Mshai Mwangola calls the 'uhuru generation'. The uhuru generation was not 'fixated on the recovery of the lost promises of uhuru', unlike the 'lost generation' that came of age after independence and had been marginalised by the 'Lancaster House generation' that brought about independence, but looked 'forward to implementing its unrealized potential' (Mwangola 2007: 135). The youth movement encompassed groups and activities ranging from youth wings to vigilante groups, such as the dreaded Mungiki, and student activism on university and college campuses (Anderson 2002; Kagwanja 2003).

It was in this climate that the opposition political parties emerged. They were comprised of disaffected renegades from KANU keen to regain their access to the spoils of state power, civil society activists committed to reforming the political system, and underground militants ready to challenge the regime openly. Respectively, the three groups sought restorative, reformative and transformative agendas. As the struggles for democratisation intensified, Western donors rediscovered the virtues of good governance and minimalist democracy and sought to channel the process by increasing political conditionalities for loans prior to the elections of 1992 and 1997 and tempering the demands of the opposition in the intervals between elections. Although the opposition won the majority in both elections, President Moi was returned to office with 36.3 per cent of the vote in 1992 and 40.1 per cent in 1997 because the splintered opposition had fielded several candidates.

The failure to dislodge KANU from power in the two elections showed the limits of the civil society organisations and opposition parties. But KANU's concession to multiparty politics and its revision of key constitutional provisions demonstrated their increasing strength and the crumbling of the authoritarian order. The pro-democracy movement suffered from a lack of clear objectives, failure to articulate a unifying ideology, crisis of leadership, inability to mobilise and retain devoted followers, and dependency on external resources, which compromised its autonomy and made it vulnerable to state attacks on its 'patriotism'. More specifically, the opposition parties were driven by factionalism, ethnocentrism and the egotistical ambitions of their founders, and debilitated by low levels of institutionalisation and internal democracy, resource shortages, and their inability to define distinctive party policies and programmes. This proved perilous in the face of continued dominance by the ruling party and its capacity to harass, intimidate and co-opt members of the opposition, and to sponsor ethnic clashes to undermine the appeal of multiparty politics and terrorise opposition supporters. In 1992, ethnic clashes ravaged the Rift Valley and in 1997 the Coast Province. Altogether, 2,000 people were killed and 500,000 displaced; in fact, the casualties were higher than those of the 2007–08 violence, at least based on the official figures of the latter (Rutten and Mazrui 2001; Throup and Hornsby 1995).

In the 2002 general elections, the opposition parties banded together into the National Rainbow Coalition (NARC), which finally dislodged KANU from office, bringing to an end nearly forty years of KANU rule. Kenyans were electrified by the potential of the new era, by the tantalising possibilities of constructing a new democratic developmental state. In short, a democratic developmental state is characterised by institutional autonomy and coherence and inclusive embeddedness operating in a democratic order marked by competitive and accountable electoral systems and has the capacity to promote development and growth (Edigheji 2005; 2010; Leftwich 2001; Mkandawire 2005; Robinson and White 1998).

The early signs seemed promising: political and civil freedoms expanded and the economic stagnation of the Moi years receded; and the country's economic growth rate jumped from 0.6 per cent in 2002 to 6.1 per cent in 2006. Buoyed by this robust growth, the government unveiled its ambitious Kenya Vision 2030, a development blueprint to turn Kenya into a newly industrialising 'middle income country providing [a] high quality of life for all its citizens by the year 2030'. This represented the fourth phase of postcolonial Kenya's development strategy, a phase that sought to reprise the ambitions of the first two and redress the lessons of the third.

But the euphoria did not last, for the social and structural deformities of the post-colony remained as entrenched as ever. Although these five years saw the growth of both democracy and the economy, the marriage between democracy and development remained unfulfilled. The chickens came home to roost following the disputed elections of December 2007 and the violent aftermath. When the presidential election results were hurriedly announced on the night of 30 December, declaring the incumbent President Kibaki the winner over the main opposition leader, Raila Odinga of the Orange Democratic Movement, election observers expressed surprise, the opposition cried foul, riots erupted, and the country teetered on the brink of an unprecedented crisis. The elections had promised to achieve an extraordinary development: the unseating of an incumbent president through the ballot box after only five years in power. This would have been unprecedented in Kenyan history, and is rare in Africa where incumbents typically serve the constitutional two terms and some even try to rig their way into illicit third terms.

The contest between the octogenarian Kibaki and the flamboyant Odinga represented a generational struggle for power. One of the ironies of contemporary Africa is that countries that have enjoyed relative political stability since independence, such as Kenya, Malawi and Senegal, were ruled by the nationalist generation that brought independence for far longer than the countries with more turbulent histories that made the generational transition much earlier. In this sense, the Kenyan election was a referendum between the older and the younger generations, between Mshai Mwangola's 'Lancaster House generation' and the 'lost generation'. President Kibaki and his Party of National Unity ran on their economic record, while the opposition claimed it could achieve even faster growth unadulterated by corruption. One sought continuity (*kazi iendelee*), the other promised change.

The electoral contest between continuity and change partly reflected the glaring mismatch between growth and development, both socially and spatially, and tapped into deep yearnings for a new socio-economic dispensation, a restless hunger for broad-based development frustrated by neoliberal growth. Kenya's economic recovery from 2002 largely benefited the middle classes rather than the workers and peasants. Even among the middle classes, the benefits flowed unequally between those in the rapidly expanding private service sectors and those in the retrenched and decapitalised public sectors, which had been under assault since the days of structural adjustment in the 1980s. For many Kenyans, therefore, the economy may have been doing well, but they were not.

If the economic growth after 2002 stoked expectations of development, the unequal distribution of wealth thwarted those expectations and engendered popular frustration, while democracy provided a new vent to express that frustration. Anti-corruption discourse and the widespread popular distaste for corruption were both real and rhetorical in so far as they reflected disgust at actual corruption scandals and invoked deep disaffection among many Kenyans who felt left out of the rapidly growing economy; it was a critique of rising economic class inequalities (Wrong 2009). In the authoritarian past, there was no political alternative to the one-party state; now, the discontented electorate could transfer its hopes for development to the opposition, even if its investment in the opposition did not promise to yield different dividends. In short, the expansion of democratic space led to rising expectations that were increasingly frustrated and manipulated by rival politicians entrenched in the divisive politics of ethno-regional mobilisation.

Class is not a reliable predictor of political loyalties and voting behaviour, even in the so-called developed countries; often, far more powerful are the constructed identities of ethnicity or race. This is not simply because politicians mobilise ethnicity for electoral purposes – which they do, and Kenyan politicians are notoriously adept at playing the ethnic card. Rather, general elections are performances played out on two different levels: elections for members of parliament are local or regional political events, while elections for the president are national events. The former tend to be characterised by intra-ethnic or intra-regional contests in which members of the same region or ethnicity compete and lose to each other; in the latter, electoral competition and behaviour mutate into inter-ethnic or inter-regional contestations. Thus, while many politicians lost in their own constituencies among their 'own' people, the presidential election inflamed regional and ethnic passions.

Ethnicity in Kenya is tied in complex and contradictory ways to the enduring legacies of colonial and postcolonial uneven regional development. The ethnic narrative of Kikuyu–Luo rivalries tends to ignore a simple fact that not all Kikuyus are dominant and not all Luos are disempowered. Colonial, neo-colonial and neoliberal capitalisms have bred class differentiations within communities as much as they have led to uneven growth between regions. In other words, Kikuyu and Luo elites have much more in common with each other than they do with their co-ethnics among the peasants and workers, who also have more in common with each other across ethnic boundaries than with their respective elites. This is a reality that both the elites and the masses strategically ignore during competitive national elections because the former need to mobilise and manipulate their ethnic constituencies in intra-elite struggles for power, and because the latter believe that elections offer one of the few opportunities to shake the elites for the crumbs of development for themselves and their areas.

The dawn of the 'Second' Republic?

Few could have predicted that a little more than two and a half years after the post-election carnage, Kenya would be celebrating the passage of a new constitution, let alone that the drive for the new constitution would be led by the protagonists of the 2007 post-electoral crisis, President Kibaki and Prime Minister Odinga. The referendum capped more than four decades of struggle for a new constitutional dispensation, which started in the dark days of the de facto, then de jure, one-party state and peaked after the 1990s as pressures escalated from an enraged and energised civil society and from emboldened, if often self-serving, opposition politicians itching to get back into the corridors of power.

The fratricidal post-election violence and explosive political stalemate was brought to an end by the National Accord and Reconciliation Act of 2008. Under the act, the position of prime minister was created and the new power-sharing government was committed to establishing a new constitution as a top priority. The new arrangements accelerated the erosion of the symbols and substance of the 'imperial presidency' (Gaitho 2010). Prodded by an anxious population fearful of a repeat of 2007 in the forthcoming elections of 2012 (that were eventually held in March 2013), and by an international community impatient with the dangerous shenanigans of the political class, an ambitious draft constitution was negotiated and agreed upon. In delivering the vote, the president assured himself a burnished legacy as the 'Father of the Second Republic', while the prime minister earned a head start to the presidency in 2012 (Mutua 2010).

The resounding victory of the 'Greens' was a tribute to the virtues of the draft constitution itself; the power of incumbency by the 'Greens', who were led by the president and prime minister; and the ineptitude and bankruptcy of the 'Reds'. The latter trotted out former President Moi, who served only to remind voters of the old Kenya of corruption, tribalism, repression, impunity and stagnation (Onyango-Obbo 2010). The 'Reds' also concentrated on blatant misrepresentations and contrived controversies over abortion from a pro-life perspective (the constitution forbids it except when 'the life or health of the mother is in danger') and the dangers of Muslim courts (Kadhi courts are not new in the country's legal system). The 'No' politicians and church leaders

34

seemed to be running a right-wing American campaign; indeed, there were accusations that some were bankrolled by American Christian fundamentalists and anti-Muslim fanatics.

The new constitution goes a long way in dealing with many of the challenges that have bedevilled Kenya since independence. Three features stand out. First, it establishes a bill of rights that recognises all the so-called three generations of rights (civil and political, social and economic, and solidarity rights, including development and environmental rights). Specific provisions are included to promote gender equality (in which women are to get a third of all leadership positions at national and county levels and in the civil service) and the rights of children, people with disabilities, the youth, older members of society, and minorities and marginalised groups. Underpinning the conception and implementation of the bill of rights is an inclusive notion of citizenship in which dual citizenship for Kenya's rapidly growing diaspora is explicitly acknowledged.

Second, the new constitution lays out a clear separation of powers between the executive, legislature and judiciary and their respective limitations. Parliament is expanded to include the national assembly and the senate, which represents the counties. The electorate is given the right of recall. The president is limited to two terms and can be removed on grounds of incapacity or by impeachment. His power to nominate cabinet secretaries, the attorney general, the director of public prosecutions and the chief justice and deputy chief justice is subject to parliamentary approval. As for the judiciary, the chief justice is limited to a maximum term of ten years and can also be removed from office under certain conditions. The constitution identifies three types of courts: the superior courts (supreme court, court of appeal and high court); special courts with the status of the high court and established by parliament to hear and determine disputes relating to employment and labour relations, the environment, and the use and occupation of and title to land; and subordinate courts including magistrates' courts, Kadhi courts and courts martial.

Third, the constitution entrenches the principles and structures of devolved government. The objectives are spelled out with admirable clarity:

> to promote democratic and accountable exercise of power; to foster national unity by recognising diversity; to give powers of self-governance to the people and enhance the participation of the people in the exercise of the powers of the State and in making decisions affecting them; to recognise the right of communities to manage their own affairs and to further their development; to protect and promote the interests and rights of minorities and marginalised communities; to promote social and economic development and the provision of proximate, easily accessible services throughout Kenya; to ensure equitable sharing of national and local resources throughout Kenya; to facilitate the

decentralisation of State organs, their functions and services, from the capital of Kenya; and to enhance checks and balances and the separation of powers.

There will be forty-seven county governments, each with an executive and an assembly headed by an elected governor and deputy governor who are also subject to removal for violation of the constitution, abuse of office, criminal acts or incapacity.

There can be little doubt that this constitution is far superior to the independence constitution. Unlike the latter, which was drawn up by the imperialists and negotiated with a handful of nationalist leaders at Lancaster House with hardly any public input, the 2010 constitution is home-grown and has involved a protracted participatory process. And if there are any external overseers at all for the new dispensation, they are eminent African leaders led by former UN Secretary General Kofi Annan (Juma 2009). While both constitutional projects were triggered by mass protests and aspirations for self-determination, development and democracy, they represent different dynamics and different historical moments and projects.

In national histories, as is sometimes the case in individual lives, moments of crisis can present new opportunities as nations are forced to confront their political and social demons and begin to muster the will to refashion themselves, to reinvent themselves as imagined national communities of citizens. One possible organised manifestation in this process of national self-reckoning is constitutional reform. Constitutions reflect the prevailing and aspirational political culture and values; they embody abstract and concrete expressions of the national imaginary, a register of the national consensus on the dos and don'ts, of collective rights and responsibilities. Constitutional documents and arrangements represent the working institutions and structures of governance, a kind of 'power map' guiding and governing the allocation of authority and duties among state functionaries as well as relations between the state and civil society (Fombad 2008; Ihonvbere 2000).

Clearly, constitutions do not guarantee constitutionalism, but without well-articulated constitutional principles and provisions there can be little prospect for constitutionalism. Many African constitutional scholars believe that the core elements of constitutionalism should include, as a minimum, the recognition and protection of fundamental rights and freedoms, the separation of powers, the rule of law, and the protection and promotion of institutions that support democracy. Like other recent African constitutions that have sought to shed their authoritarian colonial heritage, the new Kenyan constitution seeks to incorporate all these elements.

The question that has faced countries that have incorporated the second- and third-generation rights in their constitutions and in their conception of fundamental human rights and freedoms, which is often encapsulated in the notion of the right to development, centres on their justiciability: that is, their enforceability. In some narrow legalistic circles, rights only exist if they are enforceable. Others caution against excessive reliance on justiciability as the primary means to realise the progressive implementation of social, economic and solidarity rights, arguing that such rights can best be mainstreamed principally through political pressure on the elected executive and legislative branches of government (Zeleza 2006; 2007).

In other words, what is at stake is not simply enforceability but implementability, which requires the creation of effective monitoring agencies or consultative forums. This raises the question of resources, and the extent to which the realisation of the right to development should be made dependent on resource availability. To some, this underscores the inherent practical limits of economic, social, cultural and solidarity rights, while to others it is an argument for inaction. They point out that once these rights are recognised, it is the responsibility of states – individually and collectively through international cooperation – to ensure that the available resources are used effectively to safeguard their progressive realisation.

African countries differ in their views on the justiciability of economic, social, cultural and solidarity rights. In Ghana and Nigeria, for example, these rights are cast as directive principles of state policies, while in South Africa they are constitutional obligations; the state is expected to respect, protect and fulfil the right to housing, health and other elements of economic, social and cultural rights. The South African constitutional court has done much to clarify and mainstream the justiciability of these rights.

The new Kenyan constitution also reflects what has now become common practice in recent African constitution-making in the way it frames and seeks to entrench the separation of powers by providing checks and balances and curtailing the authority of the executive. The degree to which this has been achieved in practice continues to vary depending on the clarity and strength of the constitutional provisions and enforcement mechanisms, the relative independence of the judiciary in terms of both relational independence (the nature of judicial appointments and conditions of service) and functional independence, and the prevailing political culture and culture of politics. In many countries, it has proved difficult to wean politicians from the clientelist politics of 'big man' sycophancy, especially where ruling parties enjoy large parliamentary majorities.

The rule of law entails abiding by the principles of legality and protection from the arbitrary exercise of power, as well as the principle of equality before the law. Critical for constitutionalism are the methods by which the constitutionality of laws is determined. South Africa set up a constitutional court that reviews actual violations of existing laws and potential violations of legislation before it has been promulgated. In the new Kenyan constitution, judicial review 'for redress of a denial, violation or infringement of, or threat to, a right or fundamental freedom' in the bill of rights resides with the high court.

Also critical has been the question of the process by which constitutional amendments are made. In many of the new African constitutions, great efforts have been made to raise the bar for constitutional amendments to avoid abuses by would-be dictators. Quite well known are efforts to change terms of office, extending them beyond the customary two terms, by leaders who suddenly convince themselves that they are indispensable. There are other, less publicised but equally troubling threats to constitutionalism and the rule of law in many of Africa's new constitutional democracies. The Kenyan constitution provides amendatory procedures through parliament or by popular initiative.

Constitutionalism and democracy, which are not synonymous, need each other for both to thrive. In essence, constitutionalism entails the institutionalisation of respect for human worth and dignity. Crucial to forging the synergistic relationship between constitutionalism and democracy are the creation and entrenchment within the constitution of autonomous institutions whose primary purpose is the promotion of democracy. To use the example of South Africa again, six such institutions are listed, namely: the Public Prosecutor; Human Rights Commission; Commission for the Promotion and Protection of the Rights of Cultural, Religious and Linguistic Minorities; Commission for Gender Equality; Auditor General; and the Electoral Commission.

The Kenyan constitution identifies ten independent commissions specifically charged to '(a) protect the sovereignty of the people; (b) secure the observance by all State organs of democratic values and principles; and (c) promote constitutionalism.' They are: the National Human Rights and Equality Commission; the National Land Commission; the Independent Electoral and Boundaries Commission; the Parliamentary Service Commission; the Judicial Service Commission; the Commission on Revenue Allocation; the Public Service Commission; the Salaries and Remuneration Commission; the Teachers Service Commission; and the National Police Service Commission.

With the passage of the new constitution, Kenya has entered the mainstream of contemporary African constitution-making. This in itself is a welcome development for a country that is so vital for peace and stability in the East African region. It is certainly an achievement for its people in their age-old struggles for a constitutional dispensation that advances the long-cherished dreams of *uhuru* for self-determination, development and democracy. But the drafting and passing of a new constitution is only part of the struggle for a more productive future, and for creating empowered citizens and progressive governments devoted to fundamental social transformation.

In short, constitutions are not a panacea in the absence of political will, the eternal vigilance of the demos, the commitment of the political class and the existence of enforcement mechanisms. Both the rulers and the ruled, the political class and the citizens, have to believe in the legitimacy of the constitution and in the core values it espouses and represents, and there has to be institutional capacity for constitutional monitoring and implementation. We are all only too aware of African leaders who have brazenly abrogated or subverted well-crafted constitutions.

Democratisation is a work in progress all over the world, notwithstanding claims of democratic maturity in some countries. The Kenyan crisis underscores the severe challenges of democratic transition, never mind the questions it raises about the prospects of democratic consolidation. Examples abound to show that, as the suffocating lid of state tyranny is lifted during moments of democratic transition, the suppressed voices and expectations of civil society surge, but that the stresses and strains arising from the competitive grind of democracy often find articulation in the entrenched identities, idioms and institutions of ethnic solidarity. The challenges facing Kenya, and Africa's democratic experiments in general, are many and complex indeed. They include reconstructing the postcolonial state, decentralising and devolving power, embedding constitutionalism, safeguarding human rights and the rule of law, instituting structures for the effective management of ethnic and other cultural diversities, promoting sustainable growth, reducing uneven development, empowering women, promoting the youth, and managing globalisation.

All this demands a leadership that is truly up to the challenge: a leadership that pursues a *national* project of profound social transformation and that eschews narrow and short-sighted exclusionary politics and neoliberal economic growth. Kenya's contenders for power in the 2007 elections seemed keen to retain or gain power at all costs. The power struggle was as sinister as the differences between the leaders were small. But it is often the very narcissism of minor differences that breeds gratuitous violence and viciousness, as histories of genocide demonstrate. The trajectory of Kenya's recent politics is part of a much larger story. The absence of articulated and organised institutional and ideological alternatives under neoliberalism is at the heart of the political crisis facing contemporary Africa and much of the world. It has led, thus far, to the ossification of politics and, in some countries, the premature abortion or ageing of elections as instruments of transformative change. The spectre of choiceless democracies (Mkandawire 1999) is not confined to countries in the global South, for in many parts of the global North, including the United States, the ideological divide between the major parties is often indecipherable, the result of which is both political apathy and polarisation as the electoral process is left to fanatics while the majority switch off. For the more fragile postcolonial societies, the danger is not apathy but anarchy.

Having crossed this constitutional Rubicon (Ngumo 2010), Kenya has given itself a fresh start that could rescue it from the debilitating history of political instability, economic stagnation and social decay. Over the last two decades, since the onset of the current wave of democratisation, Africa has been awash with constitutional reforms, but the results have not always been edifying. As several prominent Kenyan public intellectuals warn, the people have to keep a watchful eye on the politicians as the country 'has experienced too many false starts in the past' (Mutiga 2010b).

References

Ake, C. (1995) *Democracy and Development in Africa*. Washington, DC: Brookings Institution Press.

Akonor, K. (2006) *Africa and IMF Conditionality: The unevenness of compliance, 1983–2000*. New York, NY: Routledge.

Amin, S. (1972) 'Underdevelopment and dependence in Black Africa: origins and contemporary forms'. *Journal of Modern African Studies* 10(4): 503–24.

Anderson, D. (2002) 'Vigilantes, violence, and the politics of public order in Kenya'. *African Affairs* 102(405): 531–55.

— (2005) *Histories of the Hanged: The dirty war in Kenya and the end of empire*. New York, NY: W. W. Norton.

Atieno-Odhiambo, E. S. (2003) *Mau Mau and Nationhood: Arms, authority and narration*. Athens, OH: Ohio University Press.

Berman, B. (1999) *Control and Crisis in Colonial Kenya: The dialectic of domination*. Athens, OH: Ohio University Press.

— and J. Lonsdale (1992a) *Unhappy Valley: Conflict in Kenya and Africa. Book 1: State and class*. Athens, OH: Ohio University Press.

— (1992b) *Unhappy Valley: Conflict in Kenya and Africa. Book 2: Violence and ethnicity*. Athens, OH: Ohio University Press.

Branch, D. (2009) *Defeating Mau Mau, Creating Kenya: Counterinsurgency, civil war, and decolonization*. New York, NY: Cambridge University Press.

— and N. Cheeseman (2009) 'Democratization, sequencing, and state failure in Africa: lessons from Kenya'. *African Affairs* 108(430): 1–26.

Bratton, M. and N. van de Walle (1997) *Democratic Experiments in Africa: Regime transitions in comparative perspective*. Cambridge: Cambridge University Press.

Denoon, D. (1983) *Settler Capitalism: The dynamics of dependent development in the southern hemisphere*. New York, NY: Oxford University Press.

Edigheji, O. (2005) *A Democratic Developmental State in Africa? A concept paper*. Johannesburg: Centre for Policy Studies.

— (2010) *Constructing a Democratic Developmental State in South Africa: Potentials and challenges*. Pretoria: HSRC Press.

Elkins, C. (2005a) *Imperial Reckoning: The untold story of Britain's gulag in Kenya*. New York, NY: Owl Books.

— (2005b) *Settler Colonialism in the Twentieth Century: Projects, practices, legacies*. New York, NY: Routledge.

Escobar, A. (1997) 'The making and unmaking of the third world through development'. In M. Rahnema and V. Bawtree (eds) *The Post-Development Reader*. London: Zed Books.

Eyoh, D. (1999) 'Community, citizenship and the politics of ethnicity in postcolonial Africa'. In E. Kalipeni and P. T. Zeleza (eds) *Sacred Spaces and Public Quarrels: African cultural and economic landscapes*. Trenton, NJ: Africa World Press, pp. 271–300.

Fanon, F. (1967) *The Wretched of the Earth*. Translated by Constance Farrington. Harmondsworth: Penguin.

Fombad, C. M. (2008) 'Post-1990 constitutional reforms in Africa: a preliminary assessment of the prospects for constitutional governance and constitutionalism'. In A. Nhema and

P. T. Zeleza (eds) *The Roots of African Conflicts: The causes and costs.* Athens, OH: Ohio University Press, pp. 179–99.

Gaitho, M. (2010) 'Farewell imperial presidency'. *Daily Nation*, 7 August.

Geoff, L. (1974) *Peasant Politics: Conflict and development in Murang'a.* New York, NY: St Martin's Press.

Gertzel, C. (1970) *The Politics of Independent Kenya, 1963–8.* Chicago, IL: Northwestern University Press.

Haugerud, A. (1997) *The Culture of Politics in Modern Kenya.* Cambridge: Cambridge University Press.

Himbara, D. (1994) *Kenyan Capitalists, the State, and Development.* Boulder, CO: Lynne Rienner Publishers.

Ihonvbere, J. (2000) 'Politics of constitutional reforms and democratization in Africa'. *International Journal of Comparative Sociology* 41: 9–25.

Juma, M. K. (2009) 'African mediation of the Kenyan post-2007 election crisis'. *Journal of Contemporary African Studies* 27(3): 407–30.

Kagwanja, P. (2003) 'Facing Mount Kenya or facing Mecca? The Mungiki, ethnic violence and the politics of the Moi succession in Kenya, 1987–2002'. *African Affairs* 102: 25–49.

— and R. Southall (2009) 'Introduction: Kenya – a democracy in retreat?' *Journal of Contemporary African Studies* 27(3): 259–77.

Kaiser, P. J. and F. W. Okumu (eds) (2004) *Democratic Transitions in East Africa.* Farnham: Ashgate Publishing.

Kayizzi-Mugerwa, S. (1999) *The African Economy: Policy, institutions and the future.* New York, NY: Routledge.

Kelly, K. (2010) 'Obama, Annan laud Kenyans over new constitution'. *Daily Nation*, 6 August.

Kitching, G. (1980) *Class and Economic Change in Kenya: The making of an African petite-bourgeoisie, 1905–1970.* New Haven, CT: Yale University Press.

Klopp, J. M. (2002) 'Can moral ethnicity trump political tribalism? The struggle for land in Kenya'. *African Studies* 61(2): 269–94.

Lafargue, J. (2009) *The General Elections in Kenya, 2007.* Nairobi: Mkuki na Nyota Publishers.

Lamb, G. (1974) *Peasant Politics: Conflict and development in Murang'a.* London: Palgrave Macmillan.

Leftwich, A. (2001) *States of Development: On the primacy of politics in development.* Malden, MA: Blackwell.

Leys, C. (1975) *Underdevelopment in Kenya: The political economy of neo-colonialism, 1964–1971.* London: Heinemann.

Lindberg, S. I. (2006) *Democracy and Elections in Africa.* Baltimore, MD: Johns Hopkins University Press.

Lonsdale, J. (1994) 'Moral ethnicity and political tribalism'. In P. Kaarsholm and J. Hultin (eds) *Inventions and Boundaries: Historical and anthropological approaches to the study of ethnicity and nationalism.* Roskilde: Roskilde University Press.

Mamdani, M. (1996) *Citizen and Subject: Contemporary Africa and the legacy of late colonialism.* Princeton, NJ: Princeton University Press.

Mkandawire, T. (1995) 'Fiscal structure, state contraction and political responses in Africa'. In T. Mkandawire and A. O. Olukoshi, *Between Liberalisation and Oppression: The politics of structural adjustment in Africa.* Dakar: Codesria, pp. 20–51.

— (1999) 'Crisis management and the making of "choiceless democracies" in Africa'. In R. Joseph (ed.) *The State, Conflict and Democracy in Africa.* Boulder, CO: Lynne Rienner Publishers.

— (2005) 'Thinking about developmental states in Africa'. *Cambridge Journal of Economics* 25: 289–314.

— and A. O. Olukoshi (1995) *Between Liberalisation and Oppression: The politics of structural adjustment in Africa.* Dakar: Codesria.

Mueller, S. D. (2008) 'The political economy of Kenya's crisis'. *Journal of Eastern African Studies* 2(2): 185–210.

Munene, M. (2010) 'Raila the man to beat in 2012: poll'. *Daily Nation*, 21 August.

Murunga, G. R. and S. W. Nasong'o (2007)

Kenya: The struggle for democracy. Dakar: Codesria and Zed Books.

Mutiga, M. (2010a) 'Obama: Kenya's new law a boon'. *Daily Nation*, 21 August.

— (2010b) 'Rebirth of a nation'. *Daily Nation*, 7 August.

Mutua, M. (2008) *Kenya's Quest for Democracy: Taming leviathan.* Boulder, CO: Lynne Rienner Publishers.

— (2010) 'Who won, and who lost, after the poll'. *Daily Nation*, 7 August.

Mwangola, M. S. (2007) Leaders for tomorrow? The youth and democratization in Kenya'. In G. R. Murunga and S. W. Nasong'o (eds) *Kenya: The struggle for democracy.* Dakar: Codesria and Zed Books, pp. 129–63.

Ngumo, D. M. (2010) 'Kenyans have now crossed the Rubicon; there's no turning back'. *Daily Nation*, 5 August.

Nhema, A. and P. T. Zeleza (2008a) *The Resolution of African Conflicts: The management of conflict resolution and post-conflict reconstruction.* Athens, OH: Ohio University Press.

— (2008b) *The Roots of African Conflicts: The causes and costs.* Athens, OH: Ohio University Press.

Njogu, K. (2009) *Healing the Wound: Personal narratives about the 2007 post-election violence in Kenya.* Nairobi: Twaweza Communications.

Obiero, C. (2010) *Bloodshed for Mr. President: An insight into Kenya's post election violence.* Saarbrücken: Lambert Academic Publishing.

Ochieng', W. R. (1988) *A Modern History of Kenya, 1885–1980: Essays in honor of B. A. Ogot.* Nairobi and London: Evans Brothers.

— and B. A. Ogot (eds) (1996) *Decolonization and Independence in Kenya: 1940–93.* Athens, OH: Ohio University Press.

Onyango-Obbo, C. (2010) 'Why glory of the referendum belongs to "No" campaigners'. *Daily Nation*, 7 August.

Paulson, J. A. (1996) *African Economies in Transition. Volume I: The changing role of the state.* New York, NY: Palgrave Macmillan.

Percox, D. (2004) *Britain, Kenya and the Cold War: Imperial defense, colonial security and decolonization.* London: I. B. Tauris.

Robinson, M. and G. White (eds) (1998) *The Democratic Developmental State: Political and institutional design.* Oxford: Oxford University Press.

Rothchild, D. (1973) *Racial Bargaining in Independent Kenya: A study of minorities and decolonization.* New York, NY: Oxford University Press.

Rutten, M. and A. Mazrui (2001) *Out for the Count: The 1997 general elections and prospects for democracy in Kenya.* Kampala: Fountain Publishers.

Sahn, D. E. et al. (1999) *Structural Adjustment Reconsidered: Economic policy and poverty in Africa.* New York, NY: Cambridge University Press.

Sandbrook, R. (1975) *Proletarians and African Capitalism: The Kenya case, 1960–1972.* New York, NY: Cambridge University Press.

Schatzberg, M. (1987) *The Political Economy of Kenya.* New York, NY: Praeger Publishers.

Shaw, C. M. (1995) *Colonial Inscriptions: Race, sex, and class in Kenya.* Minneapolis, MN: University of Minnesota Press.

Shimoli, E. (2010) 'The seven steps to a brave new Kenya'. *Daily Nation*, 5 August.

Swainson, N. (1980) *The Development of Corporate Capitalism in Kenya 1918–1977.* Berkeley, CA: University of California Press.

Throup, D. and C. Hornsby (1995) *Multiparty Politics in Kenya: The Kenyatta and Moi states and the triumph of the system in the 1992 elections.* Athens, OH: Ohio University Press.

van de Walle, N. (2001) *African Economies and the Politics of Permanent Crisis, 1979–1999.* Cambridge: Cambridge University Press.

Wasserman, G. (1976) *Politics of Decolonization: Kenya Europeans and the land issue 1960–1965.* New York, NY: Cambridge University Press.

Woldemariam, K. (2009) *The Rise of Elective Dictatorship and the Erosion of Social Capital: Peace, development, and democracy in Africa*. Trenton, NJ: Africa World Press.

Wrong, M. (2009) *It's Our Turn to Eat: The story of a Kenyan whistle-blower*. London and New York, NY: Harper Perennial.

Young, C. (1994) *The African Colonial State in Comparative Perspective*. New Haven, CT: Yale University Press.

Zeleza, P. T. (1993) *A Modern Economic History of Africa. Volume 1: The nineteenth century*. Dakar: Codesria.

— (1997) *Manufacturing African Studies and Crises*. Dakar: Codesria.

— (2003) 'Imagining and inventing the postcolonial state in Africa'. *Contours: A Journal of the African Diaspora* 1(1): 101–23.

— (2005) 'Democracy, Africa'. In M. C. Horowitz (ed.) *New Dictionary of the History of Ideas: Volume 2*. New York, NY: Charles Scribner's Sons, pp. 556–60.

— (2006) 'Human rights and development in Africa: current contexts, challenges, and opportunities'. In L. Wohlgemuth and E. Sall (eds) *Human Rights, Regionalism and the Dilemmas of Democracy in Africa*. Dakar: Codesria, pp. 57–96.

— (2007) 'The struggle for human rights in Africa'. *Canadian Journal of African Studies* 41(3): 474–506.

— (2008) 'The historic and humanistic agendas of African nationalism: a reassessment'. in T. Falola and S. Hassan (eds) *Power and Nationalism in Modern Africa: Essays in honor of the memory of the late Professor Don Ohadike*. Durham, NC: Carolina Academic Press, pp. 37–53.

— (2009) 'The African renaissance and challenges of development in the 21st century'. *Comparative Studies of South Asia, Africa and the Middle East* 29(2): 155–70.

— and P. McConnaughay (eds) (2004) *Human Rights and the Rule of Law in Africa*. Philadelphia, PA: University of Pennsylvania Press.

2 | Fuelling the violence: the print media in Kenya's volatile 2007 post-election violence

Sammy Gakero Gachigua

Introduction

The media in society is both an arena and an actor in the public sphere. The notion of the public sphere, which is traced to the writings of German philosopher Jürgen Habermas, refers to the existence of a social space where matters of public importance are discussed to determine the public interest (Stevenson 2002). The media accomplishes the twin roles of arena and actor in the public sphere by mediating arguments and information: in other words, facilitating discourse in the public sphere. In doing so, the media aids in enlightening and provides a forum for information exchange, as well as shaping opinion among the public. In this formulation there is a close link between the public sphere, the media, the public and democracy. The classical public sphere, as Gripsrud (2002) and Stevenson (2002) argue, is tied to the idea of the democratic public sphere, which rests on the premise that every citizen takes part in the formation of public opinion in a free and independent manner by making a judgement on the information and arguments presented on an issue. The essence of public discourse is to determine the general public good through critical reflection on issues of public concern without hindrance. This formulation of the public sphere, as both Gripsrud (2002) and Stevenson (2002) observe, is an ideal of how it might best operate and not a description of how it has operated in a real historical context.

The ideal public sphere is an important normative standard against which media in modern democratic or aspiring democratic societies can be appraised. This appraisal becomes even more pressing during critical moments, as has been the case in the recent past in Kenya during the constitutional review and in the important electioneering process. These two processes have marked an important cycle in the democratic dispensation in Kenya, in which political actors, mainly through the media, sold their socio-political and economic programmes to citizens so that they could secure the rules and their mandate to govern. The appraisal is also important as the media claims to operate on the principles of objectivity, neutrality, public good, the public's right to know and freedom of the press, among others, as well as being society's watchdog.

However, with the transformation of most media as commercial enterprises in modern societies, Habermas argues that the air has been squeezed out of the public sphere and that commercial and profit concerns increasingly override the media's contribution to enlightenment and the formation of public opinion. As Stevenson comments with regard to Habermas's writings:

> Whereas once publicity meant the exposure of domination through reason, the public sphere is now subsumed into a stage managed political theatre. Contemporary media cultures are characterised by the progressive privatisation of the citizenry and the trivialisation and glamorisation of questions of public concern and interest. The hijacking of communicative questions by monopolistic concerns seemingly converts citizens into consumers and politicians into media stars protected from rational questioning (ibid.: 50).

Political processes are therefore reported in the media as personal conflicts, emphasising the dramatic, the sensational and theatrics in what is referred to as 'tabloidization' or 'dumbing down' (Kevin 2003: 229–33). The media becomes an arena for displays, glitz and entertainment as outlets compete to capture the largest audience in order to ensure sustained profitability. Real debates of political issues are thus relegated to the periphery, as the sensational takes centre stage.

It is against this background that this chapter seeks to interrogate the Kenyan print media in the run-up to the 2007 general elections and the role the print media may have played in contributing to the violence that flared up after the elections. Specifically, the chapter focuses on an analysis of the country's two oldest and most widely circulated newspapers – the *Daily Nation* and *The Standard* – from October to December 2007, with particular reference to opinion poll reports, and on their reporting of campaign news from November to December 2007. The focus on these two media outlets is informed, firstly, by an understanding that the print media, a segment that the two papers dominate, targets the Kenyan middle class, who greatly influence the local political process, and that the papers routinely set the news agenda in the country (Ogola 2009). Thus, they form an influential public sphere in Kenya. Secondly, whereas a sizable literature is available that is critical of the conduct of the media in the run-up to 2007's post-election violence – particularly social media (see, for instance, wa-Mungai 2010; Goldstein and Rotich 2008) – the mainstream media (including these two newspapers) has either been praised for balanced reporting (BBC World Service Trust 2008; Kiage and Owino 2010: 312) or criticised in broad terms (see, for example, BBC World Service Trust 2008; Kiage and Owino 2010: 312; Makokha 2010; Ogola 2009). There is a dearth of theoretically informed in-depth analysis of the content of the mainstream media. This chapter is an attempt to fill this lacuna.

A critical appraisal of the Kenyan mainstream print media before the elections and its potential contribution to the subsequent violence is essential in the country's struggle for a new constitutional order. This is because, firstly, the mainstream print media formed an influential space in the enactment of the political battles in 2007, which graphically highlighted the need for the constitutional reforms that were mooted in the aftermath of the violence. Secondly, the appraisal of the media as an influential actor and arena in the public sphere – particularly in its performance at critical moments in Kenya's history, as was the case in the 2007 election campaigns – should offer important lessons on how the media can potentially undermine the shaping of public discourses that are invaluable in other critical political moments in a nation, such as during constitutional review and implementation processes.

Kenya's 2007 election campaigns: a brief background

The immediate historical background to what happened in the 2007 election campaigns and the seeds of the violence that rocked Kenya can be traced to the reneging on the memorandum of understanding (MoU) that led to the creation of the pre-2002 election party, the National Alliance Rainbow Coalition (NARC) (see Branch and Cheeseman 2006; 2008a; 2008b for a longer historical perspective). The MoU was signed in 2002 between the National Alliance Party of Kenya (NAK) and the Liberal Democratic Party (LDP). While the former comprised 11 major political parties, the latter was made up of disgruntled leaders who had decamped from the Kenya African National Union (KANU) in protest at President Moi's unilateral decision to pass them over as senior party leaders and choose as his successor a political novice – Uhuru Kenyatta, the son of Kenya's first president, Jomo Kenyatta. The MoU – the content of which was known at the time only to the political players involved in its negotiation – had reached the understanding that, among other things, the two partners would share cabinet and other senior government positions on an equal basis. It was also reported that the MoU stipulated the creation of a prime minister post, which would be occupied by Raila Odinga of LDP. Two deputy prime minister positions were to be created and shared equally between the partners. The presidency was to be occupied by Mwai Kibaki of NAK, while the vice presidency was reserved for Wamalwa Kijana, also of NAK. The summit, the foremost body that would bring together nine top leaders in the coalition, was to act as an oversight board directing policy and resolving conflict whenever it arose (for a full discussion of the background to the coalition and its dynamics, see Oyugi 2006; Murunga and Nasong'o 2006).

On winning the 2002 elections, Kibaki reneged on the MoU and sought to exercise presidential powers as the constitution at the time provided. Fissures emerged shortly afterwards and were starkly played out in parliament and also at many acrimonious constitutional review forums. The discussions at these forums came up with a draft constitution popularly known as the Bomas draft, named after the venue of the talks. The adoption of the final draft was marred by a walkout by the pro-Kibaki NARC faction of government in protest at alleged manipulation of the talks by the Raila-led LDP bloc. It was only later that the government formally accepted the draft. As this was playing out, KANU, the ruling party from independence in 1963 until 2002, and at the time the official opposition party, was going through a crisis and trying to reinvent itself. In this moment of crisis, two factions were emerging: one cosying up to the NAK group of the NARC government, and the other coalescing around the LDP-led NARC camp.

The introduction in parliament of the Wako draft constitution, which was a version of the Bomas draft revised under the auspices of the attorney general – Amos Wako – to suit the structure of government favoured by the pro-Kibaki NARC/KANU faction, hardened the positions of the two NARC groups and their partners from KANU. When the Wako draft was passed by parliament and put to a referendum, the ties in the two political camps were cemented, with one emerging as the pro-Kibaki group, which supported a 'yes' vote, while the Raila-led LDP-KANU supported a 'no' vote. The pro-Kibaki group was given the referendum symbol of the banana, while the Raila-led group got an orange symbol. By this time, the political alignments had already started taking ethnic hues, which later gelled in the referendum vote.

The 'no' vote won the referendum with 58 per cent compared with the 'yes' vote's 42 per cent. Riding on the success of the 'no' campaign, political parties and individuals who had supported the 'no' vote decided to register the Orange Democratic Movement Party of Kenya (ODM) as a political party. However, a Nairobi lawyer, Mugambi Imanyara, upset the 'no' team's plans by registering the acronym 'ODM', forcing the team to register as the Orange Democratic Movement-Kenya (ODM-K). Later, in 2007, when ODM-K suffered a split, Kalonzo Musyoka and his political associates took charge of ODM-K, while the group associated with Raila Odinga negotiated for the transfer of ODM from Imanyara to their ownership. These two parties, alongside the Party of National Unity (PNU) – a political coalition put together from the 'yes' campaign less than four months before elections as a platform for President Mwai Kibaki's re-election bid – were the three main political players in the 2007 general elections.

As the country approached the 2007 general elections, many individuals and institutions that would have otherwise acted as voices of reason and provided a moral compass in the disturbing moments before and immediately after the elections had been sucked into the partisan politics of the time. The media was not spared either.

The media in Kenya in the run-up to the 2007 general elections

The media in Kenya enjoyed an unprecedented boom in the fifteen years starting around 1993. In 1992, for the first time the government broke its firm monopoly of the airwaves by allowing the privately owned Kenya Television Network to broadcast. In the mid- and late 1990s, the government gave further concessions to private broadcasters, licensing more organisations and providing the media with substantial freedom. This trend was accelerated after the coming to power of the NARC government in 2002, resulting in what the BBC World Service Trust (2008: 15–16) calls 'unsophisticated liberalization of the media', while Makokha (2010: 278) terms it as 'haphazard and not guided by any constitutional, social or legal philosophy'. These views were also supported by Dr Bitange Ndemo, former Permanent Secretary in the Ministry of Information and Communication (Republic of Kenya 2008a).

The print media, on the other hand, amid concerted efforts by the political class to exert influence or to control their editorial policy, had played a critical role in the agitation for democracy by providing a forum for public discourse throughout much of the country's post-independence history, and particularly in the 1990s (Ogola 2011). Makokha (2010: 277), however, seeks to qualify this, pointing out that not all media did so. The country's two oldest and highest circulation newspapers – the *Daily Nation* and *The Standard* – played a dominant role in shaping this legacy. News magazines such as the now defunct *Weekly Review*, *Nairobi Law Monthly*, *Finance* and *Society* also made significant contributions to the fight for democracy and human rights, but most were proscribed for being too critical of the government of the day or compromised by government, as was the *Weekly Review* in its later days before it folded, citing that advertisers had abandoned them.

For nearly two decades prior to the 2002 elections, the grand project of the progressive media, and especially the print media – as indeed was the case for civil society and religious bodies – seemed clear-cut. They aimed for the establishment of a more democratic, just and public-spirited society, which was partly to be achieved by breaking the much discredited KANU hegemony. The coming to power of the NARC government presented an identity crisis for most institutions and individuals, as the KANU hegemony – the common enemy that had helped the media and civil society forge a unified front – had gone. The betrayal of the NARC dream of a united, democratic, public-spirited and responsive government when President Kibaki reneged on the NARC MoU set off bitter infighting in the party that left the Kenyan society restless. This restlessness easily found an outlet in political factions with ethnic hues, which affected the media and civil society by deepening the identity crisis that they were already facing.

In the prevailing circumstances, as the BBC World Service Trust (2008) points out, the media was not spared the factional politics playing out in the wider country. Individual media personalities and media houses supported different politicians and political parties and did not make considerable efforts to find common ground that served the greater national purpose. These media outlets and personalities aligned their journalistic practices with their preferred political outlook (Makokha 2010; Ogola 2009), although, as Ogola notes, the mainstream media did so covertly and the vernacular radio broadcasters more overtly, while at the same time maintaining an aura that suggested they were still upholding journalistic principles.

Another challenge facing the Kenyan media in the run-up to the 2007 general elections relates to their commercialisation in a competitive, liberalised economy. This meant that media outlets had to grapple with the tension between operating as commercial entities driven by the profit motive and as organisations entrusted with a vital public responsibility. Commercialisation of the media has a significant bearing on what is treated as being newsworthy, and how news is packaged and relayed. Commercialisation also incites cut-throat competition in the gathering and presentation of news, as the aim is to have the greatest appeal to the audience, an audience whose captivity easily translates into increased revenue from sales and advertising. It is against this backdrop of competitively commercialised media operating in a highly polarised political atmosphere that we now turn to an analysis of election campaign news design and the implications this may have had in Kenya's 2007 general elections and their aftermath.

Election campaign news designed as a hard news genre

A media genre is a category of media product that has particular features, codes and conventions associated with it (Burton 2002). The features of a genre have come to be well understood and recognised through being repeated over a period of time. These features act as rules both for producers to encode texts and for audiences to decode them. Because of their repetitive nature, the characteristics of a genre are reinforced and therefore become 'natural', believable, and hence amenable to ideological messages (ibid.).

Election campaign news is given extensive focus by the media 'not for impartial or neutral reasons' but, as Dennis (2003: 81) notes, 'because they believe that political power achieved through elections is a vitally important news story' – and this news story can be played out to benefit the commercial media's bottom line. The Kenyan media reaped big rewards from the 2007 election campaigns, but with the violence that followed it saw a sharp decline in revenues (Makokha 2010: 303). It is for this reason that commercial media has a desire for the electioneering process to develop dramatically over a long period because it then attracts audiences – and larger audiences have an impact on the media's profits. One way in which the media sustains the dramatic playing out of the election process is by adopting a 'hard news' approach in the reporting of election news.

Hard news, according to Jamieson and Campbell (2001), is personalised, it is dramatic and conflict-filled, and it involves extreme physical action and emotional intensity. It is also out of the ordinary and controversial, as well as being linked to issues prevalent at the time. This modelling of news, as Jamieson and Campbell argue, is not unproblematic.

Hard news is personalised and individualised because such news is appealing, attention-grabbing, interesting and easy to assimilate by a varied mass audience (Louw 2010). The notion of personalised news can be better understood if one considers the fundamental appeal that lies behind the rise and popularity of the celebrity phenomenon and how it relies almost entirely on recounting the private lives of stars and celebrities (ibid.: Chapter 6). However, the personalising of news has its drawbacks. Firstly, it means that the media has a tendency to seek out news personalities who are spectacular, flamboyant and articulate, because they convey a sense of drama and attract attention, and not for the substance of their contribution or their centrality to the issues under discussion. Secondly, the exploration of issues and ideas surrounding news items may be relegated to the periphery as focus shifts to the theatrics of individuals. Subsequently, important questions that need to be asked on an issue may be glossed over in the search for the personalised angle. Thirdly, when complex issues do not attract news coverage, politicians are likely to ignore them and focus on simpler, more dramatic issues that ensure that they receive continued coverage.

The norm that hard news is dramatic and conflict-filled, Jamieson and Campbell (2001) further contend, influences the structuring of news reports. Conflict becomes an important device for driving forward hard news stories because its unravelling is a sure attention-grabber for the mass audience as well as interesting in providing a break from the routine, everyday occurrences. In the news media's quest to re-create conflict and drama in events, accommodative and consensual approaches and issues may be disregarded or lose out. It is also the case that many issues can be seen from several viewpoints; however, it is common in the news media for two extreme perspectives to be presented as the only existing ones, since in such presentations the conflict seems more clear-cut. In this regard, election campaigns are regularly structured in the form of battles or sporting events, with metaphors from these domains employed extensively to describe the electioneering process.

A third conception of hard news is that it involves action, an event or an identifiable occurrence. Events or occurrences are tangible and distinct and therefore can be captured in a limited time or space. As Jamieson and Campbell (ibid.) point out, the notion that hard news should lend itself to this approach is appealing to news media because the events and occurrences can be captured as single instantiations – in photographs or tape recordings, for example – or, in the case of print media, because it is possible to capture them in a pyramidal structure – a one-sentence introduction conveying the essence of an entire story, which is then elaborated incrementally in the subsequent paragraphs, with information given in the order of its importance. The distinct events or occurrences are also likely to be dramatic and to involve individuals. This norm is detrimental to coverage of the ideas, patterns, structures and processes underlying the events that are depicted so graphically. The quest to capture events as distinct occurrences may also dislocate those events from their context.

A fourth feature of hard news is that it regularly seems to be about things that are out of the ordinary or novel. This idea may be problematic in that the extraordinary events may just be that – odd events, which, when looked at in terms of their substantive consequences for citizens vis-à-vis other happenings of the time, are simply inconsequential, save for their entertainment value. An awareness of this norm in news coverage may also motivate groups intending to attract media attention to create pseudo-events in order to get publicity (Louw 2010).

The fifth characteristic of hard news is that it reports events that are linked to issues prevalent in the news at the time. The idea here is to provide continuity and pattern to the complexities of modern life. This desire for continuity in news reportage explains why individuals who are recognisably newsworthy or those who have been bankable news sources in the past receive the most coverage. This approach may determine who is covered and who is not, how often, and in what ways in, for instance, election campaigns.

The downside of the hard news model for covering election news – a model that is favoured by the commercial media – is that it lends itself to manipulation by those who understand its workings, as is shown in the next section, which focuses on politicians' exploitation of the hard news arena in the 2007 Kenya election campaigns.

Manipulation of the hard news model in Kenya's 2007 general election campaign

The modelling of political campaign coverage in the form of hard news and the sensationalising of the news by the media are one side of the coin. The other side, as Jamieson and Campbell (2001) argue, is that people and groups who understand the norms of news coverage can also manipulate news reporting in their favour. Public relations practitioners and politicians are two such groups (see Louw 2010: Chapter 5). The motivation for seeking to influence the news media is tied to an understanding that the media holds the power to set the agenda for the public. As Dennis (2003: 80, citing Cohen) points out, the news media does not tell us what to think as much as it tells us what to think about.

This understanding was keenly appreciated and played out in Kenya's 2007 presidential political campaigns like at no other time in Kenya's history. There was heavy engagement of political campaign consultants, political analysts and spin doctors by all the major presidential candidates. Most spin doctors were content to work in the background, but their work was discernible in the numerous advertisements in the media as well as in news feeds. Perhaps the most widely publicised of the campaign strategists was Dick Morris, who was brought in to the ODM campaign and paraded by the party's presidential candidate, Raila Odinga, in a press conference on 13 November 2007 as the architect of former US president Bill Clinton's successful re-election in 1996. He was reported to be ready to work for ODM pro bono. Morris was to leave the country two days later after it was established that he did not have a work permit. During his short stint in Kenya, he generated negative publicity for the ODM campaign when the party's opponents and sections of the media latched on to his controversial history in the US involving a prostitution scandal, tax evasion and run-ins with the Clintons.

One area that can be, and has been, used in influencing and even controlling news media, according to Jamieson and Campbell (2001), is the manipulation of deadlines. This involves, for example, releasing controversial information by newsworthy personalities that is harmful to opponents or in favour of the source close to the media deadline, thus leaving little time for it to be verified; the controversial information is therefore likely to be reported as it has been provided. In a competitive commercial media environment, chances of the unverified material being reported are usually higher. This is because, if one media outlet fails to report the story, other media outlets will scoop it. If readers find out about the story from other sources, they may start to question the capacity of the media outlet that did not carry the story to cover news. The unverified information can easily pass unchallenged and thus be legitimised as 'factual' if the media relaying the controversial story either lacks the capacity for investigative journalism or is compromised or biased in favour of the story's source. As the BBC World Service Trust (2008) observed, this applied to the mainstream Kenyan media in the run-up to the 2007 general elections.

A lot of conspiracy theories, claims of plans to rig elections, alleged manipulation of opinion polls, secret pacts – between, for instance, the Muslim leadership and a political party to introduce sharia laws – outright misleading statements by politicians, among other things, gave a field day to the political propagandists. The media seemed content to report such claims in descriptive terms, quoting only the sources, and at times the counterarguments, and only rarely pointing out the contradictions or requiring the politicians levelling the allegations to unequivocally substantiate their claims. Although such allegations could have had some truth to them, they circulated through the media largely through descriptive reports without much analytical insight, thereby leaving the public none the wiser.

In the face of widespread claims made in a highly polarised political campaign, a fundamental question that should confront the media is how it should handle serious, unverified allegations emanating from political campaigns, whether these allegations are true or not, especially if they have grave implications for the nation.

This question seems critical when viewed against the backdrop of what happened during the post-election violence that rocked the country. Of course, seen from a long-term perspective, there would have been no reforms relating to the constitution and constitutionalism were it not for the horror of post-election violence. But in the immediate aftermath of the election, there was literally no individual or institution that could stand up as a moral voice to calm the tension and violence that was spiralling out of control. Part of the reason was, of course, that virtually the entire Kenyan citizenry and the country's institutions, including the media and religious organisations, had been sucked into the political feuds that had informed much of the political discourse during the period between 2003 and 2007. The other reason was that, led by the political class, Kenyans had been quick in labelling anybody holding a divergent view from their own as a 'traitor' or as working in the service of the differing camp – however well thought out the divergent views were. In the prevailing circumstances, perhaps many people who had the urge to speak out about the worrying situation in the country kept their thoughts to themselves for fear of being accused of belonging to one or the other political camp – a version of Noelle-Neumann's (1993) spiral of silence. Much of this labelling was communicated through the media. The media, therefore, being a critical and powerful institution in mediating public discourse, should be more keenly aware of the danger that unsubstantiated allegations, claims and conspiracies, which are reported uncritically, may pose to society in the long run, particularly during delicate moments in a nation's history.

An avenue available to broadcast media – one that relates to the manipulation of deadlines in the print media – is the stage-managing of live news coverage. Live coverage could effectively be used to insert questionable or highly controversial material into live news stories in real time in order to reach an exceptionally large captive audience. A blatant case in the 2007 general election period was that of a Mr Julius Bisen, who, in a live media broadcast on 30 December 2007, was presented at an ODM press conference as the 'returning officer' of Molo constituency, claiming that he had announced the constituency's PNU presidential candidate vote tally of 55,755, which was at variance with the 75,261 announced at the Electoral Commission headquarters at Kenyatta International Conference Centre. Mr Bisen was whisked away by ODM stalwarts immediately afterwards, before reporters could ask him questions. As reported in the *Nation* on 28 August 2008, the genuine returning officer for Molo constituency, Mr Laban Arupe Korelach, appeared before the Kriegler Independent Review Commission – which was set up to investigate the 2007 elections – and recounted how he had been queuing to make a physical presentation of Molo's results to the national tallying officials at the Electoral Commission headquarters when he heard a Mr Bisen being presented as the returning officer for Molo. This planned misrepresentation of the situation, which was carried out in the context of the tensions building up and the claims of rigged elections, definitely added fuel to the friction and violence that started around this period.

A second arena in which journalistic norms and practices can be manipulated by politicians concerns the effective and strategic use of language and symbols. 'Of particular force is the dramatic, visual symbol ... It is also possible to attract coverage by tailoring statements and events to the predispositions of the reporter or media outlet' (Jamieson and Campbell 2001: 132–6). Symbols are particularly important in visual media, such as photography and television, and may include symbolic locations, apparel, artefacts and the like. Language, for its part, can be used to manipulate coverage when it is artfully constructed and skilfully delivered in concise and dramatic statements – sound bites – that lend themselves to unedited use by the media. It is always the desire of politicians that these sound bites appear as media headlines.

In 2007, the Kenyan political parties recognised and extensively employed the strategic use of symbols to attract crowds to their rallies, as well as in media coverage. These strategies effectively offered pomp, colour and spectacle to hype the campaigns for the benefit of the live television cameras. And the competing television stations faithfully brought these spectacles to the viewers. Entertainment by musicians, political antics laced with propaganda, sharp dressing in political party regalia, traversing the country in helicopters, elaborately decorated political venues, highly choreographed political events, among countless other tricks and displays of might and glitz, constituted the menu doled out in the campaigns as politicians launched their visions and party manifestos, and held rallies and roadshows.

The print media, like the television stations, provided extensive coverage of the spectacles that attended these events, capturing them in fancy headlines and colour photographs glorifying the shows. There was also regular juxtaposition of stories and photographs of the competing candidates, re-creating boisterous battle metaphors. The following headlines taken randomly attest to this: 'Kibaki: Here I come' (*The Standard*, 1 October 2007, p. 1); 'A red blue and white affair' and 'Pomp and colour as president rolls out poll vision' (*Daily Nation*, 1 October, pp. 3 and 4 respectively); 'ODM paints the city orange' (p. 2); 'Nairobi, Nakuru in campaign frenzy' (p. 3); 'Day of thunder: "The best days of this country are not in the past. The days of this country are yet to come. They are in the future. And the future is Orange" – The pentagon team' (*The Standard*, 7 November, p. 7); 'Kibaki dangles education carrot to seduce voters' (*Daily Nation*, 3 November, p. 6); 'Bitter-sweet orange: a taste of the fruit – how ODM's harvest of technocrats, professionals, former top civil servants and experts is causing disquiet ahead of primaries' (*The Standard*, 9 November, p. 1).

With the knowledge that the hard news media prefers such dramatic presentations of news stories and the emphasis placed on the visual symbol, political campaigns are presented gleefully, taking advantage of the possibility to influence the news to their advantage through pre-packaged pseudo-events that take into account what news gatherers consider to be newsworthy. As Jamieson and Campbell (2001) argue, the ideal pseudo-event conforms to the norms of what is considered hard news. It is filled with drama and conflict, it is personalised and novel, a discrete event yet part of an ongoing theme in the news. Pseudo-events work best when timed to take place on the basis of the deadlines that the news media has to meet, and when they leave little time for any verification of the assumptions that underlie the point of view packaged by those managing the pseudo-event. A commentator observing the sensational turn that the 2007 political campaigns and their reporting in the media had taken lamented:

> A great paradox evident in Kenya's emerging democratic polity is the lack of grasp of fundamental economic issues that underpin everything else ... The majority of voters are always deeply steeped in campaign euphoria, showbiz spectacles and meaningless sloganeering and other rhetoric that have no bread and butter value (Ngugi 2007).

An additional drawback of the overemphasis on the dramatic and visual symbol in politics and its reporting is that quite a number of questions that need to be raised in such displays go unasked in the media (Louw 2010). For instance, how much did it cost to put together such spectacles? Where did the money come from? In a modest audit of money spent on the political parties' campaigns, the non-governmental organisation Coalition for Political Campaign Accountability gave an estimate in excess of 5.6 billion Kenya shillings (about US$86 million) in a report released on 23 April 2008. An earlier report published by the *Daily Nation* newspaper on 5 November 2007, under the banner 'Campaign billions', unquestioningly reported that the campaigning parties had 'set up war chests to finance the hunt for votes in readiness for poll battles'. It did not delve into the critical question about the sources of the funding, or indeed the desirability of such ostentatious displays. A further question that remained unasked was whether African states can afford to enact such showbiz politics in the face of the myriad problems that require serious political attention.

A third avenue in which politicians can, and indeed do, exploit news media routines and norms is through the understanding of the journalistic conception of the political process. The media reproduces the idea that political campaigns are contests and candidates are adversaries, and so the campaigns are reported in mainly battle metaphors. In this view, politics is seen as a bruising fight, emphasising winners and losers, divergence rather than consensus, even when divergences may be minimal. An example of such a conception was given in the *Nation* newspaper on 5 October 2007 with a subhead that read: 'President shares campaign platform with ODM pentagon William Ruto'. The sharing of a campaign platform between Kibaki and Ruto was reported as an oddity, given that the two politicians were in different political parties competing in the elections. This view ignores the fact that electoral campaigns are not meant to be a do-or-die affair between enemies. Unfortunately, and to the great detriment of nation states in Africa, this is how politics has been perceived (Ake 2002). This conception of politics also personalises what is at stake in the political process, making it seem to be a matter between individuals and parties while downplaying the fact that ideally the political process is only a means to achieving the good and the interests of the nation, not the vanquishing of political opponents. Such media reporting legitimises as the norm the notion that competing politicians should not see eye to eye, let alone share a platform.

Further examples of the media reporting campaigns as battles include the headline of a lead story that read: 'Show of might: Raila launches all-out battle for power, describing Kibaki as a failure'. Below the lead story, another headline was juxtaposed to reinforce the battle imagery: 'Kibaki digs in to stay at State House' (*Daily Nation*, 7 October 2007, p. 1). Other headlines blasted 'ODM moves to defend its turf as Kibaki casts his net for Rift Valley vote' (*Daily Nation*, 2 December 2007) and 'Raila team storms North Rift' (*The Standard*, 1 October 2007, p. 1). In another instance, the *Daily Nation* newspaper on 12 December 2007 (p. 4), reported Raila saying – apparently borrowing from Winston Churchill's declaration in World War Two – 'We shall attack the enemy from every direction. We shall launch a simultaneous attack from the land, the air and the sea until we secure victory.' This is a case of a politician using battle sound bites to describe the election process, seemingly aware that the media interprets the process in such mental frames, and thus aligning his descriptions accordingly with the knowledge that the likelihood of the sound bite being reported verbatim is almost certain.

In yet another example indicating the zero-sum game playing out in Kenya's 2007 general elections, *The Standard* on 7 December 2007 carried the headline: 'Why a win is a must: high stakes game – for Kibaki, a loss would make him the first incumbent to do so; if he doesn't win, Raila will have missed his best bet yet; if he fails, Kalonzo could be back in 2012.' The story, which was peppered with combat terms, related the reasons why the 2007 campaigns were played out using vicious propaganda, advertising blitzes and an obsession with opinion ratings. The tone of the story did not envisage the possibility of a life out of power for the two major presidential candidates, Raila and Kibaki, nor did it suggest that this was something they might countenance.

The corollary of presenting the political process as a combat is that perceived minor candidates in the process are mainly ignored and their policies, despite their merits, are also ignored. Kalonzo's case is germane here, especially his proposal to introduce a twenty-four-hour economy in the capital, Nairobi, in order to create more employment. Also relevant was the case of his public declaration of his wealth, and his proposal that other candidates do likewise – a proposal that has been resisted aggressively by the political elite although such declarations are widely acknowledged as important in stemming corruption in the public sector (see Gachigua 2012). These were potentially important campaign issues that were generally given minimal media coverage and ignored by the other major presidential campaigns.

Another effect of presenting the political process as a contest is that personal attacks rather than advocacy of policy become the defining basis of political campaigns. Policy issues in this approach are given short shrift as the dramatic and conflictual aspects are emphasised. Questions that emerge from this conception of politics include: does this notion of politics resonate with the African socio-political psyche? Does playing politics in an all-out adversarial manner not damage further the already fragile ties that make up many African societies? Does the media reporting of elections in overly antagonistic, conflictual and combative metaphors polarise fragile African societies?

Media reporting of opinion polls in Kenya's 2007 general election campaigns

In the three months before the 2007 elections, opinion polls were conducted extensively, with the media both commissioning and reporting them. Starting in late September 2007, the Steadman Group began a fortnightly poll that ran up to about eleven days before the elections. In the three months prior to the elections, the Steadman poll was almost always reported on the front pages of the two dailies under review, either as the lead story or, less often, as the second story.

The history of widely published political opinion polling in Kenya is rather brief and became both emotive and divisive in the run-up to the 2007 general elections (Kiage and Owino 2010). The first widely acknowledged political opinion polls emerged in the 2002 general elections, which rightly predicted the victory of Mwai Kibaki, the then NARC presidential candidate, and foresaw a margin of 65 per cent. The actual figure turned out to be fairly close at 62.21 per cent. The Steadman Group established its presence in opinion polling in the intervening period, most notably during the 2005 referendum on the constitutional review. After that time, the pollster affirmed its presence through a quarterly poll gauging the popularity of political players, their parties, and opinions on issues that were thought to be of concern to citizens. Critics have argued that, in concentrating on measuring the popularity of potential presidential candidates long before the elections, the polls unduly put the country in a perpetual election mood and unnecessarily fuelled competition among political players and, by extension, the communities they represented.

In addition to the Steadman Group opinion polls, Nation Media Group also commissioned a weekly opinion poll dubbed *Barometer*, which was conducted by three groups – Strategic Public Relations Research, Infotrak Harris and Consumer Insight. The results were published every Sunday; later, they appeared on Saturday, in the period between 30 September and 16 December 2007. Within this period there were also two reported polls conducted by Gallup. The first one, announced on 22 November, indicated a very tight race between the two top contenders, with Raila scoring 45 per cent, Kibaki 42 per cent and Kalonzo 11 per cent, while 1 per cent were undecided and a further 1 per cent refused to answer. The second Gallup poll, reported on 19 December, predicted a Kibaki win with 44 per cent of the vote, Raila with 43 per cent and Kalonzo at 12 per cent. A further 1 per cent was unaccounted for in the reports of both the *Daily Nation* and *The Standard*.

Philip Ochieng, a veteran *Sunday Nation* columnist, summed up the media interest in opinion polls in the following terms on 21 October (Ochieng 2007: 11):

> Whatever the political leaning of each editor, there is no way that he can ignore Mr. Steadman. For news is his stock-in-trade. And, just a few weeks to the General Election, nothing can be more 'newsworthy' than Steadman's polling figures. A commercial newspaper ignores these figures only at its own peril.

Underlying this comment is the observation that opinion polls are seen as an important attention-grabber that can offer a good storyline that will help bolster revenues, which in turn drive commercial media.

Indeed, the 2007 opinion polls consumed Kenyans' imagination as never before. The polls were the subject of heated debates among the political classes and their supporters, with those who had been rated favourably praising the polls as a 'reflection of what is on the ground', while those rated badly fervently contested the poll results or dismissed them as inconsequential. Given the interest and heat they generated, it is instructive to ask how the media treated these opinion polls? Did the media report the polls in a manner that advanced enlightened debate on the issues of the day? Could the opinion poll results have been used by interest groups and reported in a manner that would have contributed to the violence that shook the country after the 2007 elections? And, as one commentator asked (Mbugua 2007: 7): 'Are Kenyans savvy consumers of opinion polls?' In response to his question, he observed (an observation with which I concur) that 'there is a tendency in this country to view opinion poll results as an "interim election" or a "mandate from the people"'.

It is notable that, when conducted by reputable organisations in a scientific manner, opinion polls do provide a 'snapshot in time' on a particular question (Dennis and Merrill 2003: 84). However, opinion polling is not unproblematic; indeed, the conduct of the Kenyan 2007 opinion polling and reporting did raise pertinent issues. Firstly, the opinion polls and their reporting tended to personalise the campaigns, making them a dramatic popularity contest between individuals and, by extension, between the ethnic communities or coalitions of communities the presidential contestants represented. The positions and issues espoused by the candidates were given only token consideration in the polling, with reports consumed by who was ahead of whom. This was aptly captured in nearly all the opinion poll headlines, which overwhelmingly gave prominence to the ratings of the presidential candidates and very rarely, or only as a secondary issue, to policy. These headlines picked at random demonstrate this: 'Raila tips scale but Kibaki stays close', 'Raila widens gap', 'Kibaki gains two points but Raila still leads in latest opinion poll', 'Raila's third win', 'New poll shows mixed fortune for candidates', 'Kibaki narrows gap on Raila in new poll', 'The last sprint'.

Secondly, the opinion polls commissioned by the Nation Media Group, *Barometer*, despite the positive review by Kiage and Owino (2010: 312), posed some serious questions. Even though they were seemingly acknowledged by the *Daily Nation* newspaper, these questions were not addressed satisfactorily in order to offer enlightened direction. To begin with, there were quite significant disparities between the highest and lowest rating of the same candidate by the three pollsters; for instance, on 14 October 2007, the discrepancy in the rating for Raila was 8 percentage points, as was the difference for Kibaki; on 21 October, it was 9.8 percentage points for Raila and 7.2 percentage points for Kibaki; and on 11 November, it was 12.2 percentage points for Raila and 9.2 percentage points for Kibaki. There were also major discrepancies in the margins reported between the two leading candidates that should have been accounted for: for instance, on 14 October, the Strategic Public Relations Research poll reported a margin of 17 percentage points between Raila and Kibaki, Infotrak Harris gave it as 15.9 percentage points, while Consumer Insight stated that the margin was only 3 percentage points. On 21 October, Strategic Public Relations Research reported a margin of 16 percentage points between Raila and Kibaki, Infotrak Harris 21.2 percentage points, and Consumer Insight 5 percentage points. These disparities were more telling given that the same set of questions had ostensibly been asked of respondents by the three pollsters (for example, see *Sunday Nation* of 4 November 2007 – p. 13 – for an explicit statement).

There was also a revealing difference in opinion reported by the *Barometer* poll when compared with that of the Steadman Group on the controversy surrounding whether the country should adopt the *majimbo* (federal) system of government. *Majimbo* is a historically contested term (see, for instance, Anderson 2005; Odhiambo 2004; Brown 2004) but an enduring one (Anderson 2005). ODM's campaign advocated a *majimbo* system whose devolutionary structure and meaning, as reported by Anderson and Lochery (2008: 330), were 'persistently left vague', while ODM-K had a variant version dubbed 'economic *majimbo*'. However, of particular concern in this study is the way in which polling was conducted on the subject of *majimbo*. On 28 October 2007, Strategic Public Relations Research reported that 62 per cent of the people polled were in favour of *majimbo*, Infotrak Harris showed 57 per cent support, Consumer Insight had 51 per cent in favour of the system, while the Steadman Group indicated that only 44 per cent supported the adoption of *majimbo*. Given the extreme opposing passions that the *majimbo* debate generates in Kenyan politics, the fact that these varied polls showed a discrepancy between the highest and lowest reported levels of support of only 18 percentage points helped to add confusion to an already polarised discussion of the issue. It did not help matters when the same opinion polls indicated that different people had different understandings of the meaning of *majimbo*. For example, it was reported that 'a significant number were ignorant of the concept', while 'to some it meant returning land to its "original" owners'. For others it meant 'uprooting people from their land'; for yet others *majimbo* would 'come with re-allocation of land' (*Sunday Nation*, 28 October 2007, p. 13). If, then, the term *majimbo* meant different things to different people, could it have been possible to provide a common rating of support? Wouldn't it have been prudent to rate the various versions of *majimbo* separately, for example?

It would seem that the Nation Media Group was aware of the potential controversy raised by the *Barometer* polls it had commissioned, as reflected in the disclaimer printed below the poll results: 'Caution: Readers are advised that all opinion polls have a sampling error. This error is not the only source of bias.' Seemingly after the discrepancies became more stark, and possibly also because quite a number of questions could be raised regarding the commissioned polls, the media house upgraded the disclaimer from a caution to a warning, from 4 November 2007 onwards:

> Warning: Readers are advised that all opinion polls have a sampling error.
> This error is not the only source of bias in opinion polls; Readers are further
> cautioned that the *Sunday Nation* has not confirmed the accuracy of the
> findings published here. The accuracy of the data is the sole responsibility
> of the contracted polling companies. Should you have any concerns, please
> send them to Sundaynation@nation.co.ke/Saturdaynation@nation.co.ke when
> published on Saturday.

The warning carried by the Nation Media Group relating to the subsequent publication of the commissioned polls could be questioned on various accounts. To begin with, what other errors and sources of bias were to be taken into account when reading the polls? How were the readers supposed to interpret the polls? Was the warning implying that it left the responsibility of confirming the accuracy of the polls to the readers? Did the readers have the capacity to verify the findings? Was the Nation Media Group not abdicating its responsibility for investigating the accuracy of the polls, which it had taken upon itself to commission in the first place? If the accuracy of the polls seemed uncertain, of what value were they to the public? Indeed, why peg news reports to unauthenticated polls? And, more importantly, how could the polling companies be held responsible by the public? A related issue that one may raise concerns the use of disclaimers on potentially problematic or hazardous material. It has been pointed out that it is usually written in small print below the main message and, therefore, normally goes unnoticed by readers.

A third problem was that quite a number of the *Barometer* opinion polls did not provide sufficient information on the methods or procedure of the survey or give the sample questions in order to enable readers to judge the authenticity of the results. It therefore became quite problematic when the results of the polls were used to support assertions regarding campaign predictions. This was the case with, for example, a poll reported in *The Standard* on 14 December 2007, where the front page lead story read: 'Voters have decided, says opinion survey'. The story quoted pollster Infotrak Harris: 'Once again Kenyans insist they have made up their mind on who they will vote for.' The report also indicated that the new findings showed 'that most Kenyans are not ready for hereditary kind of leadership' and went on to assert that 'Kenyans have also said a thumping "No!" to a succession arrangement that would install a dynasty, with 93 per cent saying they are totally opposed to the concept'. The only background information that hinted at how the poll was conducted stated that 'at least 2,400 people were interviewed in the poll conducted between December 9 and 11, with a rural–urban split ratio of 56:44'. The colourful language used here and the scant information about the purpose of the poll made the poll questionable.

A fourth problematic issue in opinion polling in Kenya's 2007 general election campaigns concerned commentaries carried in the news sections in which some material was couched as fact but in fact sounded more like a pitch for a specific candidate. In the *Saturday Standard* (13 October 2007, p. 3), a columnist wrote, in a story following on from a Steadman opinion poll reported on the front page of the paper, which had Raila Odinga leading with a 53 per cent rating, Kibaki at 37 per cent and Kalonzo at 8 per cent:

> There are two clearly known scientific facts about political opinion polls, the world over. First, once ratings of an individual start plummeting, it is unlikely that such a politician can weave his way back to a favourable position. The

simple logic of this is that as the voting date gets closer, political players and voters want to associate with the winning side.

The columnist then offered background details on how Kalonzo Musyoka had led in the opinion polls for ten months after the referendum in 2005, Mwai Kibaki had then taken the lead from 25 July 2006 but had lost that position to Raila Odinga the previous month, 'three months away to the polls'. The columnist cited the case of the UK Prime Minister Gordon Brown and how he had lost the lead in opinion polls to the Conservatives' David Cameron, thus plunging Brown into uncertainty over calling an election for fear of the imminent loss. Although the columnist suggested that Raila's triumph in the polls was not guaranteed to translate to a victory in the actual elections, the overtones of this article seemed to leave the impression that the scientific facts alluded to were sufficient to secure Raila's triumph, and that the lessons from Gordon Brown's situation in the UK confirmed this. Bearing in mind the tendency for Kenyans, as indicated earlier, to view opinion poll results as an 'interim election' or a 'mandate from the people', this kind of commentary could prove sensitive if such predictions did not come to pass.

Some reporting of opinion polls could also be viewed as potentially inciting sentiments along ethnic lines. For instance, the *Saturday Standard* (13 October 2007, p. 2), reporting a Steadman opinion poll, wrote: 'on the negative score, 68 per cent of voters in Central Province would *never* vote for Raila, while only 43 per cent of voters in Nyanza would *not* vote for Kibaki' (italics mine). Notice the use of the negatives 'never' – denoting an extreme, permanent condition – and 'not' – a moderate, less permanent state. It is not clear what question might have been asked in order to elicit the contrasting responses offered here, nor the range of possible responses that were given. However, the media should have exercised more caution in the choice of language as it reported the polls, lest their reports aggravated ethnic hostility, given their knowledge of the ethno-political context: firstly, Central Province is predominantly composed of the Kikuyu community while Nyanza Province is predominantly Luo; secondly, the two leading presidential candidates, Kibaki and Raila, were from the two communities respectively; and thirdly, the 2007 general elections were held within an ethnically polarised atmosphere.

Conclusion

This chapter has analysed the campaign news reports in the run-up to the 2007 Kenyan elections as published in the country's two oldest and leading newspapers – the *Daily Nation* and *The Standard* – critiquing the performance of these papers against the ideal role of the media in the democratic public sphere. The analysis specifically focused on the newspapers' failure to live up to that ideal. This appraisal has been made within the context of the political environment in which the media was operating at the time. According to the perspective provided here, the media increasingly models campaign news in the form of the hard news genre, in which such news is personalised, dramatic and filled with conflict, and involves extreme physical action and emotional intensity. It is also out of the ordinary and controversial, as well as being linked to issues prevalent at the time. The motivation for structuring campaign news as hard news is that such a characterisation appeals to readers, and this appeal is desirable in order to sustain competition and media profits, which are the driving forces of media outlets operating as commercial entities in a liberalised economy.

As discussed above, this conception of news is problematic in a number of ways that undermine the ideal role of the media as an arena and actor in the public sphere. In the context of the transitions the elections were expected to facilitate, the media played a role that exacerbated tensions and made it difficult to achieve clarity on the core questions at the heart of the elections. Furthermore, I would argue that politicians' understanding of the media's hard news norms and routines allowed them to manipulate such norms in their favour. In this regard, the chapter analysed instances in which politicians in the 2007 Kenyan general election campaigns, through the engagement of media consultants and spin doctors, manipulated hard news norms to achieve the publicity they desired. In addition, some critical shortcomings in the reporting and commissioning of opinion polls by the two leading newspapers have been noted through an examination of these processes. While acknowledging that the media would not in itself have been the cause of the 2007 post-election violence, this analysis shows how media channels contributed to the polarisation of society, or, in other cases, did not do enough to steer the campaign debates in a more enlightening manner. Therefore, this study illustrates some useful lessons on how the media has the potential to undermine the promotion of public-spirited discourses in critical political moments.

At the moment, the government is hampered in fulfilling its media oversight role because of the genuine fear that most of its interventions in the past have been far from benign (see Ogola 2011). However, self-regulation and introspection by media bodies has not been very successful (Makokha 2010); for instance, despite the Media Society of Kenya resisting attempts by the government to institute a formal review of the media through claims that the body would conduct its own review, this has not happened. Furthermore, starting from the time when the major media organisations in Kenya adopted a joint editorial at the height of the post-election violence – entitled 'Save Our Beloved Country' (3 January 2008) – the media began modelling a narrative about the resolution of the escalating conflict by urging for unconditional unity, reconciliation and patriotism, and by downplaying the necessity for truth and justice and an alternative resolution of the post-election violence.

As the mediation process took off, this seemed to be the overriding narrative among the key political elite and the media. It was the same narrative that many critics view the Kenyan media as having adopted with regard to the International Criminal Court prosecution of those thought most culpable for the post-election violence, and indeed the aftermath of the contested 2013 general elections. If that is the prevailing narrative in the Kenyan media, the reasons why it is (re)produced, how this is done, and its socio-political implications in the struggle for a new political and constitutional order need to be the subject of sustained critical media scholarship.

References

Ake, C. (2002) *The Feasibility of Democracy in Africa*. Dakar: Codesria.

Anderson, D. M. (2005) 'Yours in struggle for majimbo: nationalism and the party politics of decolonization in Kenya, 1955–64'. *Journal of Contemporary History* 40(3): 547–64.

— and E. Lochery (2008) 'Violence and exodus in Kenya's Rift Valley, 2008: predictable and preventable?' *Journal of Eastern African Studies* 2(2): 328–43.

BBC World Service Trust (2008) *The Kenyan 2007 Elections and their Aftermath: The role of media and communication*. Policy Briefing No. 1. London: BBC World Service Trust.

Branch, D. and N. Cheeseman (2006) 'The politics of control in Kenya: understanding the bureaucratic–executive state, 1952–78'. *Review of African Political Economy* 33(107): 11–31.

— (2008a) 'Democratization, sequencing and state failure in Africa: lessons from Kenya'. *African Affairs* 108(430): 1–26.

— (eds) (2008b) 'Election fever: Kenya's crisis'. *Journal of Eastern Africa Studies* 2(2) (special edition).

Brown, S. (2004) 'Theorising Kenya's protracted transition to democracy'. *Journal of Contemporary African Studies* 22(3): 325–42.

Burton, G. (2002) *More Than Meets the Eye: An introduction to media studies*. 3rd edition. London: Arnold.

Dennis, E. E. (2003) 'The media influence – and often control – elections'. In E. E. Dennis and J. C. Merrill (eds) *Media Debates: Issues in mass communication*. 3rd edition. London and New York, NY: Longman, pp. 79–81.

— and J. C. Merrill (2003) 'Public opinion and the polls'. In E. E. Dennis and J. C. Merrill (eds) *Media Debates: Issues in mass communication*. 3rd edition. London and New York, NY: Longman, pp. 84–99.

Gachigua, S. G. (2012) 'Should public officers make open declarations of their wealth? Kenyan parliamentary discourse on the fight against corruption'. In J. Iwaniec and H. West (eds) *Papers from the Lancaster University Postgraduate Conference in Linguistics and Language Teaching (LAEL PG) 2011*. Volume 6. Lancaster: Department of Linguistics and English Language, Lancaster University, pp. 114–32. Available at www.ling.lancs.ac.uk/pg conference/vo6.htm.

Goldstein, J. and J. Rotich (2008) *Digitally Networked Technology in Kenya's 2007–2008 Post-election Violence*. Internet and Democracy Case Studies. Cambridge, MA: Berkman Center for Internet and Society, Harvard University.

Gripsrud, J. (2002) *Understanding Media Culture*. London: Arnold.

Jamieson, K. H. and K. K. Campbell (2001) *The Interplay of Influence: News, advertising, politics and the mass media*. 5th edition. Belmont, CA: Wadsworth.

Kevin, W. (2003) *Understanding Media Theory*. London: Arnold.

Kiage, O. and K. Owino (2010) 'History, politics and science of opinion polls in Kenya'. In K. Kanyinga and D. Okello (eds) *Tensions and Reversals in Democratic Transitions: The Kenya 2007 general elections*. Nairobi: Society for International Development and University of Nairobi, pp. 311–71.

Louw, E. (2010) *The Media and Political Process*. 2nd edition. Los Angeles, CA: Sage.

Makokha, K. (2010) 'The dynamics and politics of media in Kenya: the role and impact of mainstream media in the 2007 general elections'. In K. Kanyinga and D. Okello (eds) *Tensions and Reversals in Democratic Transitions: The Kenya 2007 general elections*. Nairobi: Society for International Development and University of Nairobi, pp. 271–308.

Mbugua, K. (2007) 'Do opinion polls inhibit choice in a democracy'. *The Standard*, 17 October.

Murunga, G. R. and S. W. Nasong'o (2006) 'Bent on self-destruction: the Kibaki regime in Kenya'. *Journal of Contemporary African Studies* 24(1): 1–28.

Ngugi, A. (2007) 'Vision 2030 neglected in campaign'. *Daily Nation*, 19 October.

Noelle-Neumann, E. (1993) *The Spiral of Silence: Public opinion – our social skin*. Chicago, IL: University of Chicago Press.

Ochieng, P. (2007) 'Why poll ratings can't be ignored'. *Sunday Nation*, 21 October.

Odhiambo, E. S. A. (2004) 'Ethnic cleansing and civil society in Kenya'. *Journal of Contemporary African Studies* 22(1): 51–79.

Ogola, G. (2009) 'Media at cross-roads: reflections on the Kenyan news media and the coverage of the 2007 political crisis'. *Africa Insight* 39(1): 58–71.

— (2011) 'The political economy of the media in Kenya: from Kenyatta's nation-building press to Kibaki's local-language FM radio'. *Africa Today* 57(3): 77–95.

Oyugi, W. (2006) 'Coalition politics and coalition governments in Africa'. *Journal of Contemporary African Studies* 24(1): 59–71.

Republic of Kenya (2008a) *Commission of Inquiry into Post-Election Violence*. Nairobi: Republic of Kenya.

— (2008b) *Independent Review Electoral Commission*. Nairobi: Republic of Kenya.

Stevenson, N. (2002) *Understanding Media Cultures*. 2nd edition. London: Sage.

wa-Mungai, M. (2010) '"Soft power", popular culture and the 2007 elections'. In K. Kanyinga and D. Okello (eds) *Tensions and Reversals in Democratic Transitions: The Kenya 2007 general elections*. Nairobi: Society for International Development and University of Nairobi, pp. 217–69.

3 | Mediating Kenya's post-election violence: from a peace-making to a constitutional moment

E. Njoki Wamai

Introduction

The mediation process led by the African Union (AU) in Kenya was initiated after the 2007–08 post-election violence. The violence was triggered by the alleged rigging of the 2007 presidential elections, and resulted in 1,133 deaths and the displacement of more than 650,000 (GoK 2008). This led to the demand for a peace-making process. As a term, peace-making was introduced into greater usage in the 1992 report *Agenda for Peace*, by the then United Nations Secretary General Boutros Boutros-Ghali. In this report the secretary general called for greater involvement of regional organisations in preventive diplomacy, peacekeeping, peace-making and post-conflict reconstruction (UN 1992). He defined peace-making as actions to bring hostile parties to an agreement, essentially through such peaceful means as those foreseen in Chapter VI of the United Nations (UN) Charter (ibid.).

Mediation is one such activity defined in Chapter VI that is carried out as part of the peace-making process to end hostilities between the antagonists and to design new governance structures that can prevent a recurrence of a similar crisis. Mediation is defined by Bercovitch as a 'process of conflict management related to but distinct from parties' own negotiations where those in conflict seek the assistance or accept an offer of help from an outsider to change their perceptions or behaviour and to do so without resorting to force or invoking authority of law' (Bercovitch et al. 1991). Mediation and negotiation in the post-conflict situation provide a transitional moment, but in this Kenyan case under study, it also provided a constitutional moment for antagonists to reorder the governance structures through the introduction of a new constitution.

The term 'constitutional moment' was popularised by Bruce Ackerman (1991) when he argued that constitutional moments in America were transformative times of political crisis in which the electorate had succeeded in effecting constitutional changes collectively as a movement through extra-constitutional means. In this respect, he argued that a 'rising political movement succeeds in placing a new problematic at the center of ... political life' (ibid.: 20). Drawing on Ackerman, this chapter defines a constitutional moment as that rare opportunity when previous forces against constitution-making converge to usher in an opportunity for the state to either revise or overhaul a constitution that cannot mediate aspirations and conflicts between different groups.

Kenya had been governed for more than four decades using the Lancaster House Constitution agreed upon in three conferences in London between 1960 and 1963. This constitution, according to Cottrell and Ghai (2007: 1–8), was premised on the protection of human rights, including those of minorities, but after several amendments to suit the Kenyatta and Moi regimes, which were increasingly authoritarian, these provisions were removed. Several civil society organisations, individual intellectuals, human rights activists and progressive parliamentarians were incarcerated by the Kenyatta and Moi regimes for agitating for the bill of rights and revision of the then draconian constitution (Mutunga 1999).

The first constitutional reforms that the government accepted were proposed by the government-led Inter-Party Parliamentary Group in 1997. This later culminated in a constitutional conference at the Bomas of Kenya which delivered the Bomas draft constitution under the chairmanship of constitutional law expert Professor Yash Pal Ghai. The Bomas draft was further amended by President Kibaki's Party of National Unity (PNU) under the leadership of the then attorney general, Amos Wako, to produce the contested Kilifi draft; this was subjected to a constitutional referendum in 2005. The draft was rejected by the electorate, bolstering political support for the 'no' campaign led by Raila Odinga of the Orange Democratic Movement (ODM). Those who rejected the draft alluded to the non-participatory nature of the post-Bomas process and they accused Kibaki of sabotaging the widely agreed Bomas draft. The constitution-making process suffered another hiatus after the referendum results of 2005. The 2008 mediation process after the post-election violence provided a ripe moment to restart a conversation about the constitution.

The Kenyan mediation was known as the Kenya National Dialogue and Reconciliation (KNDR) process. It had four mediation outcomes produced from four agenda items, including: 1) a ceasefire agreement to end the violence; 2) an agreement to support and allow for humanitarian access; 3) a political agreement to amend the constitution for power-sharing; and 4) an addressing of the structural causes of the conflict through long-term measures such as implementation of a new constitution. A new constitution was promulgated in August 2010 to address the root causes of the conflict in a number of ways: by introducing affirmative action in resource distribution to address ethnic, gender and geographic inequality; by enhancing the rule of law by reducing the powers of the executive and strengthening accountability institutions such as parliament and the judiciary; and by reducing the powers of the president and the central government by introducing devolution and encouraging public participation in governance. The chapter will focus on how the Kenyan mediation process (the KNDR) provided a constitutional moment. I argue that the Kofi Annan-led panel of eminent personalities orchestrated a constitutional moment by urging the mediation team and Kenyans at large, through parliament, to accept a constitutional amendment. This resulted in a power-sharing arrangement between former president Mwai Kibaki and the former prime minister Raila Odinga, providing another chance to jump-start the stalled constitutional reform process.

The root causes of Kenya's post-election violence

A discussion of the root causes of the post-election violence also provides both an overview of Kenya's political history and the basis of why Kenya needed a constitution that would address these causes. Scholars focusing on the background to the Kenyan crisis have pointed to several causes. These include the creation of ethnic administrative provincial boundaries by the colonial administration, which resulted in politicised ethnicity that was further encouraged by the postcolonial leadership (Oucho 2010); ethno-nationalism and diffused violence (Kagwanja 2009); diffused violence and failure to reform the security sector (Katumanga 2010; Mueller 2008); failure to deal with the land question (Kanyinga 2009; Mghanga 2010; Oucho 2010); and a centralised presidency and weak institutions, including political parties (Anyang Nyong'o 1989; Kagwanja and Southall 2009).

Kenya's first president, Jomo Kenyatta, inherited the ethnic administrative provincial boundaries and a looming land crisis in the former white highlands caused by annexing the highlands from the British (Oucho 2010: 498). Instead of reforming the flawed boundaries and land system he inherited from the British, Kenyatta skewed the system further under an imperial presidency he created after several amendments to the independence constitution. He did this to reward disproportionately his Gikuyu ethnic group, and in particular the Gikuyu elite, with *matunda ya uhuru* (fruits of independence) (see also Mueller 2008). *Matunda ya uhuru* here symbolises various socio-economic and political benefits that accrued to his cronies, such as prime land in Central, Coast and Rift Valley provinces, and political appointments and economic opportunities in government, further exacerbating horizontal inequalities between the Gikuyu and other ethnic groups (Okello and Gitau 2007; Stewart 2010); this strengthened and entrenched ethno-nationalism and political tribalism (Ajulu 2002; Leys 1975). Kenyatta is criticised for contributing to the land ownership challenges by supporting his ethnic group in acquiring land in the former Rift Valley without consultation with the locals – the Kalenjin and Maasai ethnic groups – using the 'willing buyer willing seller' slogan. This created an insider (Kalenjin) versus illegitimate outsiders (Gikuyu and others) binary on which politicians have capitalised in sponsoring violence during elections to evict the so-called 'outsiders'.

After the death of Kenyatta in 1978, his vice president, Moi, a Kalenjin, succeeded him. Moi is accused of diverting socio-economic entitlements such as infrastructure development (roads, education and healthcare provision) to his Rift Valley region (Ajulu 2002; Stewart 2010). The slogan 'It is our turn to eat' found meaning among the citizens who were convinced that the only way to access state resources was to have 'one of our own' in power. This prompted outrage from brave politicians, civil society, university students and staff. Moi responded by institutionalising repression using the security forces, who detained, tortured and assassinated any critics under the guise of 'state security' (Throup and Hornsby 1998). Internal and external pressure to reform led to the reintroduction of multiparty elections from 1992, albeit marred by state-sponsored violence resulting in the displacement of those who did not support Moi in the Rift Valley and the Coast provinces (GoK 2008: 67).

Tired of Moi's autocratic leadership, opposition parties united under one presidential candidate, Mwai Kibaki, in 2002. Moi's preferred successor lost to Mwai Kibaki, who was overwhelmingly elected on a platform to correct the horizontal inequalities between ethnic groups, reduce the powers of the president, address historical injustices, including land injustices, punish large-scale corruption and improve the economy. One of his outstanding campaign promises was a commitment to enact a new constitution within the first 100 days of his presidency in order to address these challenges.

During his first term (2002–07), Kibaki succeeded in turning around the economy, with the growth rate in GDP increasing from 0.6 per cent to 7 per cent (GoK 2007: 3). But he failed to respond to the political aspirations of Kenyans, such as delivering a new constitutional order that would punish large-scale corruption, limit presidential powers and reduce ethnic and regional inequalities (Murunga and Nasong'o 2006; Prunier 2008: 2). Prunier has asserted that, by the 2007 elections, most Kenyans were frustrated by Kibaki's politics; Odinga's ODM party easily capitalised on Kibaki's failures by invoking various types of motivation in the ODM presidential campaign (Prunier 2008: 2).

The declaration of Kibaki as the winner in the 2007 presidential election by a compromised Electoral Commission of Kenya on 30 December 2007, Odinga's refusal to concede defeat and the immediate secret swearing-in of Kibaki as the president provided the immediate trigger for the post-election violence (CCR 2014: 18). Kenya descended into anarchy as protests, riots and violence broke out nationwide, especially among ODM leadership and supporters who were outraged by what they considered electoral fraud, while PNU leadership and their supporters obstinately insisted that they had won the election fairly and Kibaki should be recognised as the president (ICG 2008: 2) The violence has since been classified in three categories: organised violence by the Kalenjin against the Kikuyu in the Kalenjin-dominated regions; retaliatory violence by the Kikuyu against other ethnic groups in Kikuyu-dominated regions; and spontaneous violence in urban centres by mainly unemployed youth (GoK 2008; Murunga 2011). Lack of a proper constitutional framework that ensured equality for all ethnic groups and equal distribution of resources (including land and economic and political appointments) only heightened the tensions that culminated in the post-election violence of 2007–08.

Mediation efforts prior to the Annan-led panel of eminent personalities

Before the Kofi Annan-led mediation process took off in February 2008, there were several attempts at mediating between Kibaki's PNU and Odinga's ODM. The first attempt was made by local mediators under the umbrella forum called Concerned Citizens for Peace. They consisted of the late Dekha Ibrahim, a renowned peace activist in Kenya, Ambassador Bethwel Kiplagat and Lazarus Sumbeiyo. These mediators had previously worked to restore peace in Somalia and Sudan. Their attempts in Kenya, however, were in vain (*East African Standard*, 12 January 2008). The next person to try was retired Archbishop Desmond Tutu from South Africa, the first international intervener; he also failed. Since Kibaki had already been declared president controversially, he was against international mediation because he saw it as an affront to his 'sovereignty', as well as to Kenya's national pride after years of mediating among its turbulent neighbours (Khadiagala 2008: 6). At the same time, external pressure to accept an AU-led mediation process increased with Gordon Brown, then British Prime Minister, British Foreign Secretary David Miliband and US Secretary of State Condoleezza Rice calling for a compromise between the two politicians that would put Kenya's interests first (*Daily Nation*, 3 January 2008).

At the regional level, a number of presidents and leaders attempted to mediate between the two: President Museveni of Uganda and the then chair of the East African Community; Colin Bruce, the World Bank country director in Kenya; and Cyril Ramaphosa, then a South African politician and business-man and the current vice president of the Republic of South Africa. However, their mediation efforts were unsuccessful due to their lack of legitimacy with the PNU and ODM parties (Khadiagala 2008: 8). In fact, President Museveni's attempts have been ridiculed as a trap designed to torpedo the Kofi Annan process, as he timed his arrival and his offer to mediate to coincide with the arrival in Nairobi of Mr Annan (Annan 2012: 191). Four other former African heads of states (Tanzania's Benjamin Mkapa, Mozambique's Joaquim Chissano, Botswana's Ketumile Masire and Zambia's Kenneth Kaunda) also joined the frantic shuttle diplomacy activity in Nairobi – but all in vain (Okello and Sihanya 2010: 675). The lack of a single legitimate authority to lead the process ensured that PNU and ODM could buy time with the different mediators.

Finally, on 15 January 2008, PNU and ODM agreed to mediation by the former UN Secretary General Kofi Annan following discussions with the then

AU chairman, and president of Ghana, John Kufuor. Despite the acceptance of international mediation, PNU continued to ignore Kofi Annan's attempts to commence discussions (*Daily Nation*, 20 January 2008). In response to this, the European Union (EU) Development Commissioner Louis Michel threatened to reduce EU aid (Okello and Sihanya 2010: 676). By mid-January, the disruption of transport networks by ethnic militias threatened to choke other economies in the region (*Africa News*, 31 January 2008), prompting Rwanda's President Kagame to suggest a military intervention if the crisis continued in order to prevent Kenya from sliding into genocide, as his country Rwanda had done in 1994 (Lindermayer and Kaye 2009: 5). Eventually the parties agreed to the Annan-led mediation panel and the process started, providing for a constitutional moment as discussed in the next section.

The Kofi Annan mediation team and creation of a constitutional moment

On 23 January 2008, Kofi Annan's three-member mediation panel, known as the 'panel of eminent personalities', began the task of resolving the conflict through a mediation process the parties called the Kenya National Dialogue and Reconciliation (KNDR) process. Apart from himself, Kofi Annan's team comprised Benjamin Mkapa, whose advantage was his familiarity as a former neighbouring president, and Graça Machel, former education minister in Mozambique and the then Kenyan Africa Peer Review Mechanism team leader, who was critical in helping the team understand the root causes of the conflict and conveying the situation of vulnerable constituencies, such as children, the displaced and women, away from the mediation table (McGhie and Wamai 2011: 10). This team largely succeeded because of the nature of the lead mediator, who had the experience (having mediated other international conflicts as the UN head), skills (strategic, manipulation and formulation), status, leverage and resources from the AU, UN and EU – and the absence of other competing centres where either protagonist could go to seek alternative support. Annan relied on the resources of the AU, EU and UN to influence the antagonists to a compromise using their expertise, sanctions and threats. Disclosing this in an interview, Annan stated:

> I came with unique skills and attributes and also the ability to pick up the phone and speak to anyone around the world. Even [George] Bush spoke to me from Tanzania next door ... That helped and they also knew that I had the entire international community behind me. It wasn't me saying that, they were the ones saying, 'We are 100 per cent behind Kofi – we support him fully.' It gave me a leverage that other mediators wouldn't have had (Griffiths 2008).

Annan's experience and skills in mediation were evident at the beginning of the process when he established three critical elements for managing it

(Khadiagala 2008: 12). The first element was ensuring that there would be only one process led by his team of eminent personalities:

> When we got there, three of the four leaders in the Africa Leaders' Forum were in town ... They thought they could stay on – they were establishing an office – to deal with the social aspects by encouraging social cohesion. And I said, 'No, I think that will lead to confusion, when you have the panel of eminent persons negotiating and three or four former heads of states leading a process that is trying to get the Kenyans to talk to each other.' ... And they understood, so they left town (Griffiths 2008: 4).

The second element that underpinned the mediation process was deliberate consultation with groups away from the mediation table through regular meetings, and using the media to inform the wider public of progress (Baldauf 2008). These groups included the business community, civil society, youth, women and religious leaders (Kenyan Women's Consultation Group on the Kenyan Crisis 2009). The third element Annan devised was the use of a two-prong mediation strategy, with the principals (Raila Odinga and Mwai Kibaki) on the one hand, and, on the other, the eight PNU and ODM negotiators appointed by the principals as the main mediation team (Khadiagala 2008: 12). The two principals were engaged only intermittently as Kofi Annan worked full time with the eight negotiators. This strategy was critical to salvaging the talks when they hit a deadlock later. Communications at a higher level during a negotiation are decisive because heads of state or other senior officials are likely to bring commitments, set agendas and reach agreements faster than the negotiators (CCR 2014; Mwagiru 2008). Annan and his team of mediators and experts also guided the negotiators to agree on the mediation process. They were directed collectively by four agenda items discussed below.

Agenda items 1 and 2: Ending violence and addressing humanitarian access
These two agenda items (ending the violence and addressing humanitarian access) were agreed upon by both the PNU and ODM sides immediately, since it was clear by early January 2008 that the state and its organs no longer had the monopoly of violence; violence was continuing to spread, making areas in the former Rift Valley, Nyanza and Coast provinces ungovernable (Kofi Annan Foundation 2009).

> Both parties had agreed very quickly on the need to address the humanitarian situation and to take measures to end the violence, despite their disagreements on the political issues. That had been particularly important in giving the people confidence to lay down their weapons and in creating a space for dialogue (ibid.: 10).

By then, ethnic militias allegedly sponsored by PNU and ODM officials had emerged and were violating civil liberties and creating no-go areas. The consequences of the alleged involvement of political leaders lies behind the ongoing trials of President Uhuru Kenyatta and his deputy, William Ruto, at the International Criminal Court following their indictment by the same court.

Agenda item 3: Resolving the political crisis using a constitutional amendment This was the most difficult and lengthy agenda item due to a stalemate when the parties failed to agree on how to resolve the political crisis. ODM and PNU could not agree on a way forward that would end the crisis, because both sides believed that they had won the elections and neither party could allow the other to form the government. The mediation team presented a number of options out of the crisis that were considered, such as re-tallying of the votes and fresh elections, but these were untenable due to the divisions among the Kenyan people at that time. Kofi Annan has reported in an interview that he proposed a power-sharing agreement through a constitutional amendment, hoping that both sides would agree since it presented the best compromise.

> I had come to an early conclusion that a rerun would be a bad decision, and bad decisions get more people killed. Enough had been killed already, and in that environment any kind of election was going to be acrimonious and was going to get people killed. So I felt that we needed to find a way of dealing with the disagreement over the election by looking forward, and not trying to rerun, repeat or something that would not give you the result you want, but may also get people killed. And when looking at the election results, it was clear to me that there was no way that either party could run the government effectively without the other. So some type of partnership/coalition was going to be necessary (Griffiths 2008).

The eight PNU and ODM negotiators he was working with refused for days to agree to this proposal, which would allow Raila Odinga to become an executive prime minister after a constitutional amendment. The PNU side was opposed to the position of a prime minister unless the prime minister position was non-executive, meaning that he would be a ceremonial head without much power in government. This stalemate threatened to trigger more violence and prompted Annan to insist that he would stay until a sustainable deal had been reached, because peace in Kenya was important. 'I will stay as long as it takes to get the issue of a political statement to an irreversible point. I will not be frustrated or provoked to leave ...' (*Daily Nation*, 16 February 2008).

Drawing on his mediation skills, status and leverage, Annan abandoned the negotiators at the mediation table to consult groups away from the table using the two-prong strategy discussed earlier. He informed the media about the state of the talks and the challenges he received from the negotiating team, and he focused on convincing Kibaki, who was already president, why

73

a constitutional amendment to allow for an executive prime minister was the best way out of the crisis. Kibaki finally agreed to this after further persuasion by the incoming AU chairman, Jakaya Kikwete, the president of Tanzania. Annan's next task was to convince parliament to introduce an amendment to the constitution that allowed for an executive prime minister. The Kenyan parliament, conscious of the situation, unanimously agreed to amend the constitution in record time to allow for the position of an executive prime minister with two deputies. PNU and ODM would share power on a fifty-fifty basis under the National Accord and Reconciliation Act, which reduced the tension that had been growing greatly. As the BBC reported, 'the legal changes will be greeted with a huge sense of relief by millions of Kenyans' (*BBC News*, 18 March 2010). This amendment led to a constitutional moment by providing for a coalition government that could initiate the reform process through a constitutional overhaul, since the two main rival parties were now in government.

Agenda item 4: Addressing long-term issues Although the flawed elections had been the immediate cause of violence, it was widely agreed that the root causes were long-term political, social and economic issues that could be resolved only through an overhaul of the constitution. The constitutional amendment discussed earlier ensured that ODM and PNU were in the same government with sufficient goodwill to ensure the constitutional review process was started and completed, since both parties in the coalition did not want to be blamed for failing the process. A Committee of Experts on the constitution was appointed to lead the process of review and a referendum was successfully carried out, leading to promulgation of the new constitution on 20 August 2010. Other reforms which were agreed upon included: electoral reforms, judicial reform, security sector reform, land ownership reform and addressing youth unemployment but the constitution was considered most fundamental in addressing the governance crisis and ending impunity.

Lessons learned from the Kenyan mediation process for constitution-making

The Kenyan mediation process was unique. Indeed, it has been touted as the first successful implementation of 'Responsibility to Protect'. Attempts to replicate it in Zimbabwe and Syria, however, came to naught. Thus, while the lauding of its success might be a little too excessive, the process has a number of lessons worth concluding this chapter with.

Keep the mediation process separate from the constitution-making process Past experience of constitution-making and peace-building by the United Nations Development Programme (UNDP 2003) demonstrates that when negotiations on a peace agreement are conflated with constitution-making processes, more often than not the principles of constitution-making are compromised. For instance, the peace processes in Bosnia Herzegovina (1995) and Zimbabwe (1980) conducted the two processes simultaneously, further entrenching the divisions between the warring parties in the new constitution. As a result, the constitutions they made lacked the capacity to ensure sustainable peace and the countries are currently in the process of revising these constitutions. Discussing the right time for constitution-making, Ludsin (2011: 241) and Samuels (2005) warn against combining constitutional drafting with peace-making processes because of the differing goals they each have. Samuels concludes that the drafting of a new constitution should wait for more peaceful, secure and stable times.

It is therefore advisable for the two processes to be separated, as in the Kenyan peace-making process in 2008 and a separate constitution-making process led by the Committee of Experts in 2009. In the Kenyan case, minimum conditions for constitution-making were already guaranteed since agenda items 1, 2 and 3 had been implemented; this allowed for negotiations on constitution-making to proceed separate from the mediation process. The importance of constitutional experts being present during the mediation process to advise the mediation team on various aspects cannot be overemphasised. Indeed, this was a critical part of the Kenyan mediation process, which involved experts on mediation and constitutional review.

Identify constitutional moments during a peace process A constitutional moment arises when all previous forces against the constitution-making process converge to deliver a constitution. Mediated peace-making presents opportunities for reconciliation and for addressing long-term issues, and a deft mediation team should take advantage of this opportunity to convince the warring parties of the need for a constitution-making process while orchestrating occasions that force the antagonists to work together for peace, as in the Kenyan case.

Emergence of a constitutional moment within peace-making is dependent on the confluence of various factors. First, there must be an agreement between the warring parties on the need for a new constitution as a way out of the crisis. Second, mediators must have a level of engagement with other stakeholders away from the mediation table. Ensuring that other parties outside the warring factions, such as civil society, have an opportunity to engage with the mediation team is critical in ushering in a constitutional moment. The Kenyan public and civil society, including the business community and religious groups, were significant in reminding the mediation team of the need for a constitution process to address the structural causes of violence. Third, the Kenyan parliament was, by force of circumstances, committed to a revision of the constitutional order, judging by its speedy action to amend the constitution for power-sharing when the National Accord and Reconciliation Act was passed in record time without disagreements.

The nature of the mediation team is critical for a constitutional moment The mediator's understanding of the root causes of a crisis is important in encouraging the conflicting parties to allow a settlement and a constitutional moment. Kofi Annan's team was comprised of three elders who had the benefit of international experience in peace-making and an understanding of Kenyan political history. In addition to a great understanding of the Kenyan crisis, the mediation team had the resources to hire constitutional experts from the AU, UN, EU, think tanks and local academics. This included, for instance, Hans Corell, the former legal counsel of the UN, and Margaret Vogt, then deputy director of the Africa I Division in the UN Department of Political Affairs, and think tanks such as the Centre for Humanitarian Dialogue. They advised the team on how to orchestrate ripe moments and convince the parties of the need for a new constitution at critical junctures.

Conclusion

This chapter has argued that the Kofi Annan-led panel of eminent personalities orchestrated a constitutional moment by ensuring that Kenyan political leaders accepted a constitutional amendment that allowed for power-sharing, guaranteeing support for a new constitution. This chapter has traced the background to the mediation process of Kenya's post-independence regimes, and further examined the efforts made by various actors before and during the process to rescue Kenya from the brink.

However, despite the success of the Kenyan government in delivering a new constitution in 2010, that constitution has been mutilated through various amendments by the former and current parliament due to the leadership's lack of political will to implement it. The Kenyan constitutional process has suffered from an absence of mechanisms to ensure full compliance with the provisions of the promulgated constitution. More vigilance from citizens is called for to ensure the implementation of Kenya's new constitution, a product of the mediation process and one that promises to address the root causes of Kenya's nationhood crisis.

Finally, this chapter, like others in the study, recognises that constitution-making processes are complex and unique, and the Kenyan case study cannot define the generic conditions that can guarantee success in capturing constitutional moments during a peace-making process. This is merely an attempt to understand the relationship between Kenya's peace-making process and the emergence of a subsequent constitutional process.

References

Ackerman, B. (1991) *We the People. Volume 1: Foundations*. Cambridge, MA: Harvard University Press.

Ajulu, R. (2002) 'Politicised ethnicity, competitive politics and conflict in Kenya: a historical perspective'. *African Studies* 61(2): 251–68.

Annan, K. (2012) *Interventions: A life in war and peace*. London: Penguin Books.

Anyang Nyong'o, P. (1989) 'State and society in Kenya: the disintegration of the nationalist coalitions and the rise of presidential authoritarianism, 1963–78'. *African Affairs* 88(351): 229–51.

Baldauf, S. (2008) 'After two months of discourse, finally a handshake'. *Christian Science Monitor*, 8 August. Available at www.csmonitor.com/World/Africa/2008/0808/p25s04-woaf.html (accessed 11 July 2011).

Bercovitch, J., J. T. Anagnoson and D. L. Wille (1991) 'Some conceptual issues and empirical trends in the study of successful mediation'. *Journal of Peace Research* 28(1): 7–17.

CCR (2014) *Towards a New Pax Africana: Making, Keeping, and Building Peace in Post-Cold War Africa*. Seminar Report 46. Cape Town: Centre for Conflict Resolution (CCR), pp. 18–19.

Cottrell, J. and Y. Ghai (2007) 'Constitution making and democratization in Kenya (2000–2005)'. *Democratization* 14(1): 1–25.

GoK (2007) *Kenya Vision 2030: A globally competitive and prosperous Kenya*. Nairobi: Kenya Vision 2030. Available at www.opendata.go.ke/download/jih3-amby/application/pdf (accessed 11 August 2014).

— (2008) *Commission of Inquiry into Post-Election Violence Report*. Nairobi: Government Printers.

Griffiths, M. (2008) *Interview: The prisoner of peace. An interview with Kofi A. Annan*. Geneva: Centre for Humanitarian Dialogue.

ICG (2008) *Kenya in Crisis*. Africa Report 137. Brussels: International Crisis Group (ICG). Available at www.crisis group.org/en/regions/africa/horn-of-africa/kenya/137-kenya-in-crisis.aspx (accessed 11 August 2014).

Kagwanja, P. (2009) 'Kenya's uncertain democracy: the electoral crisis of 2008'. *Journal of Contemporary African Studies* 27(3): 365–87.

— and R. Southall (2009) 'Introduction: Kenya – a democracy in retreat?' *Journal of Contemporary African Studies* 27(3): 259–77.

Kanyinga, K. (2009) 'The legacy of the White Highlands: land rights, ethnicity, and post-2007 election violence in Kenya'. *Journal of Contemporary African Studies* 27(3): 325–44.

Katumanga, M. (2010) 'Militarized spaces and the post 2007 electoral violence'. In K. Kanyinga and D. Okello (eds) *Tensions and Reversals in Democratic Transitions: The Kenyan 2007 general elections*. Nairobi: Society for International Development and Institute for Development Studies, University of Nairobi, pp. 533–65.

Kenyan Women's Consultation Group on the Kenyan Crisis (2009) 'Women's memorandum to the mediation team' in *Pambazuka News*, issue 340. Available at www.pambazuka.org/en/category/comment/45740 (accessed 20 May 2011).

Khadiagala, G. (2008) 'Forty days and nights of peacemaking in Kenya'. *Journal of African Elections* 7(2): 4–32.

Kofi Annan Foundation (2009) *The Kenya National Dialogue and Reconciliation: One year later. Geneva, 30–31 March 2009: Report of the meeting*. Geneva: Kofi Annan Foundation. Available at http://kofiannanfoundation.org/sites/default/files/KA_KenyaReport%20Final.pdf (accessed 18 April 2014).

Leys, C. (1975) *Underdevelopment in Kenya: The political economy of neo-colonialism, 1964–1971*, London: Heinemann.

Lindermayer, E. and J. Kaye (2009) *A Choice for Peace? The story of 41 days of mediation in Kenya*. New York, NY: International Peace Institute.

Ludsin, H. (2011) 'Peacemaking and constitution-drafting: a dysfunctional marriage'. *University of Pennsylvania International Law Journal* 33(1): 239–311.

McGhie, M. P. and N. Wamai (2011) *Beyond the Numbers: Women's participation in the Kenyan mediation process*. Geneva: Centre for Humanitarian Dialogue.

Mghanga, M. (2010) *Usipoziba Ufa Utajenga Ukuta: Land, elections, and conflicts in Kenya's Coast Province*. Nairobi: Heinrich Boll Foundation.

Mueller, S. D. (2008) 'The political economy of Kenya's crisis'. *Journal of Eastern African Studies* 2(2): 185–210.

Murunga, G. R. (2011) *Spontaneous or Premeditated? Post-election violence in Kenya*. Discussion Paper 57. Uppsala: Nordic Africa Institute.

— and S. W. Nasong'o (2006) 'Bent on self-destruction: the Kibaki regime in Kenya'. *Journal of Contemporary African Studies* 24(1): 1–28.

Mutunga, W. (1999) *Constitution-making from the Middle: Civil society and transition politics in Kenya, 1992–1997*. Nairobi and Harare: SAREAT and MWENGO.

Mwagiru, M. (2008) *'The Water's Edge': Mediating violent electoral conflict in Kenya*. Nairobi: University of Nairobi.

Okello, D. and M. J. Gitau (2007) *Readings on Inequality: Sectoral dynamics and perspectives*. Nairobi: Society for International Development.

Okello, D. and B. Sihanya (2010) 'The constitutional politics of Kenya's post elections mediation process'. In K. Kanyinga and D. Okello (eds) *Tensions and Reversals in Democratic Transitions: The Kenyan 2007 general elections*. Nairobi: Society for International Development, pp. 653–704.

Oucho, J. (2010) 'Undercurrents of post election violence in Kenya: issues in the long-term agenda'. In K. Kanyinga and D. Okello (eds) *Tensions and Reversals in Democratic Transitions: The Kenyan 2007 general elections*. Nairobi: Society for International Development, pp. 491–533.

Prunier, G. (2008) 'Kenya: roots of crisis'. *openDemocracy*. Available at www.opendemocracy.net/article/democracy_power/kenya_roots_crisis (accessed 21 May 2011).

Samuels, K. (2005) 'Post-conflict peacebuilding and constitution-making'. *Chicago Journal of International Law* 6(2): 663–82.

Stewart, F. (2010) 'Horizontal inequalities in Kenya and the political disturbances of 2008: some implications for aid policy'. *Journal of Conflict, Security and Development* 10(1): 37–41.

Throup, D. and C. Hornsby (1998) *Multiparty Politics in Kenya: The Kenyatta and Moi states and the triumph of the system in the 1992 election*. London: James Currey.

UN (1992) *Agenda for Peace*. New York, NY: United Nations (UN).

UNDP (2003) *Constitution-making and Peace Building: Lessons learned from the constitution-making processes of post-conflict countries*. New York, NY: United Nations (UN).

4 | Instrumentalism and constitution-making in Kenya: triumphs, challenges and opportunities beyond the 2013 elections

Raymond Muhula and Stephen Ndegwa

Introduction

On 5 August 2010 Kenya adopted a new constitution, the culmination of various campaigns over nearly two decades. The serious efforts to change the colonial era constitution started with the transition to democracy that was launched in 1990 and led to the multiparty elections of December 1992. The now discredited independence constitution crafted at Lancaster House, United Kingdom, on the eve of Kenya's independence from British colonial rule in 1963 had been amended nearly thirty times, establishing a legal matrix that severely constrained dissent and sustained authoritarian rule spanning nearly five decades. The 2010 constitution, a product of varied processes, themselves contentious (but all radically different from the elite negotiation under British tutelage), promises a sharp departure from the imperial characteristics of its predecessor. It both reflects and continues a transformation of the state–society compact since independence. It has a far-reaching bill of rights, provides for a devolved system of government, dissolves the provincial administration (a notoriously heavy-handed executive machinery linked to the presidency), and provides for a bicameral parliament. It has been compared with the 1996 South African constitution in its 'progressiveness'. For example, it mandates the protection of minorities, and guarantees parliamentary seats for women, the youth and the disabled.

In this chapter we seek to explain the success – i.e. the eventual completion – of the review and promulgation of the constitution in 2010. We examine both the immediate instrumentality of politics (pact-making) and the shift in structural conditions that enabled change. We argue that the resulting 2010 constitution was the result of intense elite pact-making and shifting positions in response to the political conditions of the day. We offer this Kenyan example as a lesson to enhance our understanding of the nature of political change – in particular, the tension between sharp breaks versus incremental change. Especially, we underscore the significance of intermediate events in the interregnum before changes are openly observable, a period of incomplete transition that often attracts pejorative adjectives that tend to be static and do not help us understand change.

Political activity in Kenya is usually explained in terms of ethnic dominance (for example, Ghai and Cottrell 2013; Ndegwa 1997). Yet, unpacking the ethnic argument reveals that a distinctive feature of Kenyan politics is the resilience of pact-making as an immutable part of the country's political life. Pact-making is as old as the Kenyan state – starting with the decision of the leadership of the Kenya African Democratic Union (KADU) to dissolve and join the Kenya African National Union (KANU) party in 1964. In the 1990s there were similar pacts: the Inter-Parties Parliamentary Group dialogues that led to minimum reforms in the constitution; the decision of Raila Odinga's National Develop-ment Party to enter into a working agreement to support KANU – thereby giving the ruling party a numerical advantage over the opposition; and the much referenced memorandum between Raila Odinga and Mwai Kibaki be-fore the 2002 elections which ended KANU rule and brought Kibaki to power under the National Alliance Rainbow Coalition (NARC). More recently, pact-making has led to a coalescing of political parties into two major political alliances – on the one hand, the Jubilee Coalition – bringing together Uhuru Kenyatta's The National Alliance (TNA) and William Ruto's United Republican Party (URP), and helping the pair win the 2013 presidential elections – and, on the other, the Coalition for Reforms and Democracy (CORD), which brings together three major political parties under the leadership of Raila Odinga, including the Orange Democratic Movement (ODM), FORD-Kenya and Wiper Democratic Party. Most of these pacts have not been without reversals, yet they have demonstrated the tugs and pulls that are characteristic of Kenyan politics, a trait that also influenced the behaviour of key actors during the constitution-making process.

Framing the debate: pact-making and transition politics

The literature of democratisation is replete with cases of pact-making in processes of democratic transition. These are the formal and informal pro-cesses that shape debates and help key protagonists arrive at a settlement on important questions on a political issue, such as representation, boundaries and coalition formation, among others. O'Donnell and Schmitter (1986) define pacts as:

> explicit, but not always publicly explicated or justified, agreements among a select set of actors which seeks to define (or better, to redefine) rules governing the exercise of power on the basis of mutual guarantees for the 'vital interests' of those entering into it.

Further, O'Donnell (1989) refers to pacts as agreements between incumbents and opposition actors. Notwithstanding this highly laudatory endorsement of pact-making in resolving political grievances, a section of the literature is also critical of the dampening effects of pacts on the democratic process (for example, O'Donnell and Schmitter 1986). Hagopian (1990), for instance, suggests that pacts undermine majority rule as they give voice to only the key actors engaged in making them. More importantly, as observed by Przeworski (1991), while pacts may protect emerging democratic institutions by reducing immediate conflict, they may also exact a long-term burden on emerging democracies. This is largely because of the tendency of such arrangements to exclude others and create a monopoly of a few key actors in the democratic process – thus excluding the rest of the society. These negative sentiments regarding pacts are well described by O'Donnell and Schmitter (1986) thus: pacts 'tend to reduce competitiveness as well as conflict; they seek to limit accountability to wider publics; they attempt to control the agenda of policy concerns; and they deliberately distort the principle of citizen equality' (ibid.). Recent works (such as Jamal 2010) find that inclusive political settlements have important positive effects on building representative political institutions. Additionally, Encarnación (2003) finds no evidence suggesting that pact-making 'either slowed the transition or undermined the quality of the emerging democracy' (ibid.).

We argue that the product that is the 2010 Kenyan constitution was the outcome of the contentious engagement of reform advocates and organic political processes, as well as formal debates guided by parliament and the national apparatus on constitutional reform. In the process, there were gains and losses, occasional exclusion and even subversion of other key players, yet, in spite of these tugs and pulls, emerging windows of opportunity were exploited to support the development and conclusion of the 2010 constitution. Following on from earlier works on the democratic transition debate, notably Sklar (1996), we argue that in contested political environments that are usually generated by constitution-making, institutional reforms tend to be negotiated and largely depend on instrumentalist framing and windows of opportunity (McAdam et al. 2001; Sklar 1996). We therefore call for an approach that recognises the developmental nature of such reforms (democracy in parts), rather than a focus on 'lack' and 'deficits'. In this argument, we are also influenced by the literature on contentious politics that seeks to locate popular participation – windows of opportunity and framing – as important aspects of political participation (see Giugni et al. 1998; Ibarra 2003; McAdam et al. 2001; Tarrow 1998). This literature acknowledges, much like Sklar's 'developmental democracy', the protracted nature of political processes, such as democratisation and constitution-making, principally because claims made in the name of these processes may threaten certain interests (McAdam et al. 2001). We argue further that the culmination of the constitutional reform movement in Kenya provides a useful opportunity to restate the need for caution in how analysts evaluate the performance of recent democratic transitions in Africa and elsewhere.

Thus, in the case of Kenya, despite the near consensus on the negative aspects of pact-making, the potential of pacts to move processes of constitution-making forward has emerged as the single most important contributor to the emergence of a new constitutional dispensation. This is not to say that the final product was flawless, but it recognises that in highly contested issues such as constitution-making, it is inconclusive to assign success to a single path, nor is it analytically useful to view these processes in terms of what is missing. Rather, as the case of Kenya suggests, there is a need to appreciate the value of cumulative processes of change and counter-change, of progress and reversals, and of viewing the final products as another stop in the evolution of credible institutional governance architecture.

Pact-making and promulgation of the 2010 constitution

Given the two-decade attempt to change the constitution in order to align the political apparatus with the post-1992 dispensation, it is important to explain why this effort succeeded in 2010 but not in previous periods, and especially in 2005 when a referendum on a draft constitution was conducted. Regardless of the debates and pretence around 'people-driven' processes of constitution-making, we suggest, first, that constitutions are essentially elite compacts. As such, the interesting question is why the elite were able and willing to compromise in 2010 but not earlier. We offer three reasons: first, the failure of the initial attempts to remove Moi from power in 1992 and then in the 1997 election. Although the latter ushered in a new dispensation of multipartyism, it failed to bring the expected democratic reforms, largely because opposition politicians were pulling in opposite directions, including on the question of constitutional reforms. This provided important lessons that would become useful in the later years of strategising for constitutional reform. Second, opportunities were missed during Mwai Kibaki's first term, during which time instrumentalist grandstanding led to delays in producing the new constitution. And, finally, there was the jolting effect of the post-election violence of 2008 (see also Chapter 3).

The violence stemmed directly from the nature of the existing constitution, which promoted a 'winner takes all' mentality and supported the unequal distribution of the national wealth (Muhula 2009). The violence was thus a result of disenchantment with the immediate electoral cheating overlain by deep discontent about marginalisation, brutalisation, and exclusion by the state and the narrow band of elites capturing it. The violence reflected the extent to which citizens had lost confidence in the incumbent state elites and in the regime's ability to represent and mediate between popular interests, allocate resources fairly, and act as the guardian of a representative republic. The only way to restore this confidence would be through constitutional reforms.

Second, as argued previously, the rancorous Kenyan elite are in fact given to pact-making (even if their pacts are only temporarily stable) more than to violent ruptures that would threaten a break-up of their collective privilege. From this perspective, the violence of 2007–08 was an aberration, resolved once again by a pact. Third, the negotiated end to the violence reasserted pact-making as the principal instrument of credible commitment among elites. This was underscored by the codification of the pact in the National Accord and Reconciliation Act of 2008, which also gave renewed impetus to the constitutional reform movement. We discuss each in turn.

Multipartyism without democracy: the elections of 1992 and 1997

The repeal of section 2(A) of the 1963 Kenyan constitution (as previously amended) to legalise the formation of political parties other than KANU in 1991 introduced a new era of competitive politics. The subsequent elections in 1992 and 1997, which KANU won, forced the pro-democracy forces to reassess their strategies for dislodging the former single party from power. In the run-up to both elections, political actors had been confident that only minimum reforms in the constitutional structure – basically allowing competing parties in 1992 and allowing some electoral changes in 1997 – were required to usher in a new dispensation within which they would prevail. They subsequently relaxed the push for major political reforms, which would have included the overhaul of the constitution, and agreed to reforms that were based on agreements outside parliament and sometimes, but not always, written into law. In both cases, the pursuit of electoral success – after which, it was hoped, the full dispensation would be amended via political practice rather than by constitutional prescription – failed to produce fundamental change. By 1997, even though calls for a new constitution had been intensifying in the interim, parliament agreed to basic reforms to level the playing field for the upcoming elections that year but not to adopt a new constitution. A political pact, the so-called Inter-Parties Parliamentary Group agreement, allowed the elections of 1997 to proceed, but did little to transform the institutional architecture of a basically authoritarian state run by the former single party.

After losing a second time in 1997, the opposition's lack of unity delayed the process of political reform and the attainment of a new political order.[1] This outcome, however, ignited even greater reform fervour among the public, moving both civil society and the political opposition to view constitutional reform as a prerequisite for change. The opposition parties, civil society and ordinary citizens continued to demand fundamental political reforms in the form of a new constitution, and eventually forced parliament to enact the Constitution of Kenya Review Act of 2000 to formally institute a process for writing a new constitution. The act provided for the collection of views nationwide through a travelling commission, the creation of the National Constitutional Conference to debate these views and to draft the constitution, and a subsequent referendum.

The ensuing manoeuvring after the formal commencement of this process has been documented elsewhere (for example, Cottrell and Ghai 2007; Diepeveen 2010). Nevertheless, it is worth emphasising the level of resistance that encumbered the process and demonstrated how reluctant the political elites were to facilitate a process that would upend the old older. By this time, even though it was clear that incumbent President Daniel Moi would not run, having served his second and final term, it was anticipated that, as chairman of KANU, he would still have influence over the next president, and over the government of that president. It did not help that among the proposals in the new constitution were: the possibility of recalling non-performing members of parliament (MPs); the likelihood of a new election as soon as a new constitution was adopted (thus cutting short Moi's own tenure and that of all MPs); and the possibility of a truth commission to investigate political and economic crimes, presumably since independence.

The Moi administration, extremely wary of the far-reaching proposals of the reform movement, was rightly convinced that any document coming out of this process would not be friendly to its interests as the incumbent or to those of its allied groups. It, therefore, sabotaged the process through procedural and logistical hindrances from the start. Unable to put a stop to it, Moi finally used presidential authority provided by the constitution to prorogue parliament in late October 2002, a few days before the National Constitutional Conference at Bomas of Kenya started the final discussions on the draft that would end up in parliament for review and passage and would hence structure the forthcoming elections. Not only were MPs now rendered ineligible to participate at Bomas by Moi's order, the government also sent police to guard the assembly hall when members insisted on attending to continue with deliberations. That put an end to the quest for a new constitution, at least temporarily.

However, the machinations of the incumbent were only partially to blame for the evasive tactics in the process of change. The last term of President Moi also gave the principal presidential contenders in the opposition little interest in weakening the centre of power that was now clearly within their reach. Given the presidential term limit, Moi (who had an unmatched, decades-old patronage network and a provincial administration loyal to the incumbent) was no longer a candidate and the principal contenders – Raila Odinga, Mwai Kibaki, Uhuru Kenyatta and Charity Ngilu – could imagine success. For example, Raila Odinga's recruitment into KANU before being bypassed for Uhuru Kenyatta as Moi's anointed heir – which itself triggered a new momentum for the opposition to unite under the one candidacy of Mwai Kibaki – provided an important window of opportunity for reform-minded politicians to influence Moi's decisions and, eventually, KANU's implosion. The unified opposition candidacy – long held as the only way to defeat KANU – was entirely a utilitarian and ethnically calculated agreement to create a winning coalition, rather than the result of a conjoining of coherent ideas or ideologies, much less a constitutionalist vision. An example of the pact-making at the peak of elite politics, documented in a memorandum of understanding (MoU) (never made public), this agreement for a unified candidacy allowed the opposition to prevail in the 2002 elections. The breakdown of this MoU provided the seed for the three ensuing conflicts that saddled the new coalition government: disagreement over parity between principals to the pre-election MoU (Ngilu and Odinga) and the post-election president (Kibaki); the division of government ministries among followers of each principal; and corruption within the ranks of the Democratic Party, the party that most squarely captured state power by assuming the presidency on behalf of NARC.

Regime transition without change: the NARC and Kibaki election of 2002

NARC, the multiparty coalition that swept to power with a landslide victory over KANU to make Mwai Kibaki Kenya's third president, campaigned on a reform platform. Chief among the immediate reforms that NARC promised was the completion of the constitution-making process within the first 100 days of the party coming to power. After years of stalled transition, Kenyans were hopeful that the process of enacting a new constitution would begin afresh, with a new team, a new dispensation, and a positive conclusion. The NARC government was an amalgam of characters and interests that had only occasionally converged in the decade-long reform movement: Mwai Kibaki, Raila Odinga, Kiraitu Murungi, Anyang' Nyong'o, Kivutha Kibwana and Charity Ngilu, to name a few iconic and somewhat representative figures of the reform streams and ethnic composition that emerged between 1992 and 2002. Having passed the electoral threshold and now occupying state power under the extant constitution, interests shifted. Soon, the clash of those interests, asymmetrical expectations and sectarian concerns would combine to derail the reform process, undermine the unity of the coalition and extinguish the hopes for a new constitution.

The emergence of a new anti-reform group within the newly incumbent coalition was first evident during the election of the chairman of the parliamentary select committee (PSC) on the constitution, the committee that would guide the promised constitution change effort. Raila Odinga, a key member of the coalition who had been chair of the PSC in the outgoing parliament, hoped to be re-elected following parliamentary tradition and given his status as a principal partner in NARC. This was not to be the case, as the election became so personalised that even members of his NARC coalition voted against him, eventually handing the chairmanship to Paul Muite, a member of the opposition party, Safina. More significantly, the government repeatedly plotted to take over the review of the constitution through an expert team that would circumvent popular participation through the National Constitutional Conference. At the same time, parliament was keen to stamp its authority on the new constitution, preferring to debate and pass it without a referendum – contrary to what several of the new MPs had argued for before ascending to parliament. Both attempts, including repeated court-induced delays, were defeated by a more resolute civil society, a more energised reform lobby within parliament, and a new chairman of the Constitution of Kenya Review Commission, Professor Yash Pal Ghai, who insisted that he would take his position only once consensus on the process was achieved among the contending groups.

It was not lost to observers that as early as 2004 the next elections in 2007 were now foremost in the minds of major players, and no card was too small to play. Key political players in President Kibaki's team, among whom were some Moi-era reform stalwarts such as Kiraitu Murungi, Martha Karua and Kivutha Kibwana – seemingly ironically, yet quite consistent with our argument of instrumentalist behaviour – opposed the very ideas they had supported while in opposition or in civil society. The emerging divide revolved around those for the parliamentary system of government led by Raila Odinga, and those firmly supporting a presidential system, the Kibaki-friendly team led by Justice Minister Kiraitu Murungi. Thus, grandstanding became the defining characteristic of the constitution-making process, with pro-Kibaki allies focused on blocking provisions that were deemed favourable to Raila Odinga and vice versa.

The hardening of positions continued for most of the time, with delegates aligned to the government trying every trick to derail the process, especially when it became clear that the majority of the delegates preferred the parliamentary system. For many in government (i.e. the rump NARC, essentially the old Democratic Party), the feeling was that this position would favour Raila Odinga in the very immediate future. This was exacerbated by the acrimony surrounding the pre-election MoU between Odinga and Kibaki, in which the latter was accused of reneging on his undertaking to support the creation of the post of prime minister for Odinga. It was therefore not surprising when the government side, led by Kiraitu Murungi, walked out of the National Constitutional Conference at Bomas of Kenya. The remaining delegates were not deterred, and went ahead in voting to adopt a draft constitution, later known as the Bomas draft, with sweeping changes, including the establishment of the office of an executive prime minister who would be the head of government (Republic of Kenya 2004). Following the adoption of the Bomas draft by the conference, parliamentary and executive counter-manoeuvring began. This process led to the alteration of the draft by the attorney general, Amos Wako; via a secondary process, the alteration was opposed by the Raila-led team, which favoured the Bomas draft. One of the major differences between the Bomas (conference) draft and the one submitted by the attorney general as the draft to be subject to a referendum was the watering down of the powers of the prime minister. Under the revised draft (the Wako draft), the prime minister would be appointed by the president, and would thus be accountable to him. Additionally, instead of being the leader of the government, as mandated by the Bomas draft, under the Wako draft the prime minister would merely be the leader of government business in parliament. A truly people-driven process was subverted by the dominant partner in the executive, leading to an irreconcilable split between the governing coalition partners. The Banana and Orange factions – as they were later to be known, after the electoral symbols for and against the draft constitution respectively, as assigned by the Electoral Commission – would polarise the country along the lines of the ethnic coalitions. These had once come together under NARC to fight KANU, but now were severely opposed to each other. When the outcome of the 2005 referendum was announced, the Orange side – the side opposed to the adoption of the proposed new constitution – had 58 per cent of the votes cast, and the quest for a new political dispensation premised on a new constitutional order would have to wait. The voting results reflected deep ethnic fissures, mainly pitting Kibaki's Kikuyu community against the rest of the country's other ethnic groups.[2] It was these fissures, and the coalitions arrayed against each other, that would frame the intense competition in the 2007 elections and the subsequent violence.

The post-election violence and the National Accord of 2008

The 2007 elections were largely a rerun of the factional competition ranged in the referendum two years earlier. The Orange team, which had led the onslaught against the Wako draft of the constitution, now turned itself into a political party, the ODM. The ODM was led by Raila Odinga as the presidential candidate against the incumbent, President Kibaki, whose camp had reconfigured into a new Party of National Unity. While the campaign rhetoric was centred on standard Kenyan election platform issues – services, economic opportunity, corruption, nepotism and inequality – underpinning the rhetoric were strong references to a new dispensation that would be anchored in a new constitution. In order to get the support of the populous and cosmopolitan Rift Valley Province, the ODM assured voters that a new constitution would guarantee devolution not only of fiscal resources but also of governance structures, facilitating the development of the region. Thus the discourse on the constitution took advantage of immediate local concerns, and ceased to be merely a debate on an organisational remaking of the state or the constraint of state power. In the context of election campaigns, it took on the added dimension of being regarded as a use of state power to achieve certain marginalised political interests. It was therefore not surprising that among the regions with the most intense levels of violence after the 2007 elections was the Rift Valley Province, where devolution and land are of immediate import to power relations among ethnic communities.

The 2007 election campaigns demonstrated the temporal and instrumentalist nature of Kenyan politics in the formation of alliances. The high stakes of the elections placed the country on edge during the campaign period and at the end of the voting process. After two days of waiting, the Electoral Commission of Kenya announced that Kibaki had garnered 46 per cent of the votes cast, while Raila had secured 44 per cent. Several other election observers, especially the European Union (EU), had declared in a preliminary statement that the credibility of the election process was questionable. The Electoral Commission announcement immediately stoked up violence in the entire country, violence that would last for over a month, claiming over 1,100 lives and leaving several hundreds of thousands homeless and internally displaced in several camps around Kenya. The signing of the National Accord between rivals Raila Odinga and Mwai Kibaki in February 2008 brought a halt to that violence.

The post-election violence, and the internationally mediated National Accord that followed, became a major turning point in the search for a new constitution. The violence unearthed the tensions underlying the myth of Kenyan exceptionalism (as 'an island of peace in a region awash with conflict') and of an enduring elite consensus. The accord reflected the balance between instrumentalist politics and recognition of the need for a new compact that would deal with the fundamental issues of state power, citizenship and order. For the first time, the political class was willing to accept, albeit through external prompting, that Kenya's institutions were fragile and unable to resolve historical grievances, and that the only antidote to this was a reordering of the constitution and state power rather than temporary majorities via elections.

The signing of the National Accord in 2008 was a reflection of the penchant for pact-making among the political class but also an instrument to shift the structural conditions that would constrain choice in the next stage of contests. We will revisit the logic of this instrumentalist structuring and its importance in how it influenced the range of possible options and outcomes, but also how instrumentalism determines the actual choices that emerge. For instance, the National Accord recognised that for the post-electoral moment, but also for the future, the 'winner takes all' political system was unsustainable given the tendency of Kenyan presidents to favour their generally ethnic traditional voting blocs. In addition to crafting a power-sharing formula that created the position of prime minister (the leader of the party with the majority of MPs), the National Accord also outlined a series of measures the government needed to undertake in order to fully place the country on a path to reform. Known collectively as agenda 4 items, they included, among others, the enactment of a new constitution.[3]

The panel of eminent personalities led by former UN Secretary General

Kofi Annan called for comprehensive legal and constitutional reforms within one year. And, while it would take slightly over one year for the work on producing the new constitution to begin, it is worth noting that the parliamentary process that produced the Constitution of Kenya Review Act (2008), the enabling legislation that anchored the new process, sought to shield it from political manoeuvring inside parliament of the kind that had created the conditions leading to the violence of 2007–08. For instance, apart from insisting that parliament could not change anything in the draft constitution, except by a two-thirds majority vote, the act also gave enormous powers to the newly created Committee of Experts to ignore the suggestions of both the parliament and the PSC on the Constitution.

Thus insulated from the rough and tumble of everyday short-term, advantage-seeking politics, the process was able to run its course, albeit with occasional administrative setbacks. It was also helped by the fact that the watchful eyes were on it, including those of the international community (the US government and the EU, for example), the panel of eminent personalities, Kenya's civil society, the parliamentary reform caucus and ordinary citizens. In addition, there was the spectre of International Criminal Court (ICC) indictments for the post-election violence. In the end, the newly enacted constitution covers all the areas identified in agenda 4 without any major party disagreeing with the process or the content of the changes. In this respect, while instrumentalism would have been ordinarily constrained, key political players still found opportunities to create political advantages around these episodes. Thus, the involvement of the international community, the indictment of powerful figures by the ICC and the process of implementing agenda 4 all became important points of contest among political players for their own benefit.

The 2010 constitutional referendum and the rebirth of a republic

To a limited degree, the campaigns for the 2010 constitutional referendum replayed the same political arguments that various political interests had used to undermine the search for a new constitution. The same political factions that emerged in various forms during periods of political contests emerged once more, positioning along ethnic lines and reiterating historical grievances. However, there was a display of national cohesion and a singular focus on the impending transformation. President Mwai Kibaki and Prime Minister Raila Odinga, foes in 2005–07, were now united around the draft constitution and determined to see it through. For Kibaki, it was a chance to burnish his reform credentials and salvage his legacy as a reformist president, rather than an illegitimate claimant of power, a veritable certainty given the events surrounding the disputed 2007 elections. For Odinga, the stakes of the impending elections had become increasingly clear given the constitutional limitations imposed on the incumbent president, suggesting that he was the best placed aspirant. Odinga had staked his political career and personal reputation on the passage of the draft constitution, having spearheaded the defeat of the 2005 draft and having sustained a reformist posture through the 2007 elections. Failure to enact a new constitution would have severely weakened his credentials, which were now also tied to commitments under the National Accord that had created the position of prime minister, which he held.

However, the ODM coalition that defeated the 2005 constitutional draft was no longer intact or available to support the new preferred outcome. An important realignment had arisen, partly as a result of substantive disagreements on the constitution and partly from the positioning for leadership in the coming elections. Led by renegade ODM deputy leader William Ruto, this group was supported by retired President Moi, a Ruto mentor, and fronted for the interests of Kalenjin ethnic groups, mostly resident in the Rift Valley. This group resuscitated Moi's traditional argument that a new constitution would divide the country along tribal lines and argued that the new draft was a creation of the West, had foreign backing, and did not reflect the wishes of the majority in the country. Their presumed motivation for rejecting the draft constitution was twofold. Firstly, it would ensure the personal preservation of Moi, and of some of the key figures in the opposing side. The proposed constitution would create a land commission with the mandate, among other things, to repossess all public land that may have been irregularly allocated by previous governments. The key figures in the opposing camp, who included Moi, Ruto and former Moi campaigner Cyrus Jirongo, had been among the biggest beneficiaries of Moi-era excesses, and their benefits had included huge acreages of land in Rift Valley and other parts of the country.

The second reason was political. Rift Valley, long a cosmopolitan region, was a hotbed of political conflict. The area boasts the highest number of political constituencies and was instrumental in providing the large number of votes that the ODM obtained in the 2007 general elections. In the interim years, there was a political fallout between Raila Odinga – ODM leader and 2007 presidential candidate – and William Ruto, the presumed Rift Valley king-maker. Ruto's anti-constitution posture was thus a direct rebuttal of Odinga's support for the constitution. It was also a direct repudiation of the perceived popularity of Odinga within the Kalenjin community, and, even more significantly, it was evidence of Ruto's desire to stamp his authority on the Kalenjin vote. It was therefore not surprising that Rift Valley Province had the largest percentage of votes against the adoption of the 2010 constitution.[4]

Pact-making, beneficiaries and the 2010 constitution

The instrumentalist position among key political actors that has been described above led to three main related outcomes. Each of these outcomes represented the product of intense bargaining, and sometimes internal settlements between the key political players. These outcomes were: 1) the apportioning of political power via the ways in which state structures are organised; 2) the definition of citizenship and rights, especially with respect to the state; and 3) the process used to produce a legitimate constitution. Indeed, we find that these issues dominated the process of constitution-making in Kenya to the end, and provided a template for negotiating pacts among key stakeholders. In this section, we examine how the question of the structure of the state, how power is apportioned and the question of citizenship, including representation and the rights of individuals, were settled through processes of bargaining between political elites in the process of making the constitution.

Regarding the structure of the state, the dominant narrative in Kenya's reform movement has concerned the stifling effects of unconstrained state power, especially of the executive. Like many African constitutions inherited at independence, the Kenyan constitution provided for a strong executive whose main bureaucratic apparatus, the provincial administration, ensured the ubiquity of state power all over Kenya. The provincial administration controlled access to political and development resources, determined political careers, and permanently secured order at the behest of the ruling elite. As such, it was the desire to dismantle the coercive structure of the state and its abuse of power that fuelled the demand for a new constitution.

The structure of the postcolonial state remained dominant in the post-independence constitution for several years after independence. In order to continue benefiting from it, the ruling elite in independent Kenya expanded it and insisted on maintaining its pre-eminence. Successive regimes, from Kenyatta through Moi to Kibaki, manipulated constitutional provisions, giving extensive autonomy to the president to entrench their power, counter dissent, and guarantee a stranglehold on the affairs and resources of the state. The manoeuvring over the draft constitution in 2005, which led to its subsequent defeat at the referendum, demonstrates the extent to which the ruling elite were willing to protect this apparatus. The newly enacted constitution has substantially revised the structure of the state, has put a high burden on the state to protect individual rights, and has made state organs subject to a wide range of oversight measures and sanctions. The centralised bureaucratic state, which dominated citizens' lives for a long time, has largely been replaced by a more devolved one, in which citizen participation and people's ability to restrain the state are assumed to be central to state–society relations. For example, the provincial administration that had characterised the Kenyan state has been dissolved while the executive powers of the president have become increasingly subject to parliamentary oversight and public sanction.

The second key issue in the debate on constitutional reform was the question of representation. At the core of this argument was the apparent silence of the previous constitution on minority rights and women's representation, omissions that had always been criticised. The new constitution, however, lays specific emphasis on protecting minority rights, including those of women and the disabled, and recognises the position of minorities as special groups. On the question of minority rights, apart from providing broad constitutional protection for all vulnerable groups, the constitution also allows for specific affirmative action covering minorities and marginalised groups. This includes representation in governance; special opportunities for education and employment; the development and protection of culture, values and languages; and, finally, access to basic social services (Republic of Kenya 2010). Similarly, the new constitution has robust provisions for women's representation in the affairs of governance, including representation in the national and county assemblies, as well as additional affirmative action provisions: for instance, in addition to affording protection to women as a minority and marginalised group, the constitution provides for the direct election of forty-seven women, one from each of the forty-seven counties, to the national assembly.[5] Also, sixteen women are to be nominated by political parties as members of the senate – again, this is notwithstanding the fact that women can run for any of the forty-seven seats of the senate.[6]

Finally, individual rights and the broader question of citizenship have been foremost in the quest for a new constitutional dispensation. The clamour for constitutional reform owes its origins to the emergence of an authoritarian state in the Moi era. After an abortive coup in 1982, the Moi regime severely restricted the political space. Not only did the state abrogate individual rights, it also excluded critics from participating in political contests. The emergence of the one-party state and the subsequent application of the notorious Public Order Act to detain citizens without trial increasingly impinged on citizens' rights, called into question the responsibilities and obligations of the state, and created a space in which claims for constitutional reform could be framed. At the core of these claims was whether the state had unfettered juridical powers to subvert rights granted by citizenship, such as the right to form and participate in a political party.

Here, the right to religious practice is of particular importance as it relates to Muslims and the entrenchment of Kadhi courts in the constitution. An important philosophical justification for the importance of these rights, as contained in this constitution, is that the rights belong to each individual and are not derived from the state. The bill of rights is one of the longest sections of the new constitution, and arguably one of the most far-reaching. The issues covered in the bill of rights reflect an unwavering articulation of the constitutional rights that citizenship accords to the individual. More importantly, in a clear departure from the previous constitution, it recognises the obligation of the state to provide a supportive environment for the realisation of these rights; it requires the state to respect international obligations that it is bound to by signature; and, even more importantly, it entrenches the Kenya Human Rights and Gender Commission and the National Gender and Equality Commission into the constitution.

The nature of the process of change

The see-saw of politics described above illustrates at least three lessons about change. First, the union between the pursuit of principle-based politics and instrumentalist politics can be uncomfortable. Successful political actors understand that the instrumentality of politics is what makes possible the pursuit, installation and defence of principles. However, the outcomes are not guaranteed – in part because political actors prefer the instrumental politics of winning elections, forming winning coalitions, preserving unstated rules (such as those that allow impunity in certain issues) and restricted competition over principles.

Second, the realignment of coalitions – based on issues or any other factor – occurs with such rapidity in the fluidity of transition and weak party environments that any set of constitutionalist (or any other) principles is only temporarily cohesive at best. Plural politics within shifting ethnic boundaries and the trading of bloc votes result in sharp, sudden breaks rather than subtle shifts that can benefit from incremental incentives. This also means that every major success produces a realignment that is valid until the next major contest. In this context, the interests with the best chance of surviving and being rewarded are the lowest common denominator interests of regime survival.

The third lesson about change in the turmoil of transition politics concerns the penchant for pact-making (some codified) as coalitions resolve particular contests. Pacts in Kenya have been institutionalised as a solution to the problem of weak aggregation, adjudication and execution institutions, and have become the preferred method for resolving conflicts that the established institutions are unable to solve. They also provide safe havens in which the political class can craft agreements that circumvent the press of outsiders (civil society, churches, the poor, etc.), who, by their numbers or their rhetoric, can force issues on to the agenda but cannot necessarily conclude agreements that in other circumstances would be executed by the state through, for example, national conferences.

Conclusion: challenges beyond constitution-making

In this chapter we have argued that the adoption of the new constitution in Kenya was the outcome of contentious engagement and pact-making among reform advocates at various stages of the process, as well as of formal debates guided by parliament and the national apparatus on constitutional reform. From this discussion, it is clear that game-changing political events may provide the requisite impetus for political reforms, but political gamesman-ship rather than the niceties of principle and values shapes the outcomes. For Kenya, it was the post-election violence and the overwhelming coalescing of international effort to forestall further conflagration that structured politics in a way that directed elite compacts towards a new constitutional dispensa-tion. Moreover, while it is clear that constitution-making is an inherently organic social process, political groupings must converge incrementally to provide a bulwark for a sustainable reform agenda. Clearly, the emergence of constitutionalism is a cumulative process that defies linearity. There is no single path or sequence to achieve political consensus on the need to restrain the executive exercise of power, and every step of the process contributes to the whole.

Yet theoretically – and also given the two decade-long experience of legal reform that did not induce consistent change in political practice – it is worth recognising that the adoption of a new constitution is not a sufficient catalyst for the emergence of a new dispensation. Opportunistic triggers occasioned by political actors may also act as proximate contributors to the reform agenda. As the recent history of constitution-making in Kenya demonstrates, this process is always driven or supplanted by political realities, alignments, coalitions and deal-making. In this context, we see three dominant challenges for the immediate future, including for the period after the 2013 elections. The first is the need to institutionalise constitutionalism rather than continually sub-ordinate the constitution to the dominant elite's political imperatives of the day. This includes the danger that many articles could be reversed as soon as they become inconvenient (as in 1964). Secondly, there needs to be a resolu-tion of the foundational challenge in Kenya of group versus individual rights, and of how to structure the public realm in ways that actualise these rights without mutual denigration – and especially without adding to the weight of the state or the expense of public goods. Finally, it is especially critical to establish institutional settlements that provide stable and fair outcomes, given the re-emergence of ethnicity as a superlatively salient political category, as demonstrated by the alliances formed ahead of the 2013 elections and enhanced further by the lack of aggregating and mediating non-state institutions in the weakened civil society and ineffective institutions. All these three issues, like most enduring questions relating to Kenya's political economy, are likely to be negotiated with persistent reversals, coalition formation, and ultimately some form of pact-making.

Given the path to reform laid out above, we argue that the resolution of these questions presents both an opportunity for deepening democracy and a risk of increased violence, and, we dare say, even both. This is not an argument for the preordination of violence and breakdown (on the path to or instead of) stability and progress, but rather a suggestion that precisely because of the contingent nature of change, it is both important to support the forces of change and non-violence, and to demand that the state, encased in this new constitutional form, functions according to those foundational rules.

In this chapter, we have pursued a few related arguments. First, we sought to explain the success of the constitution-making process that led to the adoption of the 2010 constitution. We have done so more in terms of the finalisation of the process than of an assessment of its implementation so far. We examined both the immediate instrumentality of politics and the shift in structural conditions that enabled change. Second, we offered this Kenyan example as a lesson to enhance our understanding of the nature of political change – in particular, the tension between sharp breaks versus incremental transformation. Specifically, we underscored the significance of intermediate events in the interregnum before changes are openly observable, a period of incomplete transition that often attracts pejorative adjectives that tend to be static and do not help us understand change. Third, we discussed the content of this constitution and its promises of fundamentally altering the political landscape. In view of the second point, we discussed the constitution not as a finished product but as a new plateau of contestation – which, we argued, is at the centre of evolving institutional governance, not static but full of tugs and pulls in the struggle to establish constitutionalism. Finally, given our analysis, we highlighted the challenges that are in store for the next decade.

Notes

1 Moi's total vote of 40 per cent was much lower than that of the three opposition candidates combined, which came to over 50 per cent.

2 Central Province recorded the highest support for the constitution, at 93 per cent, while Nyanza, Rift Valley and Coast provinces (now part of Odinga's fledgling coalition) rejected the draft with over 80 per cent voting against it.

3 Other agenda 4 items included land reforms, inequality, youth unemployment, national cohesion and transparency. See the Kenya National Dialogue and Reconciliation 'Statement of principles' of 30 July 2008 at http://peacemaker.un.org/kenya-statementlongtermissues2008 (accessed 30 July 2014).

4 Another important opponent of the draft constitution was, surprisingly, the church, which incorrectly suggested that the draft constitution allowed abortion.

5 This provision does not preclude women from running for any of the statutory 297 seats of the national assembly.

6 For a thorough discussion, see Articles 21(3), 27(3), 97(1)(b), 98(1)(b) and 100(a) of the Kenyan constitution.

References

Cottrell, J. and Y. Ghai (2007) 'Constitution making and democratization in Kenya (2000–2005)'. *Democratization* 14(1): 1–25.

Diepeveen, S. (2010) 'The Kenya we don't want: popular thought over constitutional review in Kenya, 2002'. *Journal of Modern African Studies* 48(2): 231–58.

Encarnación, O. G. (2003) *The Legacy of Transitions: Pact-making and democratic consolidation in Spain*. Working Paper 193. Madrid: Instituto Juan March de Estudios e Investigaciones, p. 15.

Ghai, Y. P. and J. G. Cotterell (eds) (2013) *Ethnicity, Nationhood and Pluralism: Kenyan perspectives*. Nairobi and

Ottawa: Katiba Institute and Global Center for Pluralism.

Giugni, M. G., D. McAdam and C. Tilly (1998) (eds) *From Contention to Democracy*. Lanham, MD: Rowman and Littlefield.

Hagopian, F. (1990) '"Democracy by undemocratic means?" Elites, political pacts, and regime transition in Brazil'. *Comparative Political Studies* 23(2): 147–70.

Ibarra, P. (ed.) (2003) *Social Movements and Democracy*. New York, NY: Palgrave Macmillan.

Jamal, M. A. (2010) 'Democracy promotion, civil society building, and the primacy of politics'. *Comparative Political Studies* 45(1): 3–31. Available at http://cps.sagepub.com/content/45/1/3.

McAdam, D., S. Tarrow and C. Tilly (2001) *Dynamics of Contention*. New York, NY: Cambridge University Press.

Muhula, R. (2009) 'Horizontal inequality and ethno-regional politics in Kenya'. *Kenya Studies Review* 1(1): 85–105.

Ndegwa, S. (1997) 'Citizenship and ethnicity: an examination of two transition moments in Kenyan politics'. *American Political Science Review* 91(3): 599–616.

O'Donnell, G. (1989) 'Transitions to democracy: some navigation instruments'. In R. Pastor (ed.) *Democracy in the Americas*. New York, NY: Holmes and Meier, p. 63.

— and P. Schmitter (1986) *Transitions from Authoritarian Rule: Tentative conclusions about uncertain democracies*. Baltimore, MD: Johns Hopkins University Press.

Przeworski, A. (1991) *Democracy and the Market*. New York, NY: Cambridge University Press.

Republic of Kenya (2004) *Draft Constitution (Bomas Draft) of Kenya, 2004*. Nairobi: Government Printers. Available at www.lcil.cam.ac.uk/sites/default/files/LCIL/documents/transitions/Kenya_4_Draft_Constitution_Bomas_Draft_2004.pdf (accessed 30 July 2014).

— (2010) *Constitution of Kenya*. Nairobi: National Council of Law Reporting.

Sklar, R. (1996) 'Towards a theory of developmental democracy'. In A. Leftwich (ed.) *Democracy and Development: Theory and practice*. Cambridge: Polity Press, pp. 25–44.

Tarrow, S. (1998) *Power in Movement*. Cambridge: Cambridge University Press.

5 | Revisiting 'the two faces of civil society' in constitutional reform in Kenya

Wanjala S. Nasong'o

Civil society has played a significant role in the push for Kenya's democratisation in general, and in constitutional reform in particular. It is credited as being the instrument behind the intellectual and political mobilisation for a new constitutional dispensation. However, civil society is encumbered by the social, economic and political cleavages that characterise Kenyan society at large. This chapter examines the role of civil society in pushing for a progressive constitution. It examines this process from the 1990s in order to longitudinally map out the multiple, and at times contradictory, roles played by civil society in this process. My main thesis is that beyond the notion of civil society manifesting the ambivalent 'two faces' is the reality of civil society as a realm of contradictory possibilities replete with actors with multiple motivations – some benign, others inherently odious and self-serving – but collectively constituting a critical actor in the country's politics of constitutional re-engineering.

Civil society and political reform: theoretical and empirical considerations

The literature on the theoretical conceptualisation of civil society, its essence and its significance to political reform and democratisation is vast and extensive (see, for example, Bayart et al. 1999; Chabal and Daloz 1999; Diamond 1999; Harbeson et al. 1994; Migdal et al. 1994; Murunga 2000; Nasong'o 2002; 2005; 2007a; 2007b; Nyang'oro 2000). Essentially, civil society is that realm of organised social life that is open, voluntary, self-generating, at least partially self-supporting, autonomous from the state, and bound by a legal order or set of shared rules (Diamond 1999: 21). In this sense, Diamond argues, civil society is different from society in general in that it involves citizens acting collectively in public spaces to express their interests, passions, preferences and ideas, to exchange information, achieve collective goals, make demands on the state, improve the structure and functioning of the state, and hold public officials accountable.

Accordingly, Diamond contends that civil society facilitates the transition from authoritarianism to democracy and helps deepen and consolidate democracy in four main ways:

- As an intermediary phenomenon located between the private sphere and the state, civil society provides the basis for the limitation of state power, for the control of the state by society, and thus for democratic political institutions as the most effective means for exercising that control.
- Civil society supplements the role of political parties in stimulating political participation, increasing the political efficacy and skill of citizens, promoting an appreciation of the obligations and rights of democratic citizenship, and articulating, aggregating and representing interests.
- Civil society promotes civic awareness through civic education for democracy and recruits and trains new political leaders.
- Civil society disseminates information widely and so empowers citizens in the collective pursuit and defence of their interests and values.

Overall, therefore, civil society strengthens the social foundation of democracy and, by enhancing the accountability, responsiveness, inclusiveness, effectiveness and legitimacy of the political system, it gives citizens respect for the state and positive engagement with it (ibid. 239–50).

It is this view of civil society as the vanguard of African democratisation that legitimised the explosion in the number of non-governmental organisations (NGOs) in Africa in the early 1990s as representatives of civil society in the struggle for political reform and democratisation. These groups thrust themselves into the political arena to help push the agenda of what was regarded as the continent's second liberation. According to one analyst at the time, John Harbeson (1994: 1), 'today, grassroots movements have arisen in nearly every sub-Saharan country to remove autocratic, repressive governments and empower African people to reclaim control over their political destinies'. In this regard, civil society was assigned a central place in the process of democratising Africa. Harbeson, for instance, argued that civil society was the hitherto missing key to sustained political reform, legitimate states and governments, improved governance, viable state–society and state–economy relationships, and the prevention of political decay. Scholars taking this view argued that the structural adjustment programmes initiated in Africa in the early 1980s did not succeed largely because they failed to emphasise the political role of civil society (see Mkandawire and Soludo 1999; Murunga 2007). Instead, they consigned civil society to the realm of market economics and private enterprise.

The central thesis of the civil society discourse in relation to democratisation is that civil society's political role is indispensable to political transformation towards greater democracy in Africa. As Thomas Callaghy (1994: 233) argues, 'Teleologically, civil society comes to stand for reinvigorated forms of participatory politics, for forces pushing toward some form of democracy. Society strikes back against oppression in the form of "civil" society.' Civil society, it is argued, is critically central to the politics of democratisation through the effective negotiation of new rules of the political game (Nasong'o 2007b). However, a review of electoral politics and regime transformation in Africa in the two decades beginning in the 1990s reveals that civil society has had an ambivalent role. In some cases, civil society is hailed as having played a central role in authoritarian regime change, as illustrated by the case of Zambia in 1991 (see Ihonvbere 1996; Nasong'o 2005). In other cases, authoritarian regimes have managed to remain in power in spite of a vibrant civil society, as was the case in Kenya (see Brown 2001; Nasong'o 2005). This eventuality points to the reality of the ambivalence and inherent contradictions within the ranks of civil society with regard to its supposed vanguard role in struggles for democracy.

Stephen Ndegwa (1996) analysed the contribution of NGOs to democratisation in Kenya, and what conditions facilitate or inhibit their contributions. His comparative analysis of two local NGOs in Kenya – the Green Belt Movement and the Undugu Society of Kenya – examined the interface between NGOs and the state in the process of democratisation, how the process unfolds, and its determinants and limitations. Ndegwa argued that for NGOs and other civil society organisations (CSOs) to advance democratisation, four conditions must exist: 1) organisation; 2) resources; 3) alliances; and 4) political opportunity. He found out, however, that these four conditions are not enough: in the cases of the two NGOs he examined, a discrepancy emerged between their actions – one actively advocated for political pluralism while the other remained politically obtuse despite the similarity of the NGOs and their circumstances.

This reality is what Ndegwa (ibid.) called 'the two faces of civil society', which, according to him, strikes at the heart of the thesis that CSOs such as NGOs necessarily invest their resources in support of democratisation efforts. He hypothesised that an important determinant of whether a well-endowed NGO is transformed into an activist organisation is whether the organisation's leadership chooses to commit its resources to a progressive political agenda. According to his study, Undugu Society of Kenya had a well-structured and institutionalised leadership and well-developed mechanisms for generating its own resources, but remained politically uncommitted to activism for good governance. Conversely, the Green Belt Movement had a highly personalised leadership in the form of its founder and coordinator, Wangari Maathai, and was highly donor-dependent, yet it was the most vocal on issues of governance and human rights. This reality is quite problematic in democratic terms, and, in Ndegwa's estimation, calls for the need to re-examine present assumptions about the real and potential contribution of organisations in civil society to democratisation in Africa.

According to Ndegwa, the thesis that civil society actors are important contributors to democratic change is essentially a statement on their positive contribution to altering power relations in Africa. He argues that analysts should raise fundamental questions about where civil society actors derive their power to oppose the state and, even more importantly, where this power resides. To Ndegwa, if power resides in grass-roots mobilisation and participation and if it resides with citizens at the local level or in representative and accountable elites, only then can civil society be said to hold the promise of democratising African states. Otherwise, he posits, it is a mistake for analysts to view CSOs as steadfast supporters of democratisation. Evidence suggests that the only interests such organisations are likely to represent forcefully are those that are intimately tied to their own institutional survival.

Nevertheless, there is no gainsaying the fact that certain CSOs have played a critical role in the democratisation process in Kenya in general and in the quest for constitutional reform in particular. In spite of such organisations' bifurcated and contradictory nature, the new constitutional dispensation in Kenya is very much a product of concerted efforts by CSOs in collaboration with other progressive forces. This eventuality in Kenya is a product of initiatives from above and from below, the former being characterised by popular demands for a people-driven broad-based constitution-making process and the latter as a reaction against procrastination from incumbent elites. The protracted nature of the process has been a consequence of a delicate balance between incumbent regimes buffeted by broad-based critiques and weakened by elite defections on the one hand, and civil society and opposition groups on the other. The latter have been emboldened by gradually widening public spaces and exemplars of democratic advances across the continent (see Nasong'o 2010: 222–4; Ndegwa 2005).

Civil society and constitutional reform in Kenya

After two decades of heightened activism for constitutional reform in Kenya, a new constitution was finally adopted via a referendum on 4 August 2010 in which 67 per cent of the voters approved the new document. It was officially promulgated soon afterwards, on 27 August 2010, heralding the dawn of Kenya's second republic (see Akech 2010). The hallmarks of the new constitution, as previous chapters have described in detail, include the creation of a two-chamber legislature with a national assembly and a senate as well as the establishment of a devolved system of governance with forty-seven counties, each with its own executive and legislative institutions. The promulgation of the new constitution was a culmination of concerted and protracted struggles for constitutional reform in which CSOs played a critical role (see Kennedy and Bieniek 2010; Maingi 2012; Vliet et al. 2012). Among the leading CSOs in the push for constitutional reform were the Citizens' Coalition for Constitutional Change (4Cs), Centre for Multiparty Democracy-Kenya (CMD-K), Kenya Human Rights Commission (KHRC), National Council of the Churches of Kenya (NCCK), Catholic Peace and Justice Commission (CPJC), Law Society of Kenya (LSK), Release Political Prisoners (RPP), Constitution and Reform

Education Consortium (CRECO) and Social Development Network (SODNET), among a host of others.

Following concerted activism for political reform on the part of CSOs, coupled with opposition political society, especially as embodied in the Forum for the Restoration of Democracy in Kenya (FORD), and the support of external forces, Section 2(A) of the Kenyan constitution was repealed in 1991, paving the way for the first multiparty elections in December 1992. In the run-up to these elections, however, the opposition was terribly splintered between Oginga Odinga's Forum for the Restoration of Democracy-Kenya (FORD-K), Kenneth Matiba's Forum for the Restoration of Democracy-Asili (FORD-A) and Mwai Kibaki's Democratic Party (DP), with each of the three leaders gunning for the presidency against the incumbent President Daniel arap Moi of the Kenya African National Union (KANU). The NCCK took the initiative to hold two symposia with a view to mobilising for opposition unity and the possibility of a single opposition presidential candidate to face the incumbent. During the second symposium, the KHRC and the RPP decided to push for the release of political prisoners and the holding of a national convention to discuss a new constitution. Although the two symposia failed to galvanise opposition unity, their major outcome was the emergence of the Coalition for a National Convention (CNC), led by KHRC and RPP, and supported by the Kenya Youth Foundation Movement (KYFM), Policy Advisory Foundation (PAF), National Union of Kenya Students (NUKS) and Students Organization of Nairobi University (SONU), among others (see Nasong'o 2010: 226; 2007b: 39–44).

From the 4Cs to the NCEC

After the victory of the incumbent in the 1992 general elections with just 37 per cent of the votes cast, the CPJC's eighteen bishops issued a pastoral letter calling for the complete overhaul of the constitution by a constituent body of competent and experienced Kenyans representing all sectors of society (see *Daily Nation*, 16 March 1994). Sixteen other CSOs, led by the KHRC, went a step further to commission a constitutional lawyer to draft a model constitution – the 'Kenya We Want Constitution' – as a basis for mobilisation (Vliet et al. 2012: 21). CSO consultations over the 'Kenya We Want Constitution' resulted in the formation of the Citizens' Coalition for Constitutional Change (4Cs). At its first meeting on 31 May 1996, the 4Cs transformed itself into the National Convention Preparatory Committee (NCPC), with the goal of facilitating a broad-based constitutional review process. The NCPC undertook the tasks of: 1) drawing up minimum constitutional, legal and administrative reforms to constitute the framework for advocacy in the run-up to the 1997 elections; 2) proposing the means and strategies for achieving these minimum reforms; 3) suggesting a framework for holding a national convention to discuss comprehensive reforms; 4) proposing modalities for participation in the constitutional review process; and 5) drafting a programme for the convention and drawing up the timeframe for holding it (Nasong'o 2010: 226–7).

At its first 'National Convention Assembly' at Limuru on 15 November 1996, the NCPC adopted a 'minimum constitutional reform agenda' to be implemented prior to the 1997 general elections. The agenda included:

- reform of the Electoral Commission of Kenya (ECK), particularly Sections 41 and 42(A) of the constitution to allow for vetting of nominees to the ECK;
- amendment of Sections 15, 16 and 19 of the constitution to allow for the formation of a coalition government;
- repeal of the Public Order Act (Cap. 56), the Chief's Authority Act (Cap. 128), the NGO Coordination Act (Cap. 19 of 1990), the Societies Act (Cap. 108), the Penal Code (Cap. 63), and the Preservation of Public Security Act (Cap. 57); and
- amendment of the National Assembly and Presidential Elections Act (Cap. 107).

This agenda constituted the basis of deliberations at the second NCPC 'National Convention Assembly' in April 1997, but was expanded to include: the Films and Stage Act, Plays Act, Public Collections Act and Election Code; resettlement of victims of ethnic clashes; prohibition of illegal presidential decrees on elections; prevention of the provincial administration from interfering with the electoral process; release of all political prisoners; registration of unregistered political parties; and replacement of the 25 per cent rule with one requiring a presidential candidate to garner at least 50 per cent plus one of the votes cast to be declared the winner. The former rule simply required a candidate to win a plurality of the votes cast plus at least 25 per cent of the votes in at least five of the country's provinces, which then numbered eight.

Predictably, the 'minimum reforms agenda' excited the political opposition, who saw it as levelling the political playing field for them vis-à-vis the incumbent. However, it did not attract much support from the more progressive wing of activist CSOs, which interpreted political change in transformative rather than mere reformative terms. This CSO wing therefore emphasised the idea of 'maximum constitutional reform' (see Yahya-Othman and Warioba 2007: 12–15). To mobilise for such fundamental reform, the second 'National Convention Assembly' converted the NCPC into the National Convention Executive Council (NCEC), which organised civil disobedience and demonstrations under the slogan 'No Reforms, No Elections' as a way of pressurising the incumbent government to adopt the comprehensive constitutional review agenda prior to the 1997 general elections.

To buttress the chances of achieving its objective of 'maximum' constitutional reform, the NCEC adopted the 'zero option' strategy. The logic behind it was that, given its intransigence, the government would implement reforms only if it were confronted with a crisis of such profundity that it would have no other option. Hence the NCEC decided to confront the regime in order to simultaneously demystify it by challenging its authority and delegitimise it by provoking its violent response to organised civil disobedience (see Katumanga 2000; Mutunga 1999). In pursuit of its strategy, the NCEC convened a mass action rally at Kamukunji Grounds in Nairobi on 3 May 1997, which the government declared illegal. Nevertheless, multitudes converged on Kamukunji for the rally and, predictably, the regime unleashed paramilitary forces on the people. By defying the ban on the rally, the NCEC succeeded in delegitimising the government in the eyes of the public. Consequently, as Katumanga (2000) points out, political elite factions both within and outside government were forced to seriously rethink their position on constitutional reform, which became an agenda that every opposition politician sought to identify with. However, the state remained intransigent with regard to commencing dialogue on constitutional reform. The NCEC quickly followed with another mass action rally on 31 May 1997. During the rally, two people were shot dead by the paramilitary General Service Unit deployed to disperse the rally.

The third NCEC mass action rally was called for 7 July 1997. More than fourteen Kenyans were killed in the ensuing demonstrations and disorder, which itself was a huge embarrassment for President Moi, given that the Inter-Governmental Authority on Development conference was taking place at the time in Nairobi. The state violence against demonstrators during this rally had the impact of legitimising the mass movement for reform while simultaneously delegitimising the state for unleashing violence against unarmed civilians. The NCEC pressed on with its constitutional reform mass action and called on Kenyans to disrupt the budget-reading ceremony scheduled for 19 July 1997. The NCEC argued that, over the years, the government had continued to read budgets without tabling its expenditure statements, and so the very action of presenting the budget was, *ipso facto*, illegal. It further contended that having refused to institute constitutional reform, the state had lost the legitimate right to table budget estimates. In doing this, the NCEC had two objectives. Firstly, it sought to put the constitutional reform debate not only before the Kenyan public and the president himself, but also the entire world, as represented by the ambassadors present in parliament for the budget ceremony. And secondly, the NCEC aimed to demonstrate to the country as a whole, and to the assembled diplomats in particular, that the president was not in charge of the political situation. The government responded to the threat of budget-reading disruption by garrisoning parliament and hiring a private vigilante group, Jeshi la Mzee, to counter pro-reform activists' attempts to assemble at parliament buildings. While the skirmishes between private thugs and pro-reform crowds went on, the government faced heckling within parliament, with opposition MPs demanding to listen to demonstrators outside parliament. For the first time in the history of the country, the budget speech was switched off from the national airwaves. The 'zero option' strategy seemed to have achieved the desired impact.

On account of its tarnished image, the regime softened and agreed in principle to constitutional reform. It convened a meeting of the ruling party's National Executive Council to deliberate the issue. The ruling party, KANU, published a list of reforms for the government to implement. These included repeal of the Public Order Act, the Chief's Authority Act and the Presidential Elections Act. Furthermore, President Moi announced that he had lifted the requirement for permits for public rallies. On the basis of these concessions, Moi appealed to religious leaders to facilitate dialogue between the government and the pro-reform movement and to persuade the NCEC to call off a national strike it had called for 8 August 1998 (Nasong'o 2010: 228–30; 2007b: 42–4). Religious leaders and the diplomatic corps viewed the reforms proposed by KANU as indicative of the government finally embracing the idea of constitutional reform, and both sectors impressed upon the NCEC to call off the scheduled national strike to 'give dialogue a chance'. Nevertheless, the NCEC forged ahead with the strike with the support of opposition leaders Raila Odinga, James Orengo and Mwai Kibaki, plus thirty other parliamentarians (see *East African Standard*, 8 August 1997). During the rally, at Nairobi's Central Park, a policeman was killed, and there followed violent demonstrations in Nairobi, Kisumu, Nakuru and Kiambu.

Against this background, the government denounced the NCEC as a lawless organisation bent on violence and thus sought to pull the reform agenda initiative from the CSOs' ranks. This was accomplished, in the run-up to the 1997 elections, by the Inter-Parliamentary Parties Group initiative, which effected the minimum constitutional reforms proposed earlier by KANU, including the requirement that, to win the presidency, one needed to garner a plurality of the votes cast as well as at least 25 per cent of the votes cast in at least five of the country's eight provinces. The reforms also included expansion of the ECK to include members nominated by parliamentary political parties on the basis of their parliamentary strength. Once these reforms were put in place, the political opposition was enticed into abandoning civil society and commenced their campaigns for the December 1997 elections, which once again were won by the incumbent party and president, with 40 per cent of the votes cast.

The Government Review Commission versus the Ufungamano Initiative

Pressure from CSOs for a comprehensive review of the constitution continued after the 1997 elections. In 1999, parliament finally enacted the Constitution of Kenya Review Act, establishing the Constitution of Kenya Review Commission (CKRC), which was to collect and collate views from Kenyans and make recommendations to parliament. On account of the fact that the review process was to be controlled by parliament, with no provision for structured, broad-based participation, CSOs led by the NCEC, KHRC, LSK, the Green Belt Movement and the Presbyterian Church contested the constitutive and procedural provisions of the Constitutional Review Act. They rejected parliament as the only forum for constitution-making, arguing that it was not representative of all the voices of Kenya, and they demanded an all-inclusive process to culminate in a national conference. Their mantra was a 'people-driven' constitutional review process. Contestations between the two sides resulted in a series of consultative meetings, from Bomas I and II to Safari Park I to IV. The government acquiesced to the establishment of the organs for constitutional review, including a commission appointed by the president, constituency deliberation forums, and a national dialogue conference, of which all sitting MPs would be members as well as two representatives from each of the country's administrative districts. This would result in the promulgation of a new constitution by parliamentary vote and presidential assent (see Vliet et al. 2012: 28–30).

Wary of the government's motivations and suspicious of its commitment to the constitutional review agenda, CSOs convened a meeting on 15 December 1999. This was attended by 400 individuals representing various CSOs and some opposition political parties. The meeting, held at Ufungamano House, Nairobi, and led by Catholic, Hindu, Muslim and Protestant clergy, initiated a parallel constitutional review process under the name of the 'People's Commission of Kenya' (PCK), popularly referred to as the Ufungamano Initiative. The PCK, chaired by the late Dr Oki Ooko Ombaka, was to use churches, mosques and temples as forums for collecting and collating views from Kenyans on the constitutional review process. Once Professor Yash Pal Ghai was appointed to chair the CKRC, he successfully negotiated a merger of the CKRC and the PCK and the review process commenced in 2000. The merged constitutional review commission announced its mandate as a 'comprehensive review' whose output would be a new constitutional order rather than a revised version of the 1963 constitution.

The CKRC published a new draft constitution (later dubbed the Bomas draft), along with its report, in 2002. This draft became the focus of a national multi-stakeholder dialogue convened at the Bomas of Kenya in Nairobi, following the historic 2002 elections that were won by the opposition alliance, NARC, and which ended KANU's forty-year rule. As Vliet et al. (2012) point out, the key political parties at Bomas soon split into two camps as the pre-election unity among opposition parties foundered. One party camp (the president's) led a walkout from Bomas in 2004 and refused to participate any further. Later that year, the Bomas talks wound up the dialogue with the Bomas draft, which was presented to the attorney general for publication and tabling in parliament. The Bomas draft proposed a bicameral legislature and a dual executive system with a prime minister as head of government and a president as head of state. It also proposed far-reaching devolution of power at three levels: regional, district and local. Although bound by the review legislation to publish the draft constitution as it emerged from Bomas, the attorney general made alterations that effectively reintroduced a presidential system of government, watered down devolution, and eliminated the provisions for dual citizenship, the creation of a senate and the protection of minorities and marginalised groups, among other changes. This draft – known as the Wako draft, named after the then attorney general – was presented to a national referendum in November 2005 and was rejected by 58 per cent of the votes cast.

Post-election violence and momentum for a new constitution

The coming to power of the NARC government following the 2002 general elections had two major consequences for CSOs. First, the new government recruited quite a number of seasoned CSO leaders into its ranks, while many others joined elective politics and ended up as parliamentarians, or were even appointed as cabinet ministers. Second, the NARC government began speaking the language of human rights, of equality, of justice and of political reform, and initiated a number of programmes that had hitherto been the province of civil society advocacy. This turn of events not only depleted the CSO sector of effective leaders experienced in the art of advocacy, lobbying and mobilisation for reform, it also seriously weakened the sector's capacity to play a watchdog role, especially given its support for the opposition NARC in the run-up to the 2002 elections (see Kanyinga 2011; Murunga and Nasong'o 2006).

Within this context of a post-transition crisis marked by a loss of leaders to political parties and to government, a high level of mistrust emerged among civil society actors. Consequently, civil society's response to fundamental constitutional issues became rather fractured and disjointed, so that, for every CSO agitating for reform, there was a corresponding one working in the opposite direction. For instance, in a call by CSOs for minimum reforms before the 2007 elections, the Catholic Church broke ranks with civil society and resorted to supporting the government (Yahya-Othman and Warioba 2007: 18–19). Part of the mistrust within civil society stemmed from the perception that there was a lack of unity of purpose and effective control over the constitutional process. As Yahya-Othman and Warioba (ibid.) note, there was no agreement on whether constitutional reforms should be minimum or comprehensive at this stage. Many perceived the constitutional issue as being used as a campaign tool for the imminent 2007 elections. Whereas traditionally civil society had been the natural ally of the political opposition, there now developed a high degree of mistrust between these two groups. CSOs saw themselves as playing an important role in checking the president and preventing him from becoming dictatorial, given the leeway provided by the constitution in place at the time. However, they viewed the political opposition as focusing too narrowly on personal rather than national interests. On the other hand, the political opposition regarded CSOs as part of the political problem, maintaining that CSOs had been taken over by the political class, especially the incumbent government, which had managed to exert great influence on civil society.

The post-2007 election violence of January and February 2008 clarified the urgent need for fundamental reform in Kenya's political architecture (see Chapter 3). Indeed, Kofi Annan, the lead mediator in the crisis, saw it both as a profound threat to the East African state, which had long been viewed as an island of peace in a region engulfed in incessant political crises, and as a great opportunity to remake the country's political institutions and address the long-held historical grievances on the part of some communities (see Annan 2012: 148–208). In the face of the post-election violence, CSOs found some semblance of common ground and rallied to contribute to the resolution of the crisis. CSOs were, however, divided on this issue and two broad groups emerged. The first, led by faith-based organisations with a smattering of former soldiers and diplomats, were more moderate in their approach, arguing for peace as an end in itself. They constituted the Concerned Citizens for Peace (CCP) to articulate their demands. On the other hand, CSOs in the human rights and governance sector were much more progressive in their approach. They held that sustainable peace could be guaranteed only by resolving the questions of justice and truth about flawed election results, truth and justice about the ubiquitous violence in the country, and justice for victims of the violence. These groups constituted the grouping Kenyans for Peace, Truth and Justice (KPTJ) to pursue their concerns (see Kanyinga 2011).

Overall, CSO diversity, strength, experience and knowledge of regional and international advocacy options, as well as credible contacts therein, proved crucial for their role in the resolution of the crisis. Of particular importance was prior work on the part of CSOs on key issues up for mediation, as well as previously established contacts with key organs of the state on those issues. Therefore, CSOs energetically contributed through monitoring and documentation to provide data and analysis of both the elections and the violence; ensured domestic contributions to and leadership of the humanitarian relief effort; generated an internal demand for peace, truth and justice; and developed scenarios and recommendations for the mediation process, even as they applied pressure for a final political settlement (see Wanyeki 2010). Vliet et al. (2012: 21) note that for many years the CMD-K had facilitated informal inter-party dialogue sessions on constitutional content and process-related matters, and, parallel to the political negotiation process led by Kofi Annan after the troubled elections, CMD-K set up a broad platform of political and civil society representatives. They successfully influenced the agenda of the final agreement, in which constitutional reform featured prominently.

The imperative need for constitutional reform was thus recognised within the National Accord brokered by the Kofi Annan-led panel of eminent personalities. Nevertheless, from previous constitutional reform experience, CSOs were alive to the fact that new efforts would require stringent safeguards against partisan manipulation of the reform process. Accordingly, a host of CSO forums emerged to help shepherd the process, sustain momentum, and ensure that the process was as comprehensive and inclusive as possible. These included, among others, the Comprehensive Constitution Reform Coalition (CCRC), the Multi-Sectoral Review Forum (MSRF), the National Dialogue Conference (NDC) and the Joint Dialogue Forum (JDF) (see Yahya-Othman and Warioba 2007: 30). Continuous efforts of inter-party dialogue and proactive lobbying culminated in the Constitution of Kenya Review Act of 2008, which identified four main institutions that would be involved in the reform process and their mutual relations: the Committee of Experts (CoE), the parliamentary select committee, the national assembly and a popular referendum.

The CoE comprised six Kenyan experts – Nzamba Kitonga (chair), Atsango Chesoni (vice-chair), Otiende Amolo, Bobby Munga Mkangi, Abdirashid Abdullah and Njoki Ndung'u (members) – assisted by three foreign nationals (Christina Murray, Chaloka Beyani and Frederick Ssepembwa), a director of the committee (Ekuru Aukot) and the attorney general (Amos Wako), the latter two as *ex officio* members. For over a year, the CoE worked hard to temper national sentiments in the post-conflict period. Its mandate was mainly to reconcile the contentious issues in the two previous constitutional drafts, the Bomas and Wako drafts. Public consultation was mandated to obtain more information on how to effect reconciliation and harmonisation of the two constitutional drafts. According to Kennedy and Bieniek (2010), the presence of the three foreign experts helped to raise the CoE's profile and reinforce its credibility as a technical rather than a political committee. A two-thirds majority in parliament was required to adopt the CoE's proposed amendments to the new constitution, thereby limiting individual politicians' and parties' ability to influence its content on the basis of their specific interests. Inter-party negotiations and consensus on two contentious issues – namely, the type of political system and the level of devolution – proved crucial in helping to generate the requisite political support base needed to ensure the new constitution's adoption by parliament.

Eventually, the new constitution was adopted in a referendum on 4 August 2010. The voter turnout was over 70 per cent, with 67 per cent, slightly over two-thirds, voting for the new constitution, which was officially promulgated on 27 August 2010. Wary of the electoral shenanigans that occasioned the conflagration following the 2007 general elections, CSOs were keen to ensure fairness in the referendum vote. They constituted themselves under the rubric of Kenyan Elections Observation Group (ELOG) and under the chairmanship of Kennedy Masime. Through ELOG, Kenyan civil society managed to play a useful and important role in the referendum process. ELOG provided diverse and bipartisan monitoring and observation and acted as a watchdog for election spoilers. In addition, the group conducted parallel vote tabulations for the referendum, constructively contributing to the success of the vote by providing a comprehensive check on the Interim Independent Electoral Commission tally (Kennedy and Bieniek 2010: 5). After two decades of troubled constitution-making, Kenyans finally had a new constitution. The challenge that lay ahead now was one of effective implementation of the new social contract and of ensuring fidelity to its provisions, especially on the part of the political class (see the extended discussions of this in Chapters 6 and 8).

The CSO imprints on the new constitution include progressive provisions in the ambitious bill of rights that protect the rights of Kenyans, especially women and the vulnerable; environmental protection; the provision for dual citizenship; and the provision for women's representation in parliament, including in the senate and national assembly, among a host of other novel and progressive provisions. It provides enhanced checks and balances in governance and facilitates broad-based participation of citizens in the decision-making process through a devolved system of county governments. It is a major source of empowerment for reform activists, within both civil society and government, who are likely to further commit themselves to ensuring its successful implementation.

Beyond 'the two faces of civil society'

From developments in the constitutional reform process in Kenya since Ndegwa's 1996 'two faces' thesis, there is ample evidence that the contradictions inherent in the realm of CSOs go beyond the fact that they manifest two faces. It is true, as Ndegwa hypothesised, that some well-endowed CSOs choose to remain politically obtuse, thereby debunking the optimistic scholarly perspective that CSOs constitute an unmitigated bastion of liberty and are steadfast crusaders for political reform and democratisation (see Barkan 2004; 2005; Callaghy 1994; Chazan 1994; Diamond 1999; Harbeson 1994; Orvis 2003). Most importantly, even CSOs that commit themselves to the struggle for political reform display contradictory tendencies with regard to the interests and motivations of actors therein. It is this reality that leads Mahmood Mamdani (1995) to conclude that civil society is a realm of 'contradictory possibilities' while I (Nasong'o 2010: 225) refer to the 'bifurcated nature of civil society'.

As argued elsewhere (Murunga and Nasong'o 2006; Nasong'o 2010: 231), Kenyan civil society is replete with actors of varied persuasions and multiple motivations. Whereas many actors within civil society were genuinely committed to the political reform agenda for the sake of advancing democracy and good governance, quite a number of others saw political activism for reform as a gateway to power, wealth and privilege. Willy Mutunga, Gladwell Otieno, Maina Kiai, John Githongo, Japheth Shamallah and John Khaminwa, among others, are good examples of civil society activists whose activism for political reform was not motivated by selfish personal gain but was premised on a genuine concern that Kenyans deserved a more open, accountable and democratic political system under a new social contract. Lawyers Khaminwa and Shamallah actively participated in the pro-reform movement of the 1990s, with the former providing legal services to activists who fell foul of the incumbent regime. Robert Press (2004; 2012) documents how Shamallah's law offices in Corner House, downtown Nairobi, were used as the planning headquarters or command post for the 'foot soldiers' of the reform movement. Yet neither of these two parleyed this role into a seat at the table of power. As for Maina Kiai, he was appointed as chair of the Kenya National Commission on Human Rights by the NARC government, but his loyalty to his progressive political ideals remained intact, his new location notwithstanding.

Willy Mutunga and John Githongo are particularly emblematic of this principled cadre of CSO activists. Mutunga began his political activism in the 1980s as a university lecturer, suffering arrest and detention without trial in the process. He was a founding member of the 4Cs and was the second executive director of the KHRC, one of the leading CSOs in Kenya. Mutunga's personal integrity and steadfast commitment to the ideals of political reform were demonstrated twice – in 1992 and in 2003. Amid a splintered political opposition that could not agree on a single presidential political candidate to face the incumbent President Moi, Mutunga was approached with the proposal to have him nominated as the opposition's compromise candidate. Whereas a self-interested individual would have readily jumped at such an opportunity for potentially becoming president, Mutunga rejected the entreaties. His argument was that the opposition, and some within the CSO ranks, were overly focused on simply replacing President Moi, when the fundamental issue was the need to reform the political system to engender and institutionalise a just and democratic order.

Following the democratic assumption of power of the opposition coalition NARC in 2003, President Mwai Kibaki appointed Willy Mutunga as a member of the council of the Jomo Kenyatta University of Agriculture and Technology. Mutunga rejected this appointment on the grounds that he had not been consulted prior to his appointment, a reality that harked back to the modus operandi of the previous Moi regime when appointments to senior state and parastatal positions – as well as dismissals from the same – were done impersonally via government-owned media broadcasts. He also wondered whether he was the best qualified person for the position (see Mutunga 2003).

For his part, John Githongo was headhunted from the Kenya chapter of Transparency International (TI) and appointed by President Kibaki as Permanent Secretary for Governance and Ethics, signalling his government's commitment to fight corruption. Githongo, dubbed the 'anti-corruption tsar' because of his impeccable credentials honed at TI, went about his new job with zeal, doggedly going after the shenanigans behind the Anglo Leasing financial scandal, as well as ministers in President Kibaki's government. Soon, Githongo realised that the new government's anti-corruption rhetoric was just that – there was neither the political will nor a firm commitment to fighting corruption. In fact, the opposite was the case. The new power elite considered their new positions as their turn to eat and could not understand why one of their own was keen on outing them for corrupt activities (see Wrong 2009). It was within this context that Githongo resigned his position and went into self-imposed exile in the UK, where he continued his anti-corruption crusade, appearing at various forums including the Cato Institute in the US.

At the other end of the scale are civil society activists who used their activism as an avenue to power and prestige, utilising their 'reform credentials' to access a seat at the table of 'eating chiefs'. Representative of this group are Paul Muite and Kiraitu Murungi, two lawyer activists who gallantly fought for human rights and good governance against the authoritarian Moi regime. Once NARC took over following the 2002 elections, Murungi was appointed Minister for Justice and Constitutional Affairs while Paul Muite was appointed to chair the parliamentary select committee on constitutional reform. In contrast to their previous calls for a people-driven process and for devolution of power from the 'imperial presidency', the two leaders now led a pro-establishment struggle to retain the powers of the presidency; they stonewalled the review process, frustrated the CKRC chair, Yash Pal Ghai, leading to his resignation, and manoeuvred the review process from Bomas back to parliamentary control. When faced with questions on this contradictory behaviour, Muite famously asserted that his new role was to protect the government of President Kibaki (Murunga and Nasong'o 2006: 25). John Githongo lamented that, after the collapse of Bomas, 'I realised we had never been serious about power-sharing. Kiraitu Murungi, the very man who had written about ethnicity, was the first to use the term "these Jaluos" in my presence' (Wrong 2009: 74).

Two other examples include academics Kivutha Kibwana and Macharia Munene. Kivutha Kibwana was deeply involved in the struggle for a new constitutional dispensation in Kenya. As leader of the NCEC, he was the face of the mass action activities of the organisation at the height of its political activism. Taking advantage of his name recognition and popular activist credentials, Kibwana parleyed these into electoral politics and easily won the Makueni parliamentary seat in the 2002 elections and was subsequently appointed Minister for the Environment in the NARC government. Unlike Maina

Kiai, however, Kibwana seems to have been effortlessly socialised into the modus operandi of the status quo and abandoned the principles he stood for while in the civil society trenches. Indeed, after losing his parliamentary seat in the 2007 elections, Kibwana was appointed as adviser to President Kibaki, demonstrating his complete metamorphosis from a reform agent to a pro-establishment operative who had secured his place at the seat of power.

Perhaps no one exemplifies the odious side of the contradictory nature of civil society actors more than Macharia Munene, professor at United States International University, Nairobi. A rabid critic of the Moi regime during its heyday, Munene became a staunch supporter of President Mwai Kibaki, a fellow co-ethnic, to the extent of being an apologist for electoral fraud. With the possibility of losing the presidency to Raila Odinga looming in the run-up to the 2007 elections, Macharia Munene quipped that '[President] Kibaki is aware that it is bad manners for a sitting president to lose [an election]' (Murunga 2011: 6; *East African Standard*, 12 July 2007). It is this win-by-all-means mentality, driven by the perception of political power through the ethnic prisms of 'us and them' that triggered the post-election conflagration, the magnitude of which pushed Kenya to the brink of collapse in 2008.

Conclusion

This chapter demonstrates that there is more to Kenyan civil society than the mere manifestation of 'two faces'. The CSO sector is a complex and dynamic one replete with multiple actors imbued with different motivations – some benign, others not so benign; most progressive, but some moderate, conservative, or even outright retrogressive. In spite of the contradictions inherent in the realm of civil society in Kenya, and despite the constrained nature of the context in which CSOs have operated over time, they have contributed immensely to the struggles for democratisation in general and for constitutional reform in particular, as the analysis here amply illustrates. When civil society first took root in Kenya in the 1990s, it reflected a narrow, relatively elite network based primarily in Nairobi. It was the examination of this nascent group of CSOs on the part of Stephen Ndegwa (1996) that yielded conclusions about the two faces of civil society. By 2002, with the assumption of power by NARC and the supplanting of the entrenched KANU ruling party, much of the leadership of this first generation left civil society to go into politics. However, a new generation of leaders is rising to forge a more grass roots-oriented network. Gaining energy after the 2007–08 post-election violence, this new cohort is transforming what was once focused on the elite into a more representative and extended civil society. Although largely dependent on international support and funding, Kenyan CSOs act as an important alternative power within the space between local communities and government.

The downside is that the CSO network in Kenya still struggles from a lack of institutional capacity, autonomy, clear vision, domestic funding, and a strong base of local support (see Kennedy and Bieniek 2010; Nasong'o 2009). CSOs thus need to build upon the momentum gained during the constitutional referendum to enhance their role in the implementation stage and in having an impact on government policy in the future. In order to do so – and, in the process, to build a concrete, sustainable, grass roots-focused civil society that represents the interests of the Kenyan people – CSOs need to do the following:

- Dedicate time, energy and resources to becoming informed advocates. This is not narrowly limited to knowing and mastering one's argument and position on a given issue. It is critical to understand all perspectives in the policy debate, the history of the issue at stake, and the current status of new thinking or positions on that issue.
- Develop a clear and coherent strategy, which is a fundamental step in effective policy work. It is critical to have clarity and coherence on the exact changes or reforms one is seeking to effect. Of crucial importance is the need to decide whether an 'outsider' or 'insider' strategy would be more effective. Adopting an insider strategy means working within the corridors of power and aligning closely with those who have significant power to influence decisions or guide behaviour in the policy process. Such strategies call for relationship-building with key state actors, stimulating empathy with governmental agencies and individuals, and creating space for dialogue and reflection wherein ideas and methods can be devised and debated to address issues of conflict.
- Develop a professional approach in all their engagements with key stakeholders and be cognisant of the appropriate policy institutions with which to engage.

Overall, therefore, there is a crucial need for CSOs to enter into effective partnerships with policy-makers and to work alongside each other, ensuring that each is aware of alternative possibilities in the multiple policy areas they address. Whereas this role is relatively new, it is the key to increasing CSO capacity for leverage and extending their power in their quest to ensure implementation of the new constitution and to effectively impact upon policy-making.

References

Akech, M. (2010) *Institutional Reform in the New Constitution of Kenya*. Nairobi: International Centre for Transitional Justice.

Annan, K. (2012) *Interventions: A life in war and peace*. London: Penguin Books.

Barkan, J. (2004) 'Kenya after Moi'. *Foreign Affairs* 83(1): 87–100.

— (2005) 'New forces shaping Kenyan politics'. *Africa Notes*, no. 18.

Bayart, J.-F., S. Ellis and B. Hibou (1999) *The Criminalization of the State in Africa*. Oxford and Bloomington, IN: James Currey and Indiana University Press.

Brown, S. (2001) 'Authoritarian leaders

and multiparty elections in Africa: how foreign donors help to keep Kenya's Daniel arap Moi in power'. *Third World Quarterly* 22(5): 725–39.

Callaghy, T. (1994) 'Civil society, democracy, and economic change in Africa: a dissenting opinion about resurgent societies'. In J. W. Harbeson, D. Rothchild and N. Chazan (eds) *Civil Society and the State in Africa*. Boulder, CO: Lynne Rienner, pp. 231–53.

Chabal, P. and J. P. Daloz (1999) *Africa Works: Disorder as political instrument*. Oxford: James Currey.

Chazan, N. (1994) 'Engaging the state: associational space in sub-Saharan Africa'. In J. S. Migdal, A. Kohli and V. Shue (eds) *State Power and Social Forces: Domination and transformation in the third world*. New York, NY: Cambridge University Press, pp. 255–89.

Diamond, L. (1999) *Developing Democracy Towards Consolidation*. Baltimore, MD: Johns Hopkins University Press.

Harbeson, J. W. (1994) 'Civil society and political renaissance in Africa'. In J. W. Harbeson, D. Rothchild and N. Chazan (eds) *Civil Society and the State in Africa*. Boulder, CO: Lynne Rienner, pp. 1–34.

— D. Rothchild and N. Chazan (eds) (1994) *Civil Society and the State in Africa*. Boulder, CO: Lynne Rienner.

Ihonvbere, J. O. (1996) *Economic Crisis, Civil Society, and Democratization: The case of Zambia*. Trenton, NJ and Asmara: Africa World Press.

Kanyinga, K. (2011) 'Stopping a conflagration: the response of Kenyan civil society to the post-2007 election violence'. *Politikon* 38(1): 85–109.

Katumanga, M. (2000) *Civil Society and the Politics of Constitutional Reform in Kenya: A case study of the National Convention Executive Council (NCEC)*. Research Report. London: Institute for Development Studies.

Kennedy, P. and L. Bieniek (2010) *Moving Forward with Constitutional Reform in Kenya: A Report of the CSIS Africa Program*. Washington, DC: Centre for Strategic and International Studies (CSIS).

Maingi, G. (2012) 'The Kenyan constitutional reform process: a case study of FIDA Kenya in securing women's rights'. *Feminist Africa* 15: 63–81.

Mamdani, M. (1995) 'A critique of the state and civil society paradigm in Africanist studies'. In M. Mamdani and E. Wamba-dia-Wamba (eds) *African Studies in Social Movements and Democracy*. Dakar: Codesria.

Migdal, J. S., A. Kohli and V. Shue (eds) (1994) *State Power and Social Forces: Domination and transformation in the third world*. Cambridge: Cambridge University Press.

Mkandawire, T. and S. Soludo (1999) *Our Continent, Our Future: African perspectives on structural adjustment*. Dakar: Codesria.

Murunga, G. R. (2000) 'Civil society and the democratic experience in Kenya: review essay'. *African Sociological Review* 4(1): 97–118.

— (2007) 'Governance and the politics of structural adjustment'. In G. R. Murunga and S. W. Nasong'o (eds) *Kenya: The struggle for democracy*. London and Dakar: Zed Books and Codesria.

— (2011) *Spontaneous or Premeditated? Post-election violence in Kenya*. Discussion Paper 57. Uppsala: Nordic African Institute.

— and S. W. Nasong'o (2006) 'Bent on self-destruction: the Kibaki regime in Kenya'. *Journal of Contemporary African Studies* 24(1): 1–28.

Mutunga, W. (1999) *Constitution-making from the Middle: Civil society and transition politics in Kenya, 1992–1997*. Nairobi and Harare: SAREAT and MWENGO.

— (2003) 'Mutunga: why I turned down university job'. *Sunday Nation*, 20 April.

Nasong'o, S. W. (2002) 'Civil society and African democratization: the flip side of the coin'. *Studies in Democratization* 1: 1–16.

— (2005) *Contending Political Paradigms*

in Africa: Rationality and the politics of democratization in Kenya and Zambia. New York, NY: Routledge.

— (2007a) 'Transition without transformation: the dialectic of liberalization without democratization in Kenya and Zambia'. *African Studies Review* 50(1): 83–207.

— (2007b) 'Negotiating new rules of the game: civil society, social movements and the Kenyan transition'. In G. R. Murunga and S. W. Nasong'o (eds) *Kenya: The struggle for democracy.* London and Dakar: Zed Books and Codesria.

— (2009) *The Human Rights Sector in Kenya: Key issues and challenges.* Nairobi: Kenya Human Rights Institute.

— (2010) 'Constitutional reform and the crisis of democratization in Kenya'. In D. Branch, N. Cheeseman and L. Gardner (eds) *Our Turn to Eat: Politics in Kenya since 1950.* Berlin: LIT Verlag, pp. 221–41.

Ndegwa, S. N. (1996) *The Two Faces of Civil Society: NGOs and politics in Africa.* West Hartford, CT: Kumarian Press.

— (2005) 'Constitutionalism in Africa's democratic transitions'. *Taiwan Journal of Democracy* 1(1): 133–68.

Nyang'oro, J. E. (2000) 'Civil society, structural adjustment, and democratization in Kenya'. In R. B. Kleinberg and J. A. Clark (eds) *Economic Liberalization and Civil Society in the Developing World.* New York, NY: St Martin's Press, pp. 91–108.

Orvis, S. (2003) 'Kenya civil society: bridging the rural–urban divide?' *Journal of Contemporary African Studies* 41(2): 247–68.

Press, R. (2004) 'Establishing a culture of resistance in an authoritarian regime: the role of individual activists in Kenya, 1987–2002'. Presented at the 47th African Studies Association Annual Meeting, New Orleans, 11–14 November.

— (2012) 'Kenya's political "transition" through the eyes of its "foot soldiers" for democracy and human rights'. *Journal of Contemporary African Studies* 30(3): 441–60.

Vliet, M., W. Wahiu and A. Magolowondo (2012) *Constitutional Reform Processes and Political Parties: Principles for practice.* Leiden: Netherlands Centre for Multiparty Democracy and Centre for African Studies.

Wanyeki, M. (2010) 'Kenyan civil society and the 2007/2008 political crisis: towards and following the Kenya National Dialogue and Reconciliation (KNDR)'. Paper prepared for the African Research and Resource Foundation, Nairobi.

Wrong, M. (2009) *It's Our Turn to Eat: The story of a Kenyan whistle-blower.* London and New York, NY: Harper Perennial.

Yahya-Othman, S. and J. S. Warioba (eds) (2007) *Moving the Kenyan Constitutional Review Process Forward: A report of the fact finding mission to Kenya.* Kampala: Fountain Publishers.

PART TWO

The content, challenges and opportunities of a new constitutional order

6 | Constitutions and constitutionalism: the fate of the 2010 constitution

Yash Pal Ghai

This chapter examines the concept of constitutionalism in order to assess the prospects for the realisation of the objectives of the 2010 constitution. Constitutionalism is a form of governance that has been credited with progress and development in the West. Not every constitution conforms to the objectives and values of constitutionalism. Indeed, before 2010, Kenya's constitutions were antagonistic to these values. Earlier constitutions were problematic for the people, as the people suffered from arbitrariness on the part of the government, and more generally from the non-recognition, and denial, of their rights and freedoms. But they were not problematic for the governments, because they were given more or less absolute power to rule the people.

The 2010 constitution represents a radical departure from the earlier constitutions. It is written to serve the people, and it puts serious restrictions on the authority of the government and prescribes how it must exercise the powers of the state. It would be inaccurate to say that it has pitted the people against the government, for people do not necessarily understand how they were exploited under the past constitutions. A major reason for this lack of awareness is the politicisation of ethnicity by 'leaders' whereby they invoke tribalism to obscure class exploitation. The ruling class is well aware of the challenge posed by the constitution to their plunder of state resources. It is therefore no surprise that the ruling class has embarked upon its sabotage.

Constitutions and constitutionalism

The constitution is a set of rules and institutions that regulate the governing of the country. Constitutionalism is an ideology based on certain values, procedures and practices. At one level, the concept of the constitution is very simple: it is a text that is the supreme law of the land. Constitutions have been a way of consolidating power – as is well illustrated by colonial constitutions, but also by experiences elsewhere. The concept of constitutionalism at first focused on the supremacy of the constitution, as a means to control the people. Later, it was used to limit the power of the state. A pioneering scholar of constitutionalism, Charles Howard McIlwain, said that 'in all its successive phases, constitutionalism has one essential quality: it is a legal limitation on government; it is the antithesis of arbitrary rule; its opposite is despotic government, the government of will instead of law' (McIlwain 1947; see also Poggi 1978). In brief, a central feature is the impersonalisation of power.

Today, constitutionalism, though focused principally on the exercise of state power, encompasses a wider set of values and principles that must regulate the governance of the country. These concern not only limits on state power, but may require that state power be exercised positively to promote objectives such as equality and human rights, social justice and fair procedures. The granting of wider powers to the government so that it may fulfil this mandate also makes the control of power harder. This is the dilemma of modern constitutionalism, which brings in the sovereignty and participation of the people, and independent institutions to reinforce the protection of constitutional values and procedures.

Constitutionalism is a complex concept, involving both the source of power and limits on that power. It transcends the text and supremacy of the constitution. The origins of the concept lie outside the legal text. Constitutions used to be largely about the allocation of public power and the structure of the state, rather than values and principles. The ideas that we now associate with constitutionalism emerged in society, not the state, and to a great extent reflected changing economic and class structures. These ideas served to mould the working of the constitution; they became the basis of conventions – that is, understandings in society on how constitutional powers and procedures would be exercised or applied. Conventions reflected public morality and values, legitimacy of the political order, relations of citizens with the state and of citizens among themselves. In a sense, the values underlying conventions became more important than the text; they were internalised and became the rules of the political game.

The idea of constitutionalism sketched out above is based on the experience of Western states, emanating from changing configurations in society. Its implementation or operation was therefore not problematic, except when fundamental changes in society took place. Then the problem was solved by another constitution imposed by the ascendant social group, assuring convergence between the new dominant social group and the constitution.

Constitutionalism began to emerge as a political and legal concept in the eighteenth and nineteenth centuries, in part due to the rise of industrialisation and the market economy. It succeeded absolutism, under which the authority of the ruler, usually a monarch, could not be challenged. Over time, civil society developed, largely as a result of economic changes towards the market economy. Constitutions increasingly replaced the royal prerogative as the ultimate source of state authority. For various well known reasons, constitutionalism or the rule of law is critical to the market, allowing people to make transactions for the future, keeping the state at a distance, protecting property and securing the impartial enforcement of agreements. Marxist and liberal scholars agree that the dominant ideology of the liberal economic order is constitutionalism or the rule of law. At first, the rule of law hid the reality of power politics and the domination over the workers, but because of the very power of this ideology, overt behaviour inconsistent with its norms raised questions about the exercise of power. In this way, constitutionalism acted to restrain government action and to secure to a significant extent the liberties and freedoms of citizens.

The experience in Africa has been quite different. Constitutionalism is not a weapon in the armoury of the ruling class. On the contrary, it is conceived of as a weapon to fight, or at least restrict, the ruling class – as is illustrated by the aspirations that led to contemporary constitutions, especially in Africa and Latin America.

Colonial and postcolonial constitutions

Colonial constitutions In Kenya, constitutions have served the function of usurping power and appropriating land and other property and other rights and liberties. They have been the means of dominating society by those in charge of the state. I look first at colonial constitutions, because in some ways the roots of colonial constitutions and state institutions, largely in violence and the selective but destructive use of armed force, continue to be the basis of state power today (Ghai and McAuslan 1970).[1]

Aside from when independence was imminent, constitutions were decided upon and enacted by the imperial power in London without any consultation with the local people, the exception being European settlers and civil servants. They were driven entirely by imperial interests. They vested the plenitude of powers in the colonial government, under the overriding power and supervision of the governor, subject only to imperial laws. They said little about the rights of indigenous peoples. They were racially structured, prescribing the unequal status and rights of the various racial groups. They, or other constitutional instruments, registered fresh acquisitions of territory – from the Sultan of Zanzibar, the protectorate of Uganda and Somalia – again without consultation with the communities who were regrouped or the people they were merged with, and with a consequent effect on local communities and their rulers, whose rights were frequently disregarded when it suited the imperial agenda.

There was no accountability of government to the people they ruled. There was virtually legal immunity for the colonial administration under the Act of State doctrine, especially in respect of liability to local people. The government was free to change the law when it suited it. Nor was the judiciary independent, since the power of appointment and dismissal rested with the governor, who, for a period, also personified legislative and executive powers – and certainly dominated these institutions until independence. When the local legislature was established (initially with a government majority and with only white representatives), its laws could be vetoed by the British government. Even as the three institutions of government emerged, there was no effective separation of powers. Franchise was at first restricted to Europeans, then other communities were given the right to elect their own representatives, but African representation came last – and late. Thereafter, the rules of franchise was changed constantly to suit local Europeans. Until the very end of colonial rule, the system of government and administration was based on what a distinguished scholar of the colonial system had described as the two great principles of subordination of the colonised: '(1) The legislature is subordinate to the executive; and (2) the colonial government is subordinate to the imperial government' (White 1952: 17).

Such a constitutional model was not calculated to inspire respect for the idea of a constitution, or to provide a training in or experience of the principles of democracy. Nor was it likely to lead to the growth of a common identity or national unity among the people – who were divided for political and administrative reasons into so many communities – as antagonists facing each other in the legislature or the executive. Any openings to democracy and grudging inclusion of human rights came too late to educate budding politicians in their values and practice. On the contrary, decisions taken under the constitutions routinely violated principles of democracy and human rights (Ghai and McAuslan 1970).[2]

The colonialists' legacy to Kenya is an oppressive state, towering over society, dependent on brute force. The nature or use of force did not feature in the colonial constitution, although it constituted an essential component of colonial rule. The police, but not other armed forces, appeared for the first time in any constitutional instrument in the *madaraka* constitution of 1963. It was placed there to allay the anxieties of the minority tribes under the umbrella of the Kenya African Democratic Union (KADU) and was part of the scheme of *majimbo* (Chapter VIII).[3] It sought to break the centralisation of control over the police by the national government and to establish a National Security Council representative of the central and all regional governments to regulate police matters. An independent police service commission was to appoint members of the police force, including the inspector general. In addition to the national police contingent, there were to be regional contingents under regional police commissioners. There was no provision for other armed forces – presumably they were part of British troops and would remain under the authority of the governor. These provisions were largely reproduced in the independence constitution (Chapter IX) – and there was still no mention of other armed forces.

The independence constitution The rest, as they say, is history. The history is the mutilation of the independence constitution – a constitution that had been agreed to by all parties after prolonged and intense negotiations. The important chapter on the independence of the police was removed, enabling the government to revert to the colonial practice of using the police to harass and subvert political and civil society organisations given protection by the bill of rights. Jomo Kenyatta's government did more. It abolished *majimbo* (devolution) and with it the senate. (The rumours were that each of the senators was bribed to vote for its abolition, in addition to being transformed into a member of an enlarged national assembly with tenure extended by two years – setting the style of political bargaining and corruption that has characterised Kenyan politics ever since.) A full-blown parliamentary system was replaced by a semi-presidential or -parliamentary system, in which the head of the government, the president, became also the head of the state. Thus, with one stroke, the contours of the state were restored to their colonial origin: a highly centralised government and administration, under the governor/president, with a firm control of provincial administration and no *majimbo* (Gertzel 1970: 23–7).[4]

As if Jomo Kenyatta had not done enough damage to the *uhuru* constitution, his successor, Daniel arap Moi, returned to the task with renewed enthusiasm, destroying the independence of many critical public bodies and officers, rigging elections, and making liberal use of laws that the departing British colonists had bequeathed to the government to fight secession and other 'terrorist' activities. Space does not permit discussion of how these presidents ravaged the framework of constitutionalism that had been crafted into the 1963 independence constitution (a good source is a 1991 report by Human Rights Watch, *Taking Liberties*). Suffice it to say that the opposition parties were harassed and a law was passed to disqualify those MPs who had crossed the floor to join the opposition (Ghai and McAuslan 1970: 321–3). In due course, Moi, with Kibaki's support, made the country into a one-party state by amending the constitution. Wide-ranging power was given to the president to detain a person without trial for long periods. There is reliable evidence that several leading politicians opposed to government policies (Pio Gama Pinto and J. M. Kariuki) or who were seen as a threat to Kenya African National Union (KANU) leadership (Tom Mboya and Robert Ouko) were assassinated on the orders of the government (Branch 2011).[5] Others, like Raila Odinga, spent long periods in detention or worse in torture chambers. Many fled the country. Civil society came under considerable pressure and harassment. The media were harassed. The judiciary was brought under the control of the president and the attorney general; it became an additional source of the harassment of government opponents, and a haven of impunity for its friends (ibid.; Human Rights Watch 1991).[6] Political rulers wanted the state to be absolutist: immune to democratic rules and practices and not accountable to anyone. All controls and scrutiny over the powers of the executive were removed.

What Britain bequeathed to Kenyans was a country with its many communities brought together under political structures and with an economy
based on their subordination, but with the additional problem of finding and
creating a common identity and destiny: a state without a nation. But it also
gave Kenyatta a constitution with a state geared to political and economic
reform and development within the framework of democracy. It represented
an opportunity to promote Kenyan identity and national unity and to pursue
consensual policies for the goals that had motivated the freedom struggle.
In his greed for accumulation of wealth and his loyalty to his tribe, Kenyatta
squandered that opportunity – and built a model for other politicians.

This was possible because of the role of the state in respect of the economy
and its control over considerable resources (Hino et al. 2012).[7] This encouraged
patronage and ethnic politics as each community focused on this vital political
prize. The centrality of the capture of the state is demonstrated by the intense
anxieties and intrigues, and shifting alliances, that attend each succession.
Combined with the lack of accountability, the system led to massive corruption, benefiting principally the president's ethnic cronies. The control of land
by the government and by county councils, and in particular the president's
power to grant land without any legal process or consultation, led to massive
abuse, illegal land transfers and the dispossession of many, widening the gulf
between rich and poor. Pervasive corruption undermined state resources, dis-
tracted the president, ministers and senior bureaucrats from their ministerial
and official responsibilities, and led to declining levels of social services, the
emergence of slums, acute poverty for many and obscene affluence for a few.
State policies and practices became exclusionary, intensifying ethnic discrimination and conflict, and encouraging the militarisation of politics and armed
tribal conflict, causing many deaths and still more displacements, together
with the assassination of a few politicians committed to reform and social
justice. The rule of law could not survive the huge powers of the president,
some under the law but many with no legal foundation. The impunity of
the president and his associates became a licence for many acts of violence,
corruption and theft of state resources.

All this made people distrust government and caused suspicion and conflict between ethnic communities, as politicians played on ethnic fears and
promoted ethnic animosities, weakening national solidarity and threatening
the very integrity of the country. The logic of these developments was fully
demonstrated in the terrible violence following what were widely perceived to
be the rigged elections of 2007.

With the end of the Cold War, the US and Britain began to put pressure
on their allies to democratise their political and governmental systems. The
new wave of democracy prompted by developments in Europe encouraged
civil society in Kenya to campaign for constitutional reform. Moi, then presi-

dent, came under intense pressure from external and national groups and had to initiate a constitutional reform process. I will not describe the long and tortuous process that led eventually to the 2010 constitution, but rather will examine key aspects of it.

Objectives of the 2010 constitution

In order to analyse the scope for, and limits to, constitutionalism after the promulgation of the 2010 constitution, a brief summary of its main objectives is necessary.[8] As analysed by the Constitution of Kenya Review Commission (CKRC), there were two major problems – a corrupt and coercive state and the lack of national identity.

The stated objectives of the new constitution with regard to nation-building and state restructuring are interconnected (Ghai and Ghai 2011). As regards nation-building, the emphasis is on unity, patriotism, equal rights, inclusiveness and social justice, which are described as national values and principles to suffuse all state institutions (Article 10). There is considerable stress on redress for past injustices (e.g. Article 67(2)(c)), positive steps to deal with the marginalisation of deprived and vulnerable communities (e.g. Articles 56, 81(b) and (c), 100 and 174(e)), respect for cultures and religions, and the promotion of local languages (Articles 11, 32 and 44). By implication, exclusionary ethnic politics are incompatible with these national values; political parties are to have a national character (Article 91(1)(a)).

As regards state restructuring, the dominant principles and objectives are integrity in public life and among state officials, transparency, accountability, people's participation, ending of impunity (Chapter 6), a greatly strengthened judiciary (Chapter 10) and reform of political parties (Article 91). Devolved government as a form of power-sharing, self-government and public participation have elements of both nation-building and state restructuring (Article 174). The constitution prescribes high standards of financial probity, including transparent and competitive processes for state procurements (Article 227) and fundamental reforms in the state's financial management (Chapter 12), and it provides for an independent commission to fix the salaries of senior officials, including legislators (Article 230). A number of independent commissions and offices are established to protect human rights; ensure fair land policies and transactions; recruit to state services on merit, while promoting equitable distribution of posts on ethnic and regional bases; conduct free and fair elections; and promote probity and accountability in public finance (Chapter 15).

The constitution also emphasises public welfare – addressing the question of poverty, essentially by the introduction of social and economic rights, health, education, housing, sanitation, food and social security (Article 43) – and measures against corruption (Article 79). It recognises the importance of land to economic development and equity, as well as the fact that the current laws on land and its administration are riddled with corruption (Article 60). In order to hide this corruption, the distinctions between different categories of land were blurred and its administration built on deliberate obscurity. Recognising also that much land has been acquired illegally, the constitution denies such land constitutional protection against state takeover and mandates an independent land commission to investigate illegal acquisitions (Articles 40 and 60). A strong bill of rights gives individuals protection against undue interference by the government and against unfair administrative practices while protecting their privacy (Chapter 4). It gives various rights to the media. The protection of individual and community rights, with an emphasis on the central values of human dignity, equality and participation, indicates that the constitution is best implemented through a 'human rights-based approach to development' (UNDP 1998).[9] Human rights constitute the parameters within which state laws and policies must be made (Article 19). The approach encompasses both procedures and goals. It empowers individuals and communities and requires that they play a central role in decision-making (Articles 10(2)(a), 118 and 174(c)).

The constitution makes a stab at regulating the coercive basis of the state. For the first time the definition of national security includes the protection of the 'people, their rights, freedoms, property, peace, stability and prosperity', and is subject to the authority of parliament (Article 238(10) and (2)). National security is to be pursued in compliance with the law and 'the utmost respect for the rule of law, democracy, human rights, and fundamental freedoms', and security forces are to respect 'the diverse culture of' Kenya's communities (Article 238(2)). Unlike past practice, security organs must 'reflect the diversity of the Kenyan people in equitable proportions' (Article 238(d)).

Together, these provisions seek to bring about a fundamental change in nation and state. The constitution defines the nature of democracy for Kenya, not as majoritarianism, but as the balance of different interests of communities, and the preservation and promotion of constitutional principles. Indeed, the constitution is rich in values and principles. It sets the objectives for which state power may be exercised. It creates a participatory democracy in which people play an important role on a continuous basis. It seeks to deal with past injustices. It addresses the issues of exclusion and poverty – and of gender inequity. It disperses the power of the state to all regions of the country, dismantling the monopolisation of its powers at the centre. The constitution addresses several sensitive and difficult balances between diversity and nationhood, which may be hard to sustain, given the strong ethnic, cultural and religious background of most communities (Ghai and Cottrell 2013). It sets high standards of integrity and fairness – and of service to the people.

People power An important strategy of the CKRC was to empower the people in order to facilitate achievement of constitutional objectives. There is a constant emphasis on the participation of the people in public affairs (e.g. Articles 10(2)(a), 118 and 196(a)); they have easy access to courts and other institutions that receive and deal with complaints; they have the right to form associations (Article 36) and to assemble, demonstrate, picket and petition public authorities (Article 37); they can recall legislators (Article 104); and, through referendums, they can protect important constitutional provisions (Articles 255(2) and 257(10)). Most importantly, every five years, the people elect the president, governors, parliament and county assemblies. And the constitution keeps reminding the people that sovereignty lies with them.

Challenge of implementation

A great deal of effort has gone into crafting the constitution so that its values and structures will impose themselves on the state and society, with much attention given to enforcement and remedies. However, the internal logic and dynamics of the constitution will have to compete with larger social forces, the most powerful of which may have little commitment to its values. The fortunes of a constitution are shaped by many factors: personalities and elites, political parties and other organisations, social structures, economic changes, traditions of constitutionalism – and by the rules and institutions of the constitution itself (Ghai 2010: 313–31).

It is important to note that this constitution was imposed on politicians and bureaucrats by the people (a revolutionary constitution but no revolution), unlike the previous ones that were imposed by politicians on the people. Those familiar with Kenya's past regimes will immediately recognise how it seeks to revolutionise state and society. A major obstacle to its implementation is that the state is the primary source of power and wealth in society. Corruption is the principal vehicle for accumulation. Since a major preoccupation of the constitution is the safeguarding of public resources from plunder, the only way in which the ruling class could achieve its objectives is by systematic violation of the constitution, benefiting from impunities that the political and legal systems have bestowed upon them. The question is whether those who are committed to the reform of the state will be able to impose the discipline of the constitution on the ruling class.

Planning implementation The drafters of the constitution were well aware of the resistance that the constitution would encounter from vested interests in state and society. They were also aware of the complexity of the political and administrative system they were recommending; the vast number of new laws to be made, and some to be repealed; new institutions to be established, while some old ones were to be dismantled; the redeployment of civil servants; reallocation of financial and other resources; a new electoral system; and a host of independent commissions to be created or modified.

A constitution's success depends both on factors internal to the constitution (its structures, incentives, enforceability, clarity, and so on) and on outside factors (social and economic classes, legitimacy of the constitution, support for and opposition to the constitution). Drafters can do something about the former, but little about the latter (see ibid.). However, the long period of the constitution-making process, during which considerable civic education as well as consultations with Kenyans took place, enabled the people to understand the objectives of the constitution. The anticipated challenges to the constitution would be both political and technical or legal, and would include:

- resistance by the political, bureaucratic and business elites to the objectives of the constitution;
- the considerable amount of legislation necessary to implement the principles of the constitution (for example, integrity, land, recall of legislators, an electoral system handling simultaneously the election of six categories of representatives, representation of marginalised groups, independence of the judiciary, parliamentary control over the security forces and oversight by an independent authority, a financial management system, and, perhaps the most difficult of all, devolution – forty-seven counties with totally new institutions, the allocation and transfer of functions, their relationship with central authorities, dispute resolution, the setting up of sub-county authorities, etc.) and the establishment of a number of new institutions, including the senate, independent commissions and office-holders, and the revenue allocation mechanism;
- issues of sequencing and coordination between different steps (for example in making major changes to the judiciary and the police);
- cooperation between and coordination of different bodies charged with implementation;
- treating the process of implementation, especially the drafting of laws, as not just a routine exercise but one that itself reflects the values and processes of the new constitution, with a new stress on participation; and
- preventing government departments, and others, from reasserting the way things have always been done.

The implementation scheme The CKRC analysed carefully the new laws and old laws to be reformed, and made it obligatory for the government and the legislature to ensure the passage of these laws within prescribed periods, as set out in the Fifth Schedule; the entire process was to be completed within five years. Failure could bring about a severe penalty – no less than the dissolution of the legislature (Article 261). The attorney general was given the responsibility for the drafting in consultation with the Commission for the Implementation of the Constitution (CIC).

The constitution establishes the CIC as a temporary, independent commission to oversee constitutional implementation, although its functions are less critical for implementation than those proposed by the CKRC. Its functions are to monitor, facilitate and oversee the development of the legislation and administrative procedures required to implement the constitution; coordinate with government bodies responsible for preparing the legislation; work with each constitutional commission (including those on human rights, elections, official salaries and remuneration, and the allocation of revenue between the nation and counties, and among counties) to ensure that the letter and the spirit of the constitution are respected; and work with constitutional commissions (clause 5 of the Sixth Schedule).

But it is to the judiciary that the drafters looked for the safeguarding of the constitution in the last resort, and on whom it placed the highest responsibility. Courts play the major role in maintaining the supremacy of the constitution. The constitution strengthens the independence of the judiciary through a more representative Judicial Service Commission (JSC) (Articles 160, 166–8 and 171–2) and through more secure financial resources (Article 173). Ample opportunities are provided for access to the courts. All human rights (including socio-economic rights) are within the jurisdiction of the courts. Every person has the right to institute court proceedings if they can claim that a right or fundamental freedom in the bill of rights has been denied, violated or infringed, or is threatened, on behalf of others (Article 22(1)), or 'acting in the public interest' (Article 22(2)(c)). Court rules must ensure that formalities relating to the proceedings are kept to a minimum, including, if necessary, beginning proceedings by 'informal documentation' (Article 22(3)(b)); no fee is charged for commencing human rights proceedings (Article 22(3)(c)); and, with permission of the court, an organisation or person with particular expertise may appear as a friend of the court (Article 22(3)(e)). Similar principles apply for non-human rights cases (Article 258).

Along with other state organs, the judiciary has a fundamental duty to 'observe, respect, promote and fulfil the rights and fundamental freedoms in the bill of rights' (Article 21(a)). The judiciary, like other state organs, has the duty to 'address the needs of the vulnerable groups within society, including women, children, youth, members of minority or marginalised communities, and members of particular ethnic, religious or cultural communities' (Article 21(3)). Courts have to develop the law where it does not reflect the protection of a right (Article 20(3)).

The constitution sets guidelines for courts in the exercise of their authority. These include that 'Justice shall be done to all, irrespective of status' (Article 159(2)). The administration of justice must be directed to the promotion of the purposes and principles of the constitution. There is protection of the right to fair administrative action (Article 47), which gives the courts a specific role in respect of administrative law and practice. It recognises the rights of due process, including the right to free legal representation if substantial injustice would result otherwise (Article 50(g) and (h)). The rules of interpretation (which bind all state and private parties, not merely the courts) require that the constitution should be interpreted to promote its purposes, values and principles, to advance the rule of law, human rights and fundamental freedoms, to permit the development of the law, and to contribute to good government.

Vetting of the judiciary In giving this key role to the judiciary, the drafters were aware of the fact that the majority of the judges at that time had become corrupt and were incompetent. They would have neither the will nor the ability to promote or oversee constitutional implementation. Consequently, the drafters recommended that every judge and magistrate in office when the constitution came into effect would be vetted for integrity and competence. With successive drafts, the mechanism for vetting became rather diluted, but it remained a key element in the reform of the judiciary. The vetting seemed to get off to a good start, but some later decisions were quite suspect (people asked whether the vetting process itself became corrupted). And although the judiciary was to be excluded from any review of the decisions of the vetting board, the Court of Appeal chose to intervene, reversing the board's decision (at the time of writing, the matter is before the Supreme Court).

The record of implementation so far

The task of the implementation is massive, given that the constitution requires a fundamental change in governance (new values, institutions and structure of power). It is impossible in the space allotted to me to discuss the manifold aspects of implementation. A radical constitution has reasonable prospects of implementation only if its makers are also radical and are in charge of the state. That was not the case in Kenya, where the vast majority of the parliamentarians and ministers – and mainstream churches – opposed the draft constitution, and where key members of the coalition voted into power in 2013 campaigned against the draft. In addition, the fact that parliament and government were only halfway through their term when the constitution was adopted and would not have agreed to immediate elections had two major consequences: firstly, the provisions for the new government system at the national level and the entire devolution system would not come into effect until after the next general elections; and secondly, the major responsibility for implementation fell effectively upon a government and parliament hostile to the constitution.

Moreover, the country was ruled by a coalition government with a huge cabinet, most ministries were fragmented, and the relations between the two sides were so bitter that few cabinet meetings were called and members were divided on many issues of implementation, such as devolution. And when elections did take place in 2013, old and old-style politicians dominated the elections. The new MPs were so obsessed with their salaries and allowances that, far from implementing the constitution, they sought to change provisions that stood in the face of this selfish agenda. The new president and deputy president were too obsessed by their trial in the International Criminal Court for crimes against humanity to pay sufficient attention to their responsibilities for the implementation of the constitution, using senior officers – including the new cabinet secretary for foreign affairs and international trade and the attorney general – and considerable state revenues to defend themselves even though they are accused as individuals, not as state officials.

On the positive side, it can be said that the government, parliament and even the bureaucrats have gone through the motions of implementation. Although the result of the presidential election as announced by the electoral commission was contested, the ruling of the supreme court was generally accepted, despite trenchant criticism by many. Many new laws were enacted in accordance with the constitutional timetable. All institutions, independent commissions and offices required by the constitution have been set up. The former chief justice and attorney general (neither of whom were known for their reformist tendencies) were removed, as required by the constitution (but the attorney general was elected as a senator, attesting to the persistence of the old order!). The vetting of the judiciary for integrity and competence started on time and led to the dismissal of several high-profile judges. Even the vetting of senior police officers has started (although not required by the constitution). Most importantly, the establishment of devolution has made progress, with the election of governors and assemblies, the appointment of officers and staff, the allocation of revenue, transfers of most prescribed functions, and bold initiatives by some governors. The judiciary seems to have come of age: many people and organisations have invoked its jurisdiction for the protection and promotion of their rights and of the constitution. Already, several critical issues about politics (including the powers of, and relationship between, key governmental institutions), society and economy (regarding gender, property, land, slums and evictions) are being decided by the courts – and, in large part, are being respected, but selectively as far as the state authorities are concerned.

Progress has been made, especially as we realise that these developments are of great importance, usually controversial, and have required a great deal of hard work. But sometimes the form and the formalities have overshadowed the spirit and objectives of the institutions, values and procedures concerned. It is to this matter that I now turn.

Institutions I discuss developments in the same order as above, beginning with institutions of government at the national and devolved levels. Critical to their establishment were general elections. An analysis of the 2013 elections provides a good perspective on politics and conformity with constitutional standards (Ghai and Cottrell 2013). There is considerable evidence that the Independent Electoral and Boundaries Commission (IEBC) failed in its constitutional and legal responsibilities (Chapter 7, particularly Articles 81, 84 and 86). It was marred by widespread corruption and inefficiency; the expensive electronic technology for registration of voters and the counting of votes broke down due to inadequate preparations and training (some believe deliberately so); it stopped registration of voters well before the elections despite a constitutional requirement of 'continuous registration' (Article 88(4)(a)); it had refused to prescribe the maximum amounts that could be spent on elections by party or candidates despite knowing the propensity towards corruption and bribery; it turned a blind eye to the fraud of parties, bribery by candidates, and failures in the party nomination of candidates; it failed to enforce the rule against change of parties three months before the elections as well as the rule about transparency; and in numerous constituencies there was confusion about the forms registering votes but it failed to provide meaningful voter education.

Political parties paid scant regard to constitutional rules governing their formation and functioning, or regarding manipulation of ethnicity, prohibition of advocacy of hatred, the use of violence or the giving of bribes (Article 91). The parties tolerated and even encouraged shifts in party allegiances, making a mockery of the concept of political parties or of democracy. Altogether, neither campaigns nor the conduct of elections were in the spirit of the constitution or the kind of democracy envisaged by it. It was politics as before, another name for tribalism and corruption.

The confidence the constitution displayed in the good sense and ability of the people to choose their representatives seemed misplaced. Few voters paid attention to the record or policies of candidates. They showed, as previously, that the fundamental criterion was ethnicity – and their vulnerability to manipulation by 'tribal' leaders. The 2013 elections have made it clear that a constitution by itself cannot create democracy from above, even if most principles, institutions, processes and practices of a democratic system are inscribed therein.

To return to institutions, the post-election period, during which the political institutions came fully into being, showed that their members had little understanding of their role or the general constitutional injunction to cooperate and coordinate. Senior politicians who preferred the senate over the national assembly expressed surprise when they found that its powers were quite limited (those same politicians and bureaucrats who had dominated negotiations on the making of the constitution). The lack of understanding of their respective roles, the struggle for perks and the resistance of the government to devolution have led to much hostility and mutual recriminations. There have been many conflicts between institutions at the same and different levels (the senate versus the national assembly, senators versus governors, governors versus the president, county assembly versus the governors), most seemingly petty, which have delayed the proper implementation of the constitution, particularly devolution.[10] Few legislators show an understanding of the constitution, for example in relation to the principle of the separation of powers, and fewer still display any loyalty or commitment to the constitution. In several instances, the issue of separation of powers had to be determined by the courts. At the same time, the principle of parliamentary consent for the appointment of state officers has been largely negated; it has become a commodity in the hands of parliamentarians. Bargaining and deals are regular features. Some key positions are held by people against whom allegations of corruption or other breaches of integrity are pending. There is no evidence that any attention has been paid to the evidence given by the people or institutions against particular nominees; perhaps the most outstanding example of this is the appointment of the director of public prosecutions.

The executive has shown even greater resistance to the constitution. As to the nature of the executive, it is not inclusionary in the composition of either the cabinet or the civil service, although it is required to be so. The situation in the security services is even worse: for example, the Kikuyu, Kalenjin, Luhya, Kamba and Luo account for 70 per cent of all service jobs. Of all government workers, 22.3 per cent are Kikuyu, 16.7 per cent are Kalenjin, 11.3 per cent are Luhya, 9.7 per cent are Kamba, 9.0 per cent are Luo and 5.8 per cent are Kisii, while twenty tribes have less than 1 per cent representation in the civil service.[11]

One of the main failures of the constitution is the failure to humanise the armed forces. The greatest user of force is the police, which thrives on the colonial mandate of 'shoot to kill'. It is not only the most violent group in the country, but also the most corrupt. The government has done little to stop this state of affairs; perhaps such is its dependence on the police to maintain its grip on society.

The judiciary Of all the institutions, the judiciary has come closest to the spirit of the constitution. The bad reputation of the judiciary before 2010 has not entirely been overcome, and there are serious doubts about the integrity of the vetting process, but some corrupt judges have been removed and some excellent new ones appointed. The judiciary was easily the most favoured and trusted institution at the start of the constitution, especially with the appointment of Dr Willy Mutunga as the chief justice and the promised reform of the judiciary.

However, the judiciary no longer enjoys the same degree of popular backing. It lost considerable support, at least among its most ardent admirers – civil society – as a result of the decision of the Supreme Court on the presidential elections in April 2013; this was due to both the conduct of the trial and the decision in favour of Uhuru Kenyatta in the face of so many irregularities. While the supreme court has rightly highlighted the transformative nature of the constitution, and consequently the need to interpret it broadly and according to its spirit and aspirations, it failed to do so in this particular case. It refused to admit the Katiba Institute (KI)[12] as an amicus because of its alleged bias, but it allowed the attorney general, well known for his support of the government. In this and many other decisions, the judiciary has not appeared fair and unbiased. It therefore failed to address KI's argument that the validity of the elections should be judged against the standards set out in the constitution, rather than simply by assessing whether Kenyatta would have won even if some irregularities were taken into account. Such an approach, which is hard to apply empirically due to differences in opinion about the scale of irregularities, negated the constitutional, ethical and integrity standards of politics and elections, and ultimately the supremacy of the constitution. However, some high court judges have realised the importance of following constitutional prescriptions on integrity and process.[13]

The second reason why the judiciary has lost significant political support is due to stories of corruption within the JSC and its staff, triggered by the conflict between the commission members and the chief registrar. Each has accused the other of corruption and other forms of misconduct. It also led to conflict between the JSC and the national assembly, whose committee on the judiciary asked the president to appoint a tribunal to investigate six members of the JSC for misconduct that would justify their dismissal. The high court in turn issued an order stopping the presidentially appointed tribunal (widely perceived to be favourable to the government) from proceeding. Therefore little can be said at this stage on this matter, save that there is no doubt that this unseemly quarrel between the three major institutions of the state has done little for the reputation of any of them.[14]

Before these two incidents, the JSC had done much to improve the image as well as the conduct of the judiciary: more training, exposure to progressive foreign experiences, internal discussions on various aspects of its work in the light of the constitution, the participation of the people in public affairs and decisions, and the generation of promising jurisprudence. The judiciary, particularly the supreme court and the constitutional division of the high court, has done much to clarify the constitutional position on controversial issues and has thus facilitated proper implementation. It has provided very useful guidance on the interpretation of the constitution, emphasising its radical and transformative character.

Laws A large number of the new laws are of uneven quality. Some are written with great care for the constitutional prescriptions, some almost in disregard of them, and some very hastily (leading to rushed voting, often late at night). The drafting of many bills made it hard to understand them and raised doubts about the quality of the drafters. Most bills were passed without proper consultation with the people, which was required. In most cases where the interests of the parliamentarians were involved, the primary consideration seems to have been their welfare (as in the legislative provisions for recall of legislators, making recall almost impossible). The CIC has commented that legislation was enacted without following due process as provided for in Article 26(4) and had fundamental constitutional flaws.

Independent commissions The record of independent commissions and officers is mixed. Unfortunately, the executive has not made it easy for some of them. The CIC believes that the government has undermined their constitutional mandates. The CIC (2013) has itself experienced difficulties despite its mandate to promote and oversee proper implementation of the constitution. It lists, for example, thirty-six laws passed in the year 2012–13 that did not follow proper process, including in most cases ignoring the CIC. The establishment of some commissions was unduly delayed, including that of the Ethics and Anti-Corruption Commission and the National Land Commission. On the whole, the government seems not to respect the role of the commissions; nowhere is this more evident than in the undermining of the Salaries and Remuneration Commission (including ignoring it completely in the enactment of the Presidential Retirement Benefits (Amendment) Act 2013) and, even more blatantly, in moves to abolish the commission altogether.

Human rights No government in Kenya has ever shown any interest in or commitment to human rights. As a consequence, the country's colonial and postcolonial history is full of a litany of violations of human rights, inequalities, brutalities wreaked on the poor and the helpless, deprivation of property (mostly land), long detentions in prisons or torture chambers – and impunity for those responsible for these atrocities or other breaches of the law or their public responsibilities. Little has changed, in either the Kibaki or the Uhuru Kenyatta regimes, despite a detailed and carefully drafted bill of rights. People still have difficulty in organising meetings, assemblies and protests – police brutality still has all the hallmarks of a colonial regime. Social and economic rights are completely ignored. Violence in society is pervasive as the poverty of millions deepens.

The CIC has noted the failure of the state authorities to engender a rights-based approach; it illustrates this by the low levels of representation of marginalised groups, particularly women and people with disabilities, in elective and appointive positions, both at national and county government level (CIC 2013: 47). Court rulings on human rights are routinely ignored, for example in the area of housing, where most destructive evictions continue despite powerful judicial decisions against such evictions. The government's hostility to human rights and democracy was manifested in its efforts to curb civil society and the media towards the end of 2013. The government has so far ignored the report of the Truth, Justice and Reconciliation Commission (the commission was part of the package of measures in the National Accord following the post-2007 election violence), and the State House altered or deleted portions of the report exposing the land-grabbing of Jomo Kenyatta (Uhuru Kenyatta's father), in complete disregard of the law.

Public participation Much was expected of the provisions that give the public the opportunity to take part in public affairs, including petitions to parliament and the right to participate in the law-making process. The fact that the public did *not* take part is due in part to their own apathy or lack of knowledge of these provisions. For their part, the executive and the legislature have done little to encourage people's participation. The CIC's assessment is that:

> [the] level of public participation in the development of policies, legislation, administrative procedures as well as in the broader context of Article 10 of the constitution remains low. There is lack of awareness among the population on the constitution and the law enacted there under. This can be attributed to: (i) the low level of awareness perhaps partially due to gaps in the development and implementation of the Kenya Integrated Civic Education (K-NICE) pro- gramme; (ii) lack of a framework to ensure structured and broad based public participation and (iii) the Government has hardly budgeted any money for civic education (ibid.).

The CIC summarised the approach of the executive to implementation in the following way: 'Regrettably, though, the Executive continues to breach these guidelines and to offend the constitutional principle of public participation by rolling out policies and publishing Bills without meaningful participation of both the Commission and the public as mandated by Articles 10 and 261(4) of the Constitution' (ibid.: 4). It also says, outlining the guidelines for the process of implementation:

> Despite the established process for the development of legislation, the Executive continued to publish Bills in breach of due process. This became rampant towards the end of the quarter, i.e., in December 2012 when 30 Bills went through Parliament and were ultimately enacted on 14 January 2013. The disregard by both the Executive and Parliament of the constitutional process continues to be a major challenge to the implementation of the Constitution (ibid.).[15]

It should also be pointed out that civil society has done too little to promote knowledge of the constitution among the people.

Devolution Preparations for the establishment of devolution started well before the 4 March 2013 elections. The Commission on Revenue Allocation (charged with recommending allocations of revenue raised nationally between national and county governments and among counties) was set up soon after the CIC. A transitional authority was established in early 2012 to make plans for gradually phasing in the powers and functions of devolved governments. The IEBC factored in county elections as it prepared for the 2013 elections. Several official and unofficial workshops were held to understand the system of devolution. Despite these preparations, the transition to devolution is difficult, confusing, painful and controversial – due not only to the technical aspects and lack of understanding of the system, but principally because of the political significance of county government: high expectations in the counties and the reluctance of the national government to devolve its power and resources.

This last factor is evident daily in the fights between the county administration and the centrally run and managed formerly provincial administration system – the linchpin of the colonial system; the quarrels between the national assembly, which is seen as belonging to the national government, and the senate, seen as belonging to the counties; and between the governor and the senators for ultimate control over the counties. There are differences of opinion on how fast the powers of counties should be transferred, whether all stipulated powers should be transferred at once or gradually, whether the more developed counties should be given greater powers than those that are less well developed, and between the Treasury and county authorities as to the amount and form of financial grants (and between the Treasury and the Revenue Allocation Commission). The lack of political will or political skills means that some disputes have to be referred to the courts; the supreme court has already had to resolve a dispute between the national assembly and the senate. The problems are compounded by the greed of members of the county assemblies, most of whom staged a boycott until their remuneration was are significantly adjusted upwards.

These developments, leading to the steady attrition of the powers and authority of counties, are most unfortunate. The constitution envisages a critical role for devolution, for enhancement of democracy and diversity, accountable exercise of power, protection of minorities, and social and economic development (Article 174). The supreme court decision tries to halt the damage to the concept and practice of devolution through its robust statement of the centrality of devolution.

In the majority decision, the court said:

> The Kenyan people, by the Constitution of Kenya, 2010 chose to de-concentrate
> State power, rights, duties, competences – shifting substantial aspects to
> county government, to be exercised in the county units, for better and more

equitable delivery of the goods of the political order. The dominant perception at the time of constitution-making was that such a deconcentration of powers would not only give greater access to the social goods previously regulated centrally, but would also open up the scope for political self-fulfilment, through an enlarged scheme of actual participation in governance mechanisms by the people – thus giving more fulfilment to the concept of *democracy* ... Devolution as a required constitutional practice runs in parallel with an attendant set of values, declared in Article 10 of the Constitution: the rule of law, democracy, participation of the people, human dignity, equity, social justice, inclusiveness, equality, human rights, non-discrimination, the protection of the marginalized (SCOK 2013: paras 136, 138).

The chief justice, in a separate concurring judgment, was even more emphatic:

The Kenyan state was founded on a partisan, sectarian, and exclusionary logic. It is this logic that the Constitution of Kenya, 2010 sought to deconstruct. There is no doubt that Kenya is a diverse and unequal country. The inequalities within groups and between regions are manifested in the class structure of society, ethno-regional differences, rural–urban divides, and gender biases ... The Constitution's provisions on *Devolution* were key pillars in the deconstruction process. Indeed, a reading of the *Final Report of the Constitution of Kenya Review Commission* (CKRC) shows that vast segments of the Kenyan population felt that they were victims of the state, either in terms of *political repression*, or in terms of *developmental exclusion*. Thus, the Constitution of Kenya, 2010 was attractive to a large number of Kenyans for many reasons. In particular, *devolution* was instrumental in mobilizing support for the Constitution in the referendum, because many people perceived its dispersal of economic and political power as an act of *liberation*. There is a large section of our society for whom the new Constitution is coterminous with *devolution*. It denotes *self-empowerment, freedom, opportunity, self-respect, dignity* and *recognition*. This perception is captured succinctly in the principles and objects of devolution, in Article 174. *Devolution* is thus a positively emotive capsule, in the political dispensation (ibid.: para. 173).

Final reflections

In conclusion, while at a formal level, many constitutional provisions have been implemented, there is scant respect for the spirit and objectives of the constitution. This is not surprising. A constitution operates within society and seeks to influence its development. The distinguished Indian sociologist Andre Beteille suggests that, while a constitution may indicate the direction in which we are able to move, the social structure will decide how far we are able to move and at what pace (Beteille 1992: 1). The constitution may set out guidelines for the exercise of power and aspirations for the state to meet. But the social reform agenda characteristic of contemporary constitutions challenges existing societal values and prejudices that for the most part favour elites. Constitutional reformers cannot assume that society is uniformly supportive of their proposals. Different sectors have different, often clashing, interests. The constitution's design of a political order competes with other political models and realities. The common constitutional value of impersonal power, for example, contradicts older ideas of how a 'chief' can and should act, ideas that may underlie the 'strong man' syndrome often found in presidential government and equally supportive of politicised ethnicity.

While the African state is strong in its subjugation of society, it is weak in its capacity to direct social change. Most politicians have little desire for social progress, concentrating on their predatory practices, protected by political fragmentation and the ethnification of society. In this vortex of constitutional values and mandates in competition with the ambitions and predations of politicians and bureaucrats, there seems no room for moral values, equality under law, or settled legal principle and practice. These types of both 'strength' and weakness or incapacity are harmful for the growth of constitutionalism. That 'strength' can lead to the disregard of values, and 'weakness' to a failure to implement them.

I have argued elsewhere that the fortunes of a constitution are influenced by three factors: the nature of the state, economy and society (Ghai 2010). The 2010 constitution has changed the form but not the reality of the state: its colonial legacy. It is still dominated by a small class, dependent heavily on armed force. The economy continues to be an administered economy, despite considerable economic development and a growing private sector. In an administered economy, the key levers are in the hands of the state executive. This increases competition for control of the state. The state becomes a major source for the accumulation of private wealth – something that can be secured only by corruption and the disregard of the rule of law or constitutionalism. The conflicts between different legislative bodies and executive authorities, particularly as manifested in the management of devolution, are not about principles but about power. The competition for the capture of the state is fought out through the mobilisation of ethnic support, which downgrades policies and robs politics of its significance. The pervasive use of corruption to buy votes for and in parliament, to secure contracts, to secure appointments, to undermine justice, and so on, negates most constitutional values and principles.

The economy feeds into this system, conforming to its imperatives rather than influencing it, as market capitalism did in Europe and the US. This weakens the challenge to the practices of the state and its disregard for the constitution.

Despite the postcolonial rise of an incipient bourgeoisie and other social forces, the overwhelming political factor is the passivity of the majority of the people. By passivity, I do not mean that they do not care – they do care, but they are at the receiving end of the predatory and violent practices of the state. Although peasants and workers constitute a majority, they cannot translate their grievances into political clout or pressure, since they have allowed themselves to be divided by ethnicity. Thus, preventing the growth of their class consciousness is a critical strategy of the political class, the one class united by its many common interests. The most active popular political actions take ethnic forms and occur most patently at election times. There are few political parties in the classical sense of aggregating, articulating and protecting the interests of key sectors of the public – despite legislation that requires these objectives, on pain of a party's dissolution. Non-governmental organisations are still pursuing the politics of the 1990s, with their decreasing relevance.

These weaknesses in civil society (see Chapter 5) make it difficult for it to put any effective pressure on the state. Politics then becomes the occupation of a few professional politicians, and results in fluid parties, few of which are based on membership. Few other voices are given expression by a media that has fallen increasingly into political hands or under their influence, notwithstanding the hostile attitude to it of the Uhuru Kenyatta government.

Finally, we return to the opening of the chapter, on the nature of constitutionalism, not just as the formal supremacy of the constitution but, more importantly, as an attitude to power, a way of thinking and acting on constitutional values as a matter of habit. I end with a quote from Austin's analysis (somewhat rosy in my view) of the Indian constitution. He says that the constitution is 'about politics and economics and conditions and culture, about politicians and civil servants and lawyers and judges and journalists and individuals, rich and desperately poor, and it is about success and failure and hope and despair and power and sacrifice and motivations, selfish and grand'. As a result:

> The Indian Constitution is a live document in a society rapidly changing and
> almost frenetically political. The touchstone for public, and many private
> affairs, the Constitution is employed daily, if not hourly, by citizens pursuing
> their personal interests or in their desire to serve the public good. The working
> of the Constitution so fully expresses the essentialness of the seamless web and
> so completely reveals the society that adopted it that its study truly is a window
> into India (Austin 2000: 10).

This is not the case in Kenya, despite a constitution resplendent in principles, values and procedure. While it is too early to despair, as the constitution is new and it is radical, a few pessimistic remarks are in order. Neither the executive nor the legislature respects the constitution, both ever ready to amend it at the slightest inconvenience. Many have not read it or do not care. The ethos of the old regime continues to dominate policies and practices, and there are few effective ways to challenge the illegalities of the state.

Notes

1 For a detailed analysis of the forms and purposes of colonial constitutions up to independence, see Ghai and McAuslan (1970).

2 See Chapter XI ('Human rights and public order') in Ghai and McAuslan (1970) for laws and practices relating to human rights, and the massive derogations from these rights and freedoms.

3 The independence constitution is available at www.lcil.cam.ac.uk/sites/default/files/LCIL/documents/transitions/Kenya_1_1963_Constitution.pdf.

4 Sir Evelyn Baring, the governor during the Mau Mau struggles, decided on increasing the size and power of provincial administration as the chief instrument of the central government to combat the Mau Mau as well as to carry out orders, and maintain the authority, of the State House. The powerful and centralised provincial administration (with full authority over the police) became the lasting legacy of Kenya's presidents, down to the present (see Gertzel 1970: 23–7).

5 See Branch (2011), who has unearthed some interesting information on these assassinations in dispatches from the British High Commission to the Foreign Office in London.

6 A readable account of the disregard for constitutional norms and the atrocities by the government is Branch (2011). For a detailed earlier record of the violation of rights and the oppression of government critics, see Human Rights Watch (1991).

7 I have discussed some points in this section at greater length (in Ghai 2012). The next three paragraphs are taken from that chapter.

8 The constitution itself uses the expression 'constitutionalism' only once, in Article 249, where it states that the

promotion of constitutionalism is among the objectives of independent commissions and offices. The expression is not defined but it is interesting that the other two objectives are the protection of the sovereignty of the people and securing the observance by all state organs of democratic values and principles.

9 'A human rights-based approach is … based on the recognition that real success in tackling poverty and vulnerability requires giving the poor and vulnerable both a stake, a voice and real protection in the societies where they live. A human rights-based approach is not only about expanding people's choices and capabilities but above all about the empowerment of people to decide what this process of expansion should look like' (UNDP 2002, based on Article 2 of UNDP 1998).

10 An example is the dispute between the national assembly and the senate as to their respective roles and powers regarding the budgetary allocation to the counties, which delayed the transfer of funds to counties and had to be resolved in court (*Speaker of Senate* v. *Attorney-General* (Petition No. 518 of 2013)). Disputes have also arisen between the executive, judiciary and legislature, so much so that the high court has proposed, in the case concerning the JSC, 'That the Executive, Legislature and Judiciary develop a Protocol for Engagement between the heads of the three arms of government to facilitate amicable discussion and resolution of issues of governance and areas of potential conflict, in the spirit of co-operation and mutual respect that underlies our Constitution' (*JSC* v. *National Assembly* (Petition No. 518/2013)).

11 See the report of the National Cohesion and Integration Commission, *Ethnic Diversity of the Civil Service,*

available at www.cohesion.or.ke/index.php/resources/downloads.

12 Katiba Institute was set up in March 2011 by Yash Ghai, Jill Cottrell Ghai and Waikwa Wanyoike in order to promote the implementation of and respect for the constitution. Among other activities, it has appeared in several constitutional cases as an amicus or a party – usually with success. Refusal by the supreme court of its application in this case was a great blow, as the institute had prepared a lengthy submission raising issues no other party had raised.

13 In *Richard Kalembe Ndile v. Patrick Musimba Mweu* [2013] eKLR [High Court], Justice Majanja emphasised the relevance of Article 81 of the constitution and said, 'Whereas the 1st petitioner emerged with the most votes after the recount, can this court shut its eyes to the evidence that may affect the authenticity of the ballot and say, "Well, the numbers say it all. It is a done deal!" This approach is not consistent with the general principles that underlie a free and fair election. Elections are not about simple arithmetic ... They are about embracing standards and values that our Constitution has ordained.' See paragraph 115 at http:kenyalaw.org/caselaw/cases/view/89879/.

14 A third factor should perhaps be mentioned – the behaviour attributed to the new and now former Deputy Chief Justice Nancy Baraza for extreme rudeness to security staff at the Village Market and refusal to be searched. The incident received much adverse publicity and a tribunal (chaired by a former chief justice of Tanzania) was set up to determine whether her behaviour was a ground for dismissal. The tribunal recommended her dismissal to uphold high standards of integrity, and her removal served to affirm high standards of conduct among judges and other public servants. In this way, the decision thus served to strengthen the image of the new judiciary. For the full report, see *Tribunal to Investigate the Conduct of the Deputy Chief Justice and Vice-President of the Supreme Court of the Republic of Kenya: Tribunal Matter No. 1 of 2012* (KLR).

15 All CIC comments in this chapter are taken from CIC 2013.

References

Austin, G. (2000) *Working a Democratic Constitution: The Indian experience*. New Delhi: Oxford University Press.

Beteille, A. (1992) *The Backward Classes in Contemporary India*. New Delhi: Oxford University Press.

Branch, D. (2011) *Kenya: Between hope and despair, 1963–2011*. New Haven, CT: Yale University Press.

CIC (2013) *Annual Report 2012–13*. Nairobi: Commission for the Implementation of the Constitution (CIC).

Gertzel, C. (1970) *The Politics of Independent Kenya*. London: Heinemann Educational Books.

Ghai, Y. (2010) 'Chimera of constitutionalism: state, economy and society in Africa'. In S. Devi (ed.) *Law and (In)Equalities: Contemporary perspectives*. Lucknow, India: Eastern Book Company, pp. 313–31.

— (2012) 'State, ethnicity and economy in Africa'. In H. Hino, J. Lonsdale, G. Ranis and F. Stewart (eds) *Ethnic Diversity and Economic Instability in Africa: Interdisciplinary perspectives*. Oxford: Oxford University Press.

— and J. P. W. B. McAuslan (1970) *Public Law and Political Change: A Study of the legal framework of government from colonial times to the present*. Nairobi: Oxford University Press.

— and G. J. Ghai (2011) *The New Constitution: An instrument for change*. Nairobi: Katiba Institute.

— (eds) (2013) *Ethnicity, Nationhood and Pluralism: Kenyan perspectives*. Nairobi: Global Centre for Pluralism and Katiba Institute.

Hino, H., J. Lonsdale, G. Ranis and F. Stewart (eds) (2012) *Ethnic Diversity and Economic Instability in Africa: Interdisciplinary perspectives*. Oxford: Oxford University Press.

Human Rights Watch (1991) *Kenya: Taking*

liberties. New York, NY: Human Rights Watch.

McIlwain, C. H. (1947) *Constitutionalism: Ancient and modern*. Ithaca, NY: Great Seal Books.

Poggi, G. (1978) *The Development of the Modern State*. Stanford, CA: Stanford University Press.

SCOK (2013) 'Advisory Opinion Reference No. 2 of 2013'. Nairobi: Supreme Court of Kenya (SCOK).

UNDP (1998) 'UN Declaration on the Right to Development 1998: General Assembly resolution 41/128 of 4 December 1986'. New York, NY: United Nations Development Programme (UNDP).

— (2002) *A Human Rights-based Approach to Development Programming in UNDP: Adding the missing link*. New York, NY: United Nations Development Programme (UNDP).

White, M. (1952) *British Colonial Constitutions, 1947*. Oxford: Clarendon Press.

7 | Elite compromises and the content of the 2010 constitution

Godwin R. Murunga

Introduction

Kenya's new constitution, like most constitutions around the world, is a compromise document. The struggle for the new constitution was fought against strong proponents of the status quo and others whose stand was not too clear. The eventual victory by the progressives was achieved after negotiations and compromises. Through vague phrasing, compounded drafting and deferred legislation, the two sides – progressive and conservative – found ways of dealing with some issues on which they could not agree, while on others the pre-eminence of one side or the other clearly shows. The imprint of these two groups is reflected in different chapters of the constitution. The progressives' greatest imprint is in the bill of rights, while the conservatives show their hand in the system of governance relating to devolution of power and security clauses. Further, cultural wars also emerged in the constitutional process, particularly with respect to sexuality and women's reproductive rights. The church took a particular position and eventually mobilised open rebellion against the constitution at the referendum.

This chapter examines the effect of these ideological divergences, tendencies and competing interests on the constitution. It appraises the implications they hold for the implementation process. Specifically, it will address two issues. One, it will characterise the forces behind these tendencies and discuss the extent to which they have changed over time and why they exhibited contradictory inclinations with regard to some elements of the constitution. Two, it will review how the different ideological tendencies influenced the drafting of the constitution and what this influence implies for implementation. This analysis is viewed through a historical lens in order to highlight the cumulative interests over time.

The historical context of constitution-making in Kenya

The nature of the state The demand for democracy in Kenya is rooted in the history of the postcolonial state under Jomo Kenyatta and later Daniel arap Moi. The authoritarian state that Kenyatta built, and that Moi inherited and perfected, embedded all the reasons that forced the demand for reforms in the early 1990s. This was especially the case with respect to the kind of politics and the nature of the elite it nurtured (Barkan 1992). Whatever discernible differences there were between the Kenyatta and Moi regimes were in their detail, not their type. The form of this state was marked by a number of features, of which three are important in understanding the character of the elite and the demands for constitutional reform that built up in the early 1990s.

The three key features of the Kenyan state were:

- the centralisation of power in the presidency and concomitant personalisation of the institution of the presidency (Tamarkin 1978);
- the dispersal of these powers in the country from top to bottom through a tightly woven and controlled network of provincial administration and an equally networked security and spying system (Branch and Cheeseman 2006; Tamarkin 1978); and
- the subsequent arbitrary, criminal and murderous deployment of this power to destabilise and neuter potential foci of organised opposition (Tamarkin 1978) and to extract compliance from citizens through the use or threat of force (Ajulu 2000; Mueller 1984).

This state was situated in a social order controlled by a political elite that perceived state power primarily in the form of 'personal gain in terms of wealth, prestige, and social status' (Mutua 2008). Thus, as in many places in Africa, central to the character of the state was its role as an instrument in the accumulation of wealth or the protection of that wealth (Ake 1978).

The exercise of state power gradually became more personalised, and personalisation of the presidency was the first step in using state power for the accumulation and protection of personal wealth. In public discourses, reference was no longer made to simply the state, but to the Kenyatta or Moi state (Murunga 2004). This naming was done in the context of the struggles over the constitution during the 'change the constitution' fights following the death of J. M. Kariuki in 1975. Not only did Kenyatta become 'the object of an official campaign of adulation', as Tamarkin (1978: 298) puts it, but this adulation went to the extreme of entrenching the idea that imagining the death of the president was a treasonable act. This was the attorney general's response to the public debate around succession that had been sparked by fears of Kenyatta's advanced age and the fact that Daniel arap Moi was constitutionally mandated to take over.

By the mid-1970s, the constitution had become a useful instrument for the elite to use to protect their accumulated wealth, but it also became the basis of divergence in their thinking and action relating to the national question. Those in power sought to entrench constitutional provisions that protected their hold on that power, while those outside struggled for change. Quite often, those in power were defined by their close affiliation to Mzee Kenyatta, either as relatives, allies or friends, to the extent that they were commonly referred to as the 'family'. They were largely Kikuyu, mainly but not exclusively from Kiambu, and understood that they drew their privileged elite status from their closeness to a Kenyatta presidency. This core group of insiders constructed a patronage network of allies, drawn largely from ethnic groups perceived to be acquiescent to a Kenyatta presidency. Those outside the corridors of power were defined by default following their articulation of opposing views to those of the government and by their ethnic distance. The resulting conflict between the insiders and the outsiders was played out in many realms, one of which was the debate about and application of the constitution. Since divergence and convergence in the different camps was not neat, there was always the occasional insider who took a divergent position, as the attorney general did when he warned fellow insiders within the Kenyatta government about imagining the death of the president. In effect, this order went against the wishes of the 'family' and paved the way for Moi's assumption of power, even though it was uttered by someone very close to, and indeed a member of, Kenyatta's inner group.

The constitution therefore became a central cog in elite machinations to reproduce their position in the postcolonial state. The constitution was remade in the image of the elite. The provisions on state security came in handy and were repeatedly used to thwart attempts at organised opposition to the government (see Chapter 8). Where constitutional provisions could be instituted to provide cover for the elite to realise their objectives, amendments were rushed through to serve that specific purpose. In cases where they were not sufficient, extrajudicial means were employed, including the assassination of key opposition voices.

The contour of the Kenyan elite's behaviour mirrors that of elites elsewhere in Africa. A theory of the elite is therefore important in understanding the African experience with constitutions. Makau Mutua has concluded that the Kenyan elite is 'beholden to political myopia and moral bankruptcy' and is incapable of imagining 'a larger national interest' beyond their personal interest (Mutua 2008: 3). Mutua instead vouches for civil society, which he characterises as the 'only sector that can fundamentally renew the political class' (ibid.: 3). He forgets that civil society is interwoven with political class in complex ways and often reinforces the myopia and bankruptcy of the Kenyan political elite of which it is an integral part. The Kenyan elite, like its other African counterparts, is a product of colonial schooling and postcolonial politics. It seeks to reproduce itself in the context of that schooling, politics, and the specific country's socio-economic structures, but all this is within their neo-colonial socialisation and ties. Thus, Frantz Fanon's characterisation of the elite as steeped in conspicuous consumption still carries analytical force in the Kenyan instance (Fanon 1963).

The character of the elite The elite see power as a means to an end. But the end, for them, is not national well-being, it is personal gain. Founded on a colonial system that was repressive, violent and exploitative, the political elite in Africa reproduced that same logic in postcolonial times. Their key difference from the colonial elite, whom they sought to mimic, was their nationalist cloak. But the colonial schooling system that produced them, the institutions of governance they inherited and the logic of power they understood all pointed to a postcolonial dispensation in which the independence social contract, expressed in constitutions, and the popular aspirations of the majority of citizens, represented by that contract, would be disregarded in favour of a culture of political unanimity (Laakso and Olukoshi 1996: 14–16). Quite often, this was justified in the interests of state security and national development. The preference for national development in exchange for national unanimity was the first sign of a looming dictatorship.

Marxist theories of elites account for this kind of elite behaviour from a structuralist perspective (Nwonwu and Kotze 2008: 4). Elite behaviour is explained in terms of the material conditions of its production and reproduction. These theories therefore pay inadequate attention to the decisions the elites make in the everyday exercise of power that might reflect their material conditions but are nevertheless largely and primarily also the product of individual choice. Liberal elite theories, on the other hand, treat as inevitable the 'emergence or presence of a small group, who will inevitably control political power in society' (ibid.: 3). Precisely because of this inevitability, class dominance is treated as normal, and the desire on the part of the elite to consolidate and protect its power and reproduce itself through exploitation, alienation and violence is excused as being true to its historical mission.

Given the conservative context within which African politics is conducted, liberal postulations of the inevitability of elite existence are often taken for granted in actual practice. The truism, aptly restated by Mutua (2008: 3), asserts that 'although many a society has failed with a visionary elite, not a single one has ever prospered without one since the beginning of recorded history'. This reality has conferred a sense of elite entitlement, on display in their everyday practice of politics and their disregard for constitutionalism. In practice, elites tend to think of themselves as an inevitable part of the architecture of state power in Africa but misinterpret their historic role to assert a level of self-importance that leads them into insecure acts to protect and reproduce themselves. Power has consequently been deployed to assert not just their inevitability but also their sense of self-importance.

Thus, although constitutions in independent Africa represented the contractual 'basis for controlling state power and involving the people in the political process' (Ihonvbere 2000: 343), ultimately this contract was weighted in favour of the elite wielders of state power. In most of the postcolonial experience in

Africa, this contract was negotiated, amended and used in the image of the elite. By the early 1990s, the Kenyan constitution had not only been extensively amended, the amendments had mutilated it and created a document that lacked legitimacy in the eyes of the people. How was this done?

The Kenyatta and Moi state

The Kenya African National Union (KANU) accepted the constitution negotiated at Lancaster House only to facilitate a transition to independence in a classic case of 'seek ye first the political kingdom'. KANU's statement, made in 1961, conceding to that constitution made it clear that 'we might be forced to accept a constitution we [do] not want, but once we [have] the government, we [will] change it' (cited in Ngunyi 1996: 196). Soon after independence, the struggle shifted. The first aim was to take control and construct the state desired by the KANU elite. The second was to entrench that state to secure the interests of that elite. These aims called for a shifting of alliances and restructuring of the architecture of state power in significant ways. The focus of the struggle therefore moved from alliances cobbled together in the fight for independence to new ones designed to secure the interests of the emerging elite. The biggest pivot for this struggle was within KANU, but mainly as it sought to use its newly acquired power to ensure a political rearrangement that suited its core elite group built around Kenyatta and the 'family' (Ajulu 2002; Nyong'o 1989).

To this end, several amendments, facilitated by certain events, were effected on the independence constitution soon after Kenya became a republic. The first phase of these amendments, which lasted roughly until 1965, focused on clauses on power limitation contained in provisions on the regional system. The amendments were facilitated or preceded by the dissolution of the Kenya African Democratic Union (KADU) in 1964. They destroyed the regionalist framework entrenched in the independence constitution and centralised power, mainly in parliament. They especially focused on relocating financial arrangements, including taxation, to the centre and reducing the threshold required for a constitutional amendment from 90 per cent in the senate and 75 per cent in the lower house to 65 per cent across the board. Regional 'presidents' were renamed 'chairmen', 'regions' became 'provinces', while 'regional assemblies' became 'provincial councils'. In effect, the amendments shifted the axis of political action and debate to the centre, where political discussions were now conducted in parliament (Okoth-Ogendo 1972: 19–21).

The method of amending the constitution had two consequences. The first was to centralise politics in Nairobi. This realigned politics in a new arrangement defined by the provincial administration and centralised in the presidency, and therefore working in favour of the elite at the centre. The second was to empty subsequent debate on this issue of any ideological content, eventually personalising politics and political debate. It shifted the earlier focus from ideological debates on the nature of the state, the national question and the vision of independence development to a debilitating emphasis on individuals. The amendments were made in an ad hoc manner, often simply designed to respond to emerging, mundane everyday 'political problems'. While some of these problems were public and defensible, many others were private and indefensible (ibid.: 11).

But the constitutional amendments failed to stem rivalries within KANU. Instead, parliament became a new site of protest and challenge to the presidency with factional rivalries within KANU assuming prominence. This, it has been argued, was characterised by a lack of political ideology and ethics within KANU, a party in which old rivalries that pre-dated independence were re-emerging in independence with new virulence (Ajulu 2002; Nyong'o 1989; Okoth-Ogendo 1972). Clearly, the shift from regional politics to parliament failed to instil and ensure conformity. Instead, parliament became the site of debate and attack on the state. These debates pitted those on the ideological left against those on the right, but eventually, when Oginga Odinga was 'neutralised' through amendments to the KANU constitution and a declaration of a de facto one-party state, the axis of suspicion shifted to target the ambitious Tom Mboya, leading to his murder in 1969. This paved the way for the 'change the constitution' movement in the later part of the 1970s, this time with Daniel arap Moi as the target.

Throughout this period, the Kenyatta state treated the problem of party indiscipline as a constitutional problem rather than a political challenge. A series of challenges resulted in constitutional amendments being designed; although this was meant to address the challenges, instead these amendments were critical in building an authoritarian one-party state. Among them, the practice that required members of parliament who switched parties to seek a fresh mandate from voters proved very critical. This constitutional amendment was instrumental in reducing Oginga Odinga's party, the Kenya People's Union, into an ethnic outfit and in making it impossible after the 1966 'little general elections' for there to be any effective political opposition in Kenya. This is the context within which Daniel arap Moi assumed state power and went on to use existing practices and provisions to build a dreaded system of rule.

Moi had learned eagerly from the Kenyatta regime, having served under Kenyatta for more than a decade. From 1978, when he assumed power, to 1982, when the attempted coup occurred, Moi was keen to accommodate his erstwhile enemies in KANU, including members of the 'family' and their clients in the police network who had humiliated him during his time as Kenyatta's vice president (Karimi and Ochieng 1980; Morton 1998). However, following the attempted coup in 1982, he moved deftly to dismantle not only the power of the 'family' around Kenyatta and its Kiambu allies, but also their extended ethnic base and patronage networks. One way of doing this was to create an alternative Kalenjin base for his rule, which he started to assemble in cabinet in 1979. This became one key element of Moi's strategy from 1982 onwards. The other was to construct a network of alliances anchored in the regions with which he felt comfortable, including power bases in western Kenya created around Moses Mudavadi, among the Maasai around Justis ole Tipis and later William ole Ntimama, and on the coast around Noah Katana Ngala and Sheriff Nassir (Ajulu 2002: 262). To this was added the Asian business class, which was deployed to check the economic power of the Kikuyu entrepreneurs and simultaneously grow Kalenjin capital by commandeering state resources to support joint business ventures between Asians and top Kalenjin politicians (Chege 1998: 225).

In 1982, Moi firmly locked the political system by passing the amendment that turned Kenya into a *de jure* one-party state. Subsequently, he targeted independent offices by eliminating their security of tenure and locating the judiciary as a mere department in the office of the attorney general. Finally, he moved to consolidate the power of the executive over the legislature by, first, enhancing the power of KANU's disciplinary committee and, second, by using the party to eliminate from parliament politicians considered vocal against his government. This culminated in the 1988 general election, which achieved the target of getting rid of politicians not found amenable to Moi's authoritarian designs, such as Martin Shikuku and Joshua Angatia, to name but two.

By 1988, the Moi government had effectively closed all avenues of political expression except KANU. He had driven all opposition forces underground or into exile and had dismantled public avenues for mobilising to challenge his government. The government moved decisively to punish non-conforming politicians. Initially, this included only vocal opposition figures such as Oginga Odinga and Raila Odinga, but it expanded to target others including James Orengo, George Anyona, Koigi wa Wamwere, Chelagat Mutai, Mashengu wa Mwachofi, Lawrence Sifuna and Chibule wa Tsuma. The president went further, dismantling the network of critics within trade unions, universities and civil society. So dire was the situation in the early 1990s that a systematic demand was launched by an incipient team of opposition figures for the repeal of constitutional provisions that limited Kenya to a *de jure* one-party state.

The demand for reform initially emanated from the church, the one remaining space the state could not easily muzzle. Reverend Timothy Njoya and David Gitari pioneered the onslaught against the one-party state, leading a segment of the faith-based groups to support a return to multiparty politics. Their key demand was the repeal of Section 2(a) of the constitution that mandated a *de jure* one-party state, and they soon attracted allies, with many other people and forces joining them. These included those dubbed the 'Young Turks', who coalesced around the historic opposition led by Odinga. Others were new entrants into the opposition, such as Kenneth Matiba and Charles Rubia, who quit or were expelled from KANU and decided to plunge into opposition politics. There were also members of the old but re-emerging professional organisations, including the Law Society of Kenya, and new organisations like Kenya Human Rights Commission (KHRC), which gradually took a leading role within civil society in mobilising the energies of articulate lawyers and human rights defenders such as Maina Kiai, KHRC's founding director. Initially housed in the law firm of Kiraitu Murungi, Aaron Ringera and Gibson Kamau Kuria, KHRC grew to become a key player in the struggle for constitutional reform.

More troubling for the ideological sustainability of the demands for constitutional reform was the alliance of these forces with the historic, largely non-Kalenjin capital dominated by the Kikuyu elites. These had been the target of Moi's vicious post-Kenyatta-era backlash against the Kikuyu; he had worked tirelessly to destroy them. Some, such as Mwai Kibaki, himself a key ally of Tom Mboya in destroying the independence regionalist constitution, had survived in KANU until it was safe to decamp. He left KANU to form the Democratic Party of Kenya (DP) once Moi acceded to multiparty politics in 1991. Feeling distant from the Moi state, or having been forced out of KANU, like Matiba and Rubia, this segment joined the movement for democracy; ironically, it allied itself with the neoliberal World Bank agenda that mandated the retrenchment of the state under structural adjustment programmes – programmes that were to be implemented by the same state that had created this segment of the elite upon which it relied for largesse (Murunga 2007). The problem is that these Kikuyu elites had a minimalist democratic agenda designed to serve their own interests in re-accessing the state, rather than to fight for a total overhaul of the unfair, dictatorial and socially unjust state system. It was in the hands of this segment of the opposition that 'the social and even radical political potential of democracy was diluted, if not repudiated' (Holmquist et al. 1994: 97), leading, in several instances, to abortions in the struggle when success seemed close.

Ultimately, the groupings that developed into a new opposition pressure group, and later a party – the Forum for the Restoration of Democracy (FORD) – were not united by their ideological commitment to reforms or a desire for a new constitutional dispensation. The segments of an incipient civil society had this as their ultimate focus (see Chapter 5), but others, especially the elite recently kicked out of KANU, postured within the realm of the opposition while harbouring a self-serving minimalist reform agenda. Consequently, Kenya's opposition movement was strong only in the superficial sense of being united by a commonality of grievances against President Moi and KANU. This agenda was aptly summed up in the slogan 'Moi must go', but their unity could not survive the removal of President Moi since their grievances were too personalised.

From 'Moi must go' to 'No reforms, no elections' Knowing that a constitutional amendment freeing politics in Kenya from the *de jure* one-party era was a prerequisite to unlocking KANU's hold on power, the emerging opposition movement, FORD, defined its agenda around the repeal of Section 2(a) of the constitution. This conditioned the strategy and priority advanced by this fragile opposition coalition, which focused on demanding a multiparty dispensation and on minimal constitutional reforms, in that order. Its demand for multiparty politics, articulated through press statements, street protests and lobbying foreign embassies, among other tactics, was granted in 1991. But soon after Moi had acceded to the repeal of Section 2(a), the fragile FORD coalition not only splintered into several groupings (FORD-Kenya, FORD-Asili) but the sphere of opposition politics was also invaded by new but opportunistic entrants such as Kibaki's DP, which became the preferred home for a huge segment of that old Kikuyu capital. The DP lost the first multiparty election to Moi in 1992 but went on to play complicated, if contradictory, roles in the constitutional review process.

The second major reform thrust was started in 1995 but reached a climax in 1997. Here, the forthcoming elections framed the nature of the demands for minimum constitutional reforms before the elections. If in the 1992 context the slogan had been 'Moi must go', in this instance the slogan became 'No reforms, no elections'. This was the subject of the 1997 protests, street skirmishes and Inter-Party Parliamentary Group (IPPG) discussions (Mutunga 1999).

The demand for a new constitutional dispensation had preceded the 'No reforms, no elections' sloganeering. In fact, this slogan represented a step back from the original civil society-led struggles around constitutional reforms as described in Chapters 5 and 6 in this volume. Not only had civil society organised meetings in Limuru to galvanise support for the new constitution and placed on the table the demand for a people-driven constitutional review process, it had even drafted a model constitution that was shared extensively in many forums, including being widely available on the streets of Nairobi. The people who provided the brain power for these initiatives, including Kathurima M'Inoti, Wachira Maina and Davinder Lamba, among others, remain largely unacknowledged. A decision to mobilise the masses for public protests was adopted and the need to enter an alliance with opposition political society was accepted.

Thus, the struggle for constitutional reform was largely led by civil society from the mid-1990s. Partly, this was due to the fragility of the existing opposition, which had cost them the 1992 elections. The fact that this opposition still held a minimalist agenda for democratic reform, focusing simply on accessing the state, remained a major limitation to sustaining the struggle. By allying with the opposition in the new demand for minimum reforms, civil society was able to mobilise huge demonstrations. But this alliance, and the limited focus on the political elite within the opposition, came back to hurt civil society and its agenda. The mobilisation for street protests in 1997 was successful, but only temporarily. Among its key gains were two: first, it forced the Moi regime into a reactive position, unfamiliar ground for the then president; and second, it shifted the discussion on constitutional review from parliament to the streets. Once in the public domain, the elite instinct for self-preservation was halted temporarily. This turned the struggle for constitutional review into a popular exercise, with street demonstrators being attacked violently by the police in the full glare of the local and international media. Moi eventually acceded to the demand for minimum reforms, stepping back from his preferred expert-driven process. This was a major, though short-lived, victory.

While Moi was acceding to a popular constitutional review process, the elite instinct for self-preservation lurked behind the scenes both within the ruling coalition and among the opposition allies of civil society. Having consented to the IPPG discussion on minimum constitutional reforms before the elections, Moi planned to abort the process midway. Not only did he do so, he also encouraged the opposition to disengage from civil society, arguing that the latter were not elected representatives of the people. When word came through that an agreement on minimum reforms had been reached and a few of the targeted reforms had been passed in parliament – including the Constitution of Kenya (Amendment) Bill, a Statute Law (Repeals and Miscellaneous Amendment) Bill and the Constitution of Kenya Review Commission Bill 1997 – Moi suddenly dissolved parliament on 10 November and set the general election for 29 December 1997. Most opposition politicians went into election campaigns, leaving a fuming James Orengo, Paul Muite, Gibson Kamau Kuria and Kivutha Kibwana abusing defectors from IPPG as 'idiots and cowards' and 'political prostitutes' (ibid.: 237).

Clearly, there was no unanimity within the ranks of the political opposition on the fundamental reforms needed and what sustainable form they should take. Such unanimity was, however, very evident among those opposed to any reforms. Two key issues were clear and formed the subject of extended debate: the nature of presidential powers and the issue of devolution. Debates between those who preferred a unitary as opposed to a devolved system of government had been ongoing for quite some time. This issue touched directly on the centralised state, the presidency and its power over resource allocation. While the elite in power preferred to retain a unitary state, the opposition fragmented into those in favour of or against a devolved government. The other area of debate, connected to the above, was the bill of rights and the nature of the rights it aimed to guarantee Kenyans. While those opposed to reforms grudgingly accepted new freedoms, subject to state security, those in favour were unclear about how far the reforms should go. Surrounding these two major reform issues were others that fragmented the opposition and rendered their collective voice weak. The resulting discussions reflected the fragile alliance that civil society and the opposition had created after losing the 1997 elections to Moi.

Elites and the tribulations of a constitutional commission

The constitutional reform process after 1998 followed the framework elaborated in the Constitution of Kenya Review Commission Act of 1997. Civil society and opposition forces that had fallen out following the aborted IPPG meetings reconvened in 1999 when parliament jump-started the review process. But they came back less in the form of a formalised alliance for constitutional review than as different factions each bumping into the review process through a series of coincidences. Some of these coincidences thrust the groups together while others divided them. This is a familiar story that has defined elite behaviour in Kenya in or out of power, and one that has been told in greater detail in numerous publications by participants in the review process, including Yash Pal Ghai (Chapter 6 in this volume), P. L. O. Lumumba (2008) and Zein Abubakar (2013).

From 1999, the political manoeuvring and elite interests of the time shifted politics in a different direction. The first change was apparent in the context of political realignment, with Raila Odinga's National Democratic Party (NDP) joining an alliance with KANU to give that coalition a majority in parliament. KANU's ability to control the legislative agenda that had been whittled down at the election was re-established. As a consequence, a parliamentary motion was passed in 1999 that set up the parliamentary select committee for constitutional review, on which Raila Odinga was appointed chair. Subsequently, the committee issued a report recommending that a fifteen-member committee be appointed by parliament and chaired by someone to be selected by the president to commence the review process. It seemed at this point that Raila Odinga was amenable to an expert-driven review process. Eventually, it was through this process that Professor Yash Pal Ghai was approached to chair the Constitution of Kenya Review Commission (CKRC).

The faith-based groups, on the other hand, led by the secretary general of the National Council of the Churches of Kenya, Mutava Musyimi, was organising an alternative review process around the Ufungamano Initiative. They were supported by broad segments of the opposition and civil society, especially those politicians in DP such as Kiraitu Murungi who had boycotted the Raila Odinga-led select committee. They in turn established a People's Commission of Kenya, dubbed the Ufungamano Initiative, led by Dr Oki Ooko Ombaka.

When the two parallel commissions were amalgamated under the leadership of Ghai, deputised by Oki Ooko Ombaka, they proceeded in an uneasy manner to conduct a people-driven constitutional review process. The uneasiness stemmed from several sources, partly because of the difficulties in merging the two initiatives, but also because of the interests, actions and behaviour of some of the commissioners. Some of the commissioners had avaricious intentions, insisting on huge allowances and overly comfortable travel conditions and filing exaggerated travel claims. In addition, it soon became clear that some commissioners were in fact moles planted within the CKRC by different elite interests seeking to subvert the process in order to ensure their own survival. It is no secret that segments of the ruling elite in KANU and its allies remained strongly opposed to this people-driven process, dismissing it as a waste of resources. They sought out any information they could use to cast the commission in a bad light and launched attacks that were diversionary and aimed at sidetracking the review process to benefit the ruling elite's desire for self-preservation. The views collected in the wide national exercise and the elements of information leaking from the private discussions of the commission clearly suggested a draft constitution that would torpedo the elite from power. To facilitate a counterattack and delegitimise the CKRC, the elite relied on their spies within the commission who leaked private discussions and documents to stay abreast of developments.

Several notable figures within the review commission, including P. L. O. Lumumba and Yash Pal Ghai, have directly and publicly singled out Keriako Tobiko for 'constantly report[ing] to the President and some ministers [CKRC's internal discussions], in clear breach of confidentiality and impartiality' (Ghai 2011). These leaks served the political elite well, for example former cabinet minister Mr Julius Sunkuli. In one bizarre incident, the commission was in private session, proofreading the draft constitution, when it was reported in the news that President Moi, at a public rally in Kajiado, had dismissed the draft as terrible and had claimed that it contained un-African things. This theme of un-African clauses was picked up later by William Ruto and the faith-based organisations when they mobilised against the draft constitution during the referendum in 2010. But in this particular instance, Moi had dismissed a draft that was not yet complete and not yet in the public domain (Ghai 2012; Lumumba 2008: 84). Many other politicians went on to mount sustained attacks not just on the draft but also on some commissioners who were perceived as resisting elite attempts to torpedo the process. Yash Pal Ghai, for example, was attacked by no less a person than President Moi for being a foreigner, despite the fact that he held a valid Kenyan passport issued by Moi's government. In a strange turn of events, he was also later fervently attacked by Kiraitu Murungi and Paul Muite when the National Alliance Rainbow Coalition (NARC) was in power for refusing to alter the provisions of the draft constitution (Murunga and Nasong'o 2006: 18).

The attempts by the political elite to interfere with and ultimately scupper the constitutional review process did not end with KANU. By the second half of 2002, the focus had shifted, once again, to elections. The review process did not register on the radar. Instead, what did register were the elite interests that elections channelled and the opportunities they could open up for those in opposition. The signs were clear: KANU's alliance with NDP was faltering in the face of Moi's attempt to unilaterally nominate his heir, Uhuru Kenyatta. That eventuality gave hope to the emerging opposition alliance crafted around Mwai Kibaki, Charity Ngilu and Wamalwa Kijana. Instincts for self-preservation were high, and both opposition politicians and KANU were united in seizing the moment. While KANU saw the chance to halt the review process by dissolving parliament on 27 October 2002, the opposition was clear that it was not going to offer KANU another extra day in power. Both, however, were driven by the desire to benefit from an old constitutional dispensation and were united in halting the National Constitutional Conference set for 28 October.

NARC turncoats and the content of the 2010 constitution

The 2002 elections were won by NARC, an alliance that brought together the old Kikuyu capital coalescing around Kibaki's DP, the historic opposition led by Raila Odinga, and a splinter group from KANU led by George Saitoti and supported by earlier rebels such as Simeon Nyachae who felt ignored when Moi unilaterally anointed Uhuru Kenyatta as his heir. This group formed a fragile coalition united by their grievances against Moi and little else. The old Kikuyu capital, however, had the upper hand given the endorsement of Mwai Kibaki as presidential candidate and his eventual win against Uhuru Kenyatta with a huge margin. In this group were the old elite of the Kenyatta era, including John Michuki, who had made a name for himself and a fortune as a colonial loyalist and a key part of the Kenyatta-era provincial administration structure discussed earlier.

Once Kibaki was sworn into power, two things became clear. First, signs of internal conflicts emerged within the coalition that touched directly on the constitution-making process. Second, these conflicts would soon be exacerbated by the return of the old Kikuyu capital that Kibaki represented. The reconciliation between Kibaki and Njenga Karume, Kibaki's friend and former ally in the DP, was an initial sign. Later, when Kibaki fell out with Raila Odinga, he went to form an alliance with Nyachae and a segment of KANU that included Nicholas Biwott. Thus, the constitution-making process would soon face challenges similar to those the exiting KANU had generated in order to torpedo the process, thereby influencing the content of the constitution delivered in 2010.

NARC had promised to deliver a new constitution to Kenyans within the first 100 days of their government. Aspects of this promise were entrenched in the gentlemen's memorandum of understanding between coalition members. But signs that this would not happen emerged when a portion of the ruling coalition, led primarily by Kiraitu Murungi, manoeuvred to replace Raila Odinga, a key member of the coalition, with Paul Muite, an outsider who belonged to the Safina party and had campaigned against NARC as chair of the parliamentary select committee. Muite assumed the leadership of the committee, and for a while he warmed up to this role by vocally supporting the Kikuyu right to power, for example at a public rally in Kiambu (Murunga and Nasong'o 2006: 13–15). But he soon fell out with the old Kikuyu capital and re-emerged as a strong proponent of the new constitution.

In spite of a pre-election agreement on shared appointments of people into public office, the Raila-led side of the coalition was short-changed. This was facilitated by the return to prominence of the old Kikuyu capital, which was driven by a hatred of Moi, not by a desire for constitutional reform. As such, it was in their interests to preserve, as much as possible, the structure that Moi had created. All indications therefore suggested that they would be resistant to any radical change of the constitution. Indeed, this became apparent when there was little movement on the promise to deliver a new constitution within 100 days. Subsequently, the Kibaki government procrastinated repeatedly and eventually ignored the process as 2004 came to an end.

Instead, the elite began to restructure the state in their own image, with complete disregard for the promise of constitutional review. In an article entitled 'Queries on Kibaki's "wise men"', published in the *Daily Nation* on 8 February 2003, David Makali raised this issue. He named Harris Mule, Joe Wanjui and George Muhoho directly as Kibaki's 'wise men', sitting on the tenth floor of the president's office at Harambee House and 'sifting through curriculum vitae to fill key parastatal and other offices' that were being created in a one-sided NARC restructuring of the sector. With respect to civil service appointments, he concluded that there was a danger that this process would 'leave some communities and the segments of the population feeling slighted'. Makali was on firm ground because, in the previous week, the Kibaki government had appointed permanent secretaries in a manner that did not indicate a break with the old KANU kleptocratic behaviour. Some of the appointments sidestepped the Public Service Commission, which 'is mandated to recruit civil servants'. Singling out the appointment of Mr Matere Keriri as controller of State House and private secretary to the president, Makali pointed out that he was well over the mandatory retirement age. In fact, this appointment represented the return to power of Kibaki's old boy network. Not only was Keriri a member of the old Kikuyu elite, who 'was in the public service as far back as 1968, along with Kenneth Matiba, John Michuki, Joab Omino and Mwai Kibaki', he was also 'a business associate of the President' (Makali 2003).

In other words, the elite in power under the Kibaki regime was not new. Rather, it was very much a 'power elite who were weaned on the KANU way of politics, and [were] set to ensure continuity rather than a clean break with the past' (Murunga and Nasong'o 2006: 12). In their hands, the constitutional review process suffered even greater disruptions. It was no longer in their self-interest to devolve power from the presidency. Thus, whereas Kibaki and Kiraitu Murungi had condemned the presidency as 'imperial' when they gave their views on behalf of DP to the CKRC, on their assumption of power, Murungi became a key defender of the imperial presidency. And the cabinet arrangement worked well to frustrate the CKRC, with the Finance Minister, the Minister for Internal Security (with responsibility for the provincial administration) and Minister for Constitutional Affairs being turncoat apologists for the imperial presidency. Eventually, Murungi led the team that blocked the Bomas draft constitution and launched a vicious campaign to humiliate Ghai.

Most delegates at Bomas, and Kenyans in general, had no problem with more than three-quarters of the provisions of the Bomas draft constitution. The issues that emerged as contentious were largely those engineered by those in government who reversed their position on the provisions they had recommended when the CKRC was collecting views. By March 2004, those contentious issues had narrowed to three: executive authority, the devolution of powers, and transitional and consequential arrangements. While one side preferred an executive president who was head of state and government and who in turn appointed a prime minister, others preferred a prime minister as head of government. While some wanted a government centralised in Nairobi, others preferred a devolved system in which regional governments enjoyed a modicum of control over regional resources. Eventually, the government rejected the Bomas process and walked out. They went on to rework the draft through a process led by Amos Wako, then attorney general, and presented what was known as the Wako draft at a referendum in 2005. The draft was roundly defeated.

The challenge of developing elite consensus continued to stalk the constitution-making process until the post-election violence woke them from their slumber. In the wake of the constitutional moment presented by the mediation process that followed on from the post-election violence (see Chapter 3), the elite were forced by the prevailing circumstances to the negotiating table to cobble together a document that broadly reflected their divergent interests on the key contentious issues. Four are of immediate interest here: the issue of executive authority, devolution, the bill of rights and security. To ensure the conclusion of this process, an act of parliament was enacted with self-triggering clauses that could not be ignored or halted. This forced the recalcitrant elite into compromises. At the end of the process, the task fell on the Committee of Experts and the parliamentary select committee to mediate competing interests and to produce the document that was put to a referendum in 2010.

The effects of elite interests on content The provision on executive authority was, for instance, traded off with that on devolution. The progressive forces conceded to an executive presidential system in exchange for the conservative groups accepting the retention of a devolved system of government. As such, these two provisions have continued to sit uncomfortably together in the constitution, even during implementation. This situation represented a major victory for the conservative forces because it allowed them to retain a number of key controls over the devolved system. After they won the 2013 general elections, that control proved useful as it has been used whenever opportunity allows to claw back the independence of the county governments. A variety of tricks have been used to do this, such as rendering the transitional authority ineffective and seeking to exercise financial oversight and control over counties, including through the appointment and entrenching of executive powers in county commissioners. The unease generated by these provisions of the constitution continues to fuel debate over the independence of the county governments, the role of the senate, and the implications of the new constitution for the wage bill.

The bill of rights was obviously a major victory for the progressive forces. It contributes greatly to the possibility of making Kenya a democratic state by recognising the human rights and fundamental freedoms of all Kenyans. More importantly, it confers and defends the rights of a diversity of Kenyans in a way that was not possible in the previous constitutions. The greatest scar of the old constitution was the enactment in 1966 of the Preservation of Public Security Act, under whose authority people were detained and their rights abused. The new constitution enjoins all government institutions to respect, defend and protect these rights. The conservative forces attempted to reduce these rights in three main ways: first, by reference to the bogeymen of gays and lesbians, whom they dubbed un-African and a threat to family values. In the 'no' campaigns, this was cited as a reason not to vote for the whole constitution, even though this constitution is more explicit in its definition of marriage as being between a man and a woman. Second, the faith-based organisations, in addition to speaking out on the gay and lesbian issue, attempted to incite people regarding the so-called dangers of Islamisation, as the constitution conceded the rights of the Kadhi courts. Three, the political elite in power, together with the 'securocrats', tried, but failed, to limit the bill of rights by insisting that it should be subject to state security considerations.

Elite interests regarding security have loomed large in the discussions on the constitution, from its draft form to the promulgated version. To date, not too many Kenyans can fathom the idea of a security arrangement independent of everyday control by the president, as has been articulated within the provincial administration framework discussed earlier. For instance, writing in the *Daily Nation*, a senior media personality complained about rampant insecurity and associated it with the fact that the new security architecture does not give the president powers to hire and fire. He argued that 'the very notion of a commander-in-chief who can't command, hire and fire is ridiculous', and concluded that the constitution has 'made the president very close to power-less' (Mathiu 2014). This obvious misreading of the security architecture of the new constitution reflects the nature of elite debates relating to the security sector during the process of constitution-making and represents a continuing mobilisation to put security matters in the unilateral hands of the president.

In fact, elite trade-offs during the constitution-making process left rather progressive provisions for the security sector (see also Chapter 8). First, it subordinated national security organs to civilian authority and required them to perform their functions with the utmost respect for the rule of law, demo-cracy, human rights and fundamental freedoms. These provisions borrow from the bill of rights, which sets the spirit of the constitution on the issue of basic freedoms. To achieve this, a security architecture that facilitates those freedoms was needed, and therefore the constitution mandates reforms in the security sector. For a start, it establishes the National Security Council with the president as its head and allocates it 'supervisory control' over national security organs. However, it accords the inspector general of police independent com-mand over the National Police Service, while at the same time locating some of his administrative tasks within the framework of the National Police Service Commission. Finally, it also establishes the Independent Policing Oversight Authority, through which civilian oversight is exercised.

Conclusion

This chapter has attempted a historical reflection on the nature of elite interests, their shifting nature, and how they have had an impact on the constitution-making process leading to the 2010 constitution. Kenya's politi-cal elites have permanent interests, which are framed in personal terms and constantly refer to personal gains. They have a sense of entitlement to power in Kenya and treat their presence in national circles as a right. While they express group interests, there is no consensus on what interests they front collectively. As a result, they often operate through factions. However, their desire to acquire power and retain it are permanent features of elite interests. The constitution in Kenya has historically facilitated such access; when it did not, the Kenyan elite has historically used extra-constitutional means to further their interests. This framework of operation explains Kenya's many attempts at constitutional review, which often suffered from procrastination due to conflicting elite interests. Eventually, when a constitution was cobbled together and promulgated, the imprint of elite machinations remained clear. In this chapter, we have used four areas of contention to illustrate this influence.

The examples of provisions on executive authority, devolution, the bill of rights and security reforms illustrate the way in which elite compromises gave varied outcomes in terms of the content of the 2010 constitution. Other areas reflect the imprint of trade-offs and compromises resulting from entrenched or shifting interests. For instance, whereas some elite groups had initially supported the draft policy on land, an important core issue in the welfare of the people they represented, they lined up to reject the constitution by erroneously citing non-existent clauses mandating that women must inherit land from their parents. However, this example of women and land reveals the character of elite views on gender. Closely associated with this retrogressive thinking on gender are numerous citations of un-African clauses that threaten family values. These were used to mobilise against the draft during the referendum. The arguments presented by religious groups on this subject reveal how individual and institutional interests influenced the final draft of the constitution.

References

Abubakar, Z. (2013) 'Memory, identity and pluralism in Kenya's constitution building process'. In Y. P. Ghai and J. C. Ghai (eds) *Ethnicity, Nationhood and Pluralism: Kenyan perspectives*. Ottawa and Nairobi: Global Centre for Pluralism and Katiba Institute, pp. 21–45.

Ajulu, R. (2000) 'Thinking through the crisis of democratisation in Kenya: a response to Adar and Murunga'. *African Sociological Review* 4(2): 133–57.

— (2002) 'Politicised ethnicity, competitive politics and conflict in Kenya: a historical perspective'. *African Studies* 61(2): 251–68.

Ake, C. (1978) *Revolutionary Pressures in Africa*. London: Zed Books.

Barkan, J. D. (1992) 'The rise and fall of a governance realm in Kenya'. In G. Hyden and M. Bratton (eds) *Governance and Politics in Africa*. Boulder, CO: Lynne Rienner Publishers, pp. 167–92.

Branch, D. and N. Cheeseman (2006) 'The politics of control in Kenya: understanding the bureaucratic–executive state, 1952–78'. *Review of African Political Economy* 33(107): 11–31.

Chege, M. (1998) 'Introducing race as a variable into the political economy of Kenya debate: an incendiary idea'. *African Affairs* 97(387): 209–30.

Fanon, F. (1963) *The Wretched of the Earth*. New York, NY: Grove Press.

Ghai, Y. P. (2011) 'Is Tobiko fit to be director of public prosecutions?' *The Star*, 17 May. Available at www.the-star.co.ke/news/article-63417/tobiko-fit-be-director-public-prosecutions.

— (2012) 'Exercising power under constitution'. *The Star*, 17 January. Available at www.the-star.co.ke/news/article-33899/exercising-power-under-constitution.

Holmquist, F. W., F. S. Weaver and M. D. Ford (1994) 'The structural development of Kenya's political economy'. *African Studies Review* 37(1): 69–105.

Ihonvbere, J. (2000) 'How to make an undemocratic constitution: the Nigerian example'. *Third World Quarterly* 21(2): 343–66.

Karimi, J. and P. Ochieng (1980) *The Kenyatta Succession*. Nairobi: Transafrica.

Laakso, L. and A. Olukoshi (1996) 'The crisis of the post-colonial nation-state project in Africa'. In A. Olukoshi and L. Laakso (eds) *Challenges of the Nation-State in Africa*. Uppsala: Nordiska Afrikainstitutet, pp. 7–39.

Lumumba, P. L. O. (2008) *Kenya's Quest for a Constitution: The postponed promise*. Nairobi: Jomo Kenyatta Foundation.

Makali, D. (2003) 'Queries on Kibaki's "wise men"'. *Daily Nation*, 8 February.

Mathiu, M. (2014) 'Why elect a president and then deny him the powers to protect Kenyans?' *Daily*

Nation, 6 March. Available at http://
mobile.nation.co.ke/blogs/Why-
elect-a-president-and-then-deny/-/
1949942/2233714/-/format/xhtml/-/
jacjelz/-/index.html.

Morton, A. (1998) *Moi: The making of an
African statesman*. London: Michael
O'Mara Books.

Mueller, S. D. (1984) 'Government and opposition in Kenya, 1966–1969'. *Journal of
Modern African Studies* 22(3): 399–427.

Murunga, G. R. (2004) 'The state, its
reform and the question of legitimacy
in Kenya'. *Identity, Culture and Politics*
5(1&2): 179–206.

— (2007) 'Governance and the politics
of structural adjustment in Kenya'.
In G. R. Murunga and S. Nasong'o
(eds) *Kenya: The struggle for democracy*.
London and Dakar: Zed Books and
Codesria, pp. 263–300.

— and S. Nasong'o (2006) 'Bent on
self-destruction: the Kibaki regime in
Kenya'. *Journal of Contemporary African
Studies* 24(1): 1–28.

Mutua, M. (2008) *Kenya's Quest for Democracy: Taming leviathan*. Boulder, CO:
Lynne Rienner Publishers.

Mutunga, W. (1999) *Constitution-making
from the Middle: Civil society and
transition politics in Kenya, 1992–1997*.
Nairobi and Harare: SAREAT and
MWENGO.

Ngunyi, M. (1996) 'Resuscitating the
Majimbo project: the politics of decon-
structing the unitary state in Kenya'.
In A. Olukoshi and L. Laakso (eds)
Challenges of the Nation-State in Africa.
Uppsala: Nordiska Afrikainstitutet,
pp. 183–212.

Nwonwu, F. and D. Kotze (2008) 'Introduc-
tion'. In F. Nwonwu and D. Kotze (eds)
African Political Elites. Pretoria: Africa
Institute of South Africa.

Nyong'o, P. A. (1989) 'State and society
in Kenya: the disintegration of the
nationalist coalitions and the rise of
presidential authoritarianism, 1963–78'.
African Affairs 88(351): 229–51.

Okoth-Ogendo, H. W. O. (1972) 'The politics of constitutional change in Kenya
since independence, 1963–69'. *African
Affairs* 71(282): 9–34.

Tamarkin, M. (1978) 'The roots of political stability in Kenya'. *African Affairs*
77(308): 297–320.

8 | Security and human rights in the new constitutional order in Kenya

Mutuma Ruteere

The meaning of security and the conduct of security agencies have been part of the struggles for democratisation in Kenya since the formation of the Kenyan state. From colonial times, through the successive presidencies of post-independence Kenya, security has been central to the organisation, exercise and distribution of political and economic power in Kenya. Security agencies have also been the instrument through which the governing elites have guaranteed their survival and secured their privileges. Domination, demo-cratisation and change in Kenya cannot be adequately understood without an examination of the ideas and practices of the governance of security. From colonialism to contemporary Kenya, continuity rather than change describes the dominant security mentalities of the political elites and the practices of the institutions of security. The unfettered powers of the colonial institutions of domination were happily inherited by the leaders of postcolonial Kenya. Consequently, the struggles for democracy and human rights that define the recent history of Kenya have aimed to dismantle the logic, the laws and the institutions that had been deployed against the people for decades.

This chapter examines the changes in the security sector as a lens for understanding how struggles over human rights have shaped public policy in light of the new constitution adopted in 2010. That constitution has been described as one of the most progressive in Africa with regard to human rights provisions. The chapter locates the official framings of security and resistance to this within the context of the construction and operations of the repressive Kenyan state. The chapter provides a critical assessment of the reforms occasioned by a new constitutional order in Kenya and offers tentative conclusions about the policy implications of the expected reconfigurations of security governance.

Punitive security and the legacies of colonialism

Questions of security cannot be separated from questions of the political theory of the state, the chosen ideology of its elites and the political economy of the society in question. In Hobbesian terms, it can be said that security is the very first moment of state formation. In any state, security is a reflection

163

of how power is organised, distributed and exercised. Ideas and values of democracy and rights are therefore inextricably bound with security in the modern nation state. Security is a useful analytical entry point into how power is exercised and governed in a society.

In most parts of Africa, and in Kenya specifically, colonial state formation was a violent project. The order of the colonial state was established not by the consent of the African natives, but by the threat and often actual deployment of brutal and punitive violence. Law and order in the colonial state were maintained through the menacing threat and the deployment of actual violence by the colonial police and military forces. As Sir Frederick Lugard, the architect of British imperial policy of indirect rule in Africa, pointed out: 'The maintenance of law and order depends in every country on the power of coercion by force, and is supported by force if collectively defied' (Lugard 1922: 578). As Bruce Berman has noted, the prestige of the colonial state had to be established through numerous pacification expeditions (Berman 1999).

Police forces in the colonies were essentially militarised: the Kiswahili word for both soldier and police officer in Eastern Africa was *askari*. Because British indirect rule in colonies such as Kenya was erected on a framework of governance of the African as a subject of their traditions and ethnic groups, even the recruiting of Africans into the security forces was logically ethnicised. In Kenya, the colonial state recruited heavily from those communities that were seen as less hostile to the colonial project (Throup 1992: 127–57). Ordinarily these militarised police were not deployed to serve in their own areas to avoid the possibility of their loyalties shifting to their ethnic kin.

Like everything else under colonialism, security in colonial Kenya was racialised. From its very beginnings as a trading company, the colonial state administration was constructed on the logic of containment of the African populations in order to protect white settler interests. Indeed, the very first act of colonial conquest, in the form of the construction of the Uganda railway, depended on a mobilisation of violence and force against the resisting African populations. Unsurprisingly, therefore, the police force was among the earliest state institutions established in colonial Kenya; it began in 1896 in the coastal town of Mombasa as a squad to pacify Africans and to pave the way for the construction of the railway (Clayton and Killingray 1989).

The colonised Africans were not allowed into the domain of civil rights – which was reserved for the white settlers – but were ruled through a legal despotism enforced through native authorities by the ever-present threat of the tribal police and other instruments of colonial coercion (Mamdani 1996). According to colonial law and security ideology, the African was a threat to the civil rights and physical security of the white settler. Law and its enforcement were therefore designed to contain the Africans in the rural reserves, away from the urban areas.

This meant that settlement and movement in the urban areas was racialised and closely policed (Mitullah 2003; Omenya and Lubaale 2012). In Nairobi, Africans were restricted to the eastern suburbs of the city, while the more affluent and planned western suburbs were reserved for the whites. The Asians, who were second in the racial colour bar, were restricted to the northern parts of the city, specifically the Parklands area. Police stations were erected in the more wealthy white settlements to protect them from threats from the poor African sections.

Control was exercised both directly and indirectly. In most instances, the colonial administration depended upon the native administration to enforce its domination. Indirect domination depended on the provincial administration through a system of district commissioners, district officers and chiefs. This form of governance sought to legitimise itself as being rooted in tradition, but the indigenous system of control was as brutal as that unleashed directly by the colonial state forces: 'more than the force of tradition, the colonial legacy came to signify a tradition of force' (Mamdani 1996: 52).

To support the provincial administration there was the native police force – in Kenya called the administration police – which was largely located in rural areas. The police agency invested with responsibility for investigating crime – the Kenya Police Force, through its criminal investigations department – was essentially an urban force. The administration police was not engaged in investigating crime, unlike conventional police forces; its role was rather to enforce order.

Colonial mentalities in postcolonial contexts

The brutal nature of the colonial security forces was further amplified during the conflict at the peak of the independence struggles in the 1950s. In particular, the Mau Mau struggle for independence in the 1950s brought out the worst excesses of the colonial security agencies (Anderson 2005; Elkins 2005).[1] As has been noted by many scholars, while independence provided the opportunity for dismantling the colonial state, the new leadership in Kenya was not keen on this course of action. The independent state inherited and perfected the institutions of the colonial state along with the idea of security being the privilege of a select group of elites to the exclusion of the vast majority of the population.

While independence marked the formal end of the colonial state in Kenya, the mentalities of security of the colonial state survived the transition to independence. In fact, the independence government of President Jomo Kenyatta did not produce any new policy document on its vision of security for the citizens of a newly independent state. That policy silence in effect meant that the logic of security remained much the same as it was in colonial times, as did the security infrastructure. The only significant change was the Africanisation of many of the officer positions in both the police and the military that had initially been reserved for the British under colonialism (Katumanga 2010; Tamarkin 1978: 297–300).[2]

Within the first year of independence, a secessionist movement led by the Somali in the Northern Frontier District, who sought to be part of the greater Republic of Somalia, provided the first opportunity for the government to deploy punitive military and police force. For the next three decades, the violence and brutality visited on the residents of the region would become the exemplification of the dominant conception of security (Sheikh 2007).[3] In the name of national security, the Northern Frontier District (renamed the North Eastern Province after independence) would experience massacres and the collective punishment of entire communities by the security forces, recurrent detentions of individuals without trial and an almost total suspension of human rights. This was underpinned by the state of emergency imposed on the region in 1966, turning the region into a police state (KHRC 2009).[4] The complete impunity of the security forces was guaranteed by the enactment of the Indemnity Act of 1970 that indemnified them against any claims arising from their actions in the region.

It is tempting to see the situation in the North Eastern Province as a state of exception, particularly in light of the legislation mentioned above. While legalised state violence was restricted to the region, this practice of security quickly became the reality for the rest of the country too, albeit on a smaller scale. Security officers who had experimented with brutality in the North Eastern Province often found a use for their expertise in the policing of other regions.

Under colonialism, state security had been invoked in the service of a racial elite; after independence, it was now invoked and deployed in the service of the governing elite. Although not explicitly stated, at the core of this governing elite was the ethnic elite from the president's community. The genuine challenges of constructing a nation out of the mosaic of different ethnicities, coupled with the infancy of state institutions, became the cover under which the post-independence leadership transformed security into a weapon for the domination and decimation of legitimate political opposition. Governing through the claims of security allowed the state to introduce detention without trial through a 1966 amendment to the Preservation of Public Security Act. The first victims of the introduction of preventive detention were the supporters of the Kenya Peoples Union, the party of the first vice president, Jaramogi Oginga Odinga, who had fallen out with President Kenyatta and resigned in 1966. The clawback of the rights set out in the independence constitution allowed both Kenyatta and his successor, Daniel arap Moi, to silence political opposition through preventive detention. As in the colonial period, law was therefore deployed to give the colour of legitimacy to the violence of the state in the name of security. Even in the management of ordinary crime, violence was the preferred policy intervention, as demonstrated by the tough and violent police responses to armed robberies from the 1970s onwards. Highly publicised executions of suspected armed robbers in Nairobi became the preferred way of dealing with rising crime in the form of bank robberies. Patrick Shaw, the police officer mostly associated with these killings, became lionised in media coverage, not for solving the crimes but for accumulating an impressive body count of suspected criminals (Smith 2013).

The consolidation and expansion of the repressive roles of security forces in the 1980s and 1990s set the stage for the confrontations between the public and the police in the 1990s, as Kenyans took to the streets to agitate for a multiparty system of government. At the dawn of the 1990s, and as the mobilisation for political reforms gained momentum, the police were increasingly deployed by the Moi government to stop public protests. In many of the street protests of the 1990s, the police often worked hand in hand with militias, such as Jeshi La Mzee, which were mobilised by ruling party officials to mete out violence against critics of the Moi government. The 1990s also marked the emergence of the phenomenon of ethnic violence, particularly in the multi-ethnic regions of the Rift Valley and the coast. When the violence broke out in Rift Valley in 1991, it targeted members of ethnic communities seen as sympathetic to the multiparty agitation and in opposition to President Daniel arap Moi and the ruling party, Kenya African National Union (KANU). Reports by human rights groups, religious organisations and even an official parliamentary inquiry concluded that the police forces were complicit in the violence against members of these ethnic groups. On the whole, the police either provided protection to groups of attackers or failed to protect the victims of the ethnic attacks.

Security reforms in the post-Moi period

Given the extent of the implication of the police and intelligence services in political repression, the reform of these institutions was top of the priority demands of the reform movement of the 1990s. Owing to this pressure, the Special Branch (officially known as the Directorate of Security Intelligence and formally a department of the police) was delinked from the police in 1998 through the enactment of the National Security Intelligence Act and renamed the National Security Intelligence Service (NSIS). This delinking removed the arrest powers of the NSIS that had allowed intelligence officers to arrest political critics of the government of the day. Only in a very limited number of cases would the director of the NSIS now have powers to order the arrest of an individual. A complaints mechanism was also created through which aggrieved citizens could seek redress for actions by the intelligence service.

Substantive reforms of the police, however, remained elusive until the retirement of President Daniel arap Moi in 2002. Among the signature reform pledges of the government of Mwai Kibaki, who succeeded Moi as president, was the reform of security institutions and the promotion of human rights.

Indeed, the idea of reforming the police force found its way into the new government's policy plans. In particular, the government's economic recovery and wealth creation strategy of 2003 identified police reforms as integral to economic reforms. The aim was to improve the effectiveness and efficiency of the police in dealing with crime and to enhance the accountability of the institution over a five-year period. The reforms also stressed the need to improve the welfare and working conditions of police officers. A community policing programme was also initiated in 2004 but was not developed much beyond the production of booklets on the importance of a partnership between the police and the public in dealing with crime. In reality, the police continued to view community policing as a tool for recruiting police informers from within the community. Accountability was marginal to this conception of community policing. As earlier studies have concluded, community policing was a complete failure in the Kenyan context (Ruteere and Pommerolle 2003: 587–604).

The appointment of Major General Mohamed Hussein Ali as the new commissioner of the Kenya Police Force in 2004 was billed as marking a new beginning in the management of security in Kenya. The choice of a career military officer was viewed by the public and reform advocates as key to bringing a new decisiveness and discipline to a police force that was widely identified with ineffectiveness and corruption. Within a short time, however, it was clear that a military man was not a good choice for a civilian service that urgently needed to improve its relationship with the public. Under Ali, policing became increasingly militarised in its command. It was also under Commissioner Ali that the extrajudicial elimination of criminal groups was allowed to proliferate. The state human rights body, the Kenya National Commission on Human Rights, reported that in a five-month period in 2007, the police under Ali were responsible for the killing or disappearance of 500 suspected Mungiki members (KNCHR 2008). The existence of police death squads was also confirmed by the United Nations Special Rapporteur on Extrajudicial, Summary or Arbitrary Executions at the conclusion of his 2008 visit to Kenya.

The collapse of the delicate political coalition that had propelled Kibaki to power doomed any prospects for a radical reform of the police, and Kibaki increasingly ethnicised the leadership of the security agencies as a form of insurance against the perceived threats from the opposition, now led by Raila Odinga of the Liberal Democratic Party. Even more than his predecessor, president Kibaki treated the security of his government as only being guaranteed if his ethnic kin led the security organs. The public perception of the police as a partisan force in the service of the ethnic elites around President Kibaki considerably sharpened the ethnic divisions precipitated by the political fallout in the ruling National Alliance Rainbow Coalition (NARC) coalition. It did not help that, in the run-up to the 2007 elections, some police officers had allegedly been found distributing leaflets against Raila Odinga. Consequently, by the time the country went to the 2007 elections, which were followed by ethnic violence over the disputed presidential results, the role of the police as neutral bureaucratic actors had all but collapsed.

The official inquiry into that violence – the Commission of Inquiry into Post-Election Violence (CIPEV) – found that the police were largely unprepared, uncoordinated, and also not impartial in dealing with the violence (CIPEV 2008). The report of the commission was highly critical of the police and the failures in intelligence coordination and utilisation. The Waki report (named after the chair of the commission, Justice Philip Waki) called for radical reforms of the Kenyan police force and set the ball rolling for security sector reforms.

The post-election violence precipitated far-reaching reforms of the country's governance architecture, with police reforms as a key priority, among others. More significantly, the government established the National Task Force on Police Reforms to examine and make proposals on how to transform the Kenya Police Force into an effective, efficient and accountable service. The task force, led by retired justice Philip Ransley, made several recommendations in its report, among them the need to ensure that the police reflect a proper mix of Kenyan communities, exercise impartiality, respect human rights, and adopt a decentralised style of policing (Republic of Kenya 2009). The report also noted that, in order to recover public confidence, the police needed to adopt policing approaches that involved the community and therefore needed to build on the community policing approach that it had already adopted. So far, the report has been the most important blueprint for the transformation of the police in post-independence Kenya. To implement the recommendations of the report, a Police Reforms Implementation Committee was established.

Security reforms after the 2010 constitution

The post-election violence also injected new effort into the finalisation and enactment of a new constitution. In 2010, a new constitution was promulgated following its approval in a national referendum. The constitution provided a new framework for governance in Kenya, introducing new values and ideals, restructuring the system of government, and creating new institutions and new protections of rights. Security governance in Kenya therefore needs to be seen against the new constitutional order.

Although security is specifically addressed in Chapter 14 of the new constitution, a better way of understanding how the values of rights have shaped security under the new constitutional order is by examining the constitution in its entirety, as security concerns are scattered in various chapters. Chapter 4 provides for an elaborate bill of rights that seeks to protect Kenyans from the arbitrary use of security agency powers. In particular, the strong protections against arbitrary arrests (Article 49) and the provisions for the rights of those detained in custody or in prison (Article 51) seek to remedy the past history of violations in the name of national security, as well as the misuse of power by the security agencies. In addition, the independent judiciary that the constitution provides for is meant to tame the appetites of the security actors to curtail freedoms and rights. Parliament has also been invested with an oversight role over the security agencies.

The constitution has devoted a chapter to the issue of national security (Chapter 14); for the first time, the principles guiding the promotion of national security have been spelled out (Article 238). Of particular note is the fact that the constitution stresses that the pursuit and promotion of national security must be 'subject to the authority of this Constitution and Parliament' (Article 238(2)(a)). The constitution also stresses that national security promotion must be in conformity 'with the law and with the utmost respect for the rule of law, democracy, human rights and fundamental freedoms' (Article 238(b)).

The new constitution has led to a reformed judiciary that has demonstrated assertiveness in holding the security forces to account, in many cases releasing individuals held in custody beyond the period allowed by the constitution. The accountability expectation has also shaped the state framing of security sector reforms by political leaders. In many of the policy discussions in much of the period from 2010 to 2012, the late minister for internal security, George Saitoti, often made references to the establishment of the Independent Policing Oversight Authority (IPOA) as central to the police reforms agenda. This was a marked departure from the past, when policy discussions on police reforms were largely confined to improving the efficiency and effectiveness of the force. While the IPOA has already been established through an act of parliament, challenges remain for its operationalisation and in the fact that it is too limited a mechanism to be expected to fundamentally change the decades-long police culture of unaccountability. Moreover, with the death of Minister George Saitoti, the issue of accountability appears to have taken a back seat in police reforms.

Oversight mechanisms over security organs are now part of the new constitutional architecture of security governance. All national security organs – National Police Service, Kenya Defence Forces and the National Intelligence Service (NIS) – are 'subordinate to civilian authority' (Article 239(5)) and parliament has been given the authority to legislate on their functions, organisation and administration. This oversight is now to be found in the implementation legislation that parliament has enacted according to the constitution. As already noted, the IPOA has already been established to provide oversight over serious violations by the police, such as deaths through police action and torture by police officers.

Unlike in the case of the police, however, the oversight mechanisms over the rest of the security agencies remain potentially weak and less visible in policy discourse. The only mechanism for civilian oversight of the military remains the parliamentary departmental committees. In the past, however, these committees have proved to be largely ineffective, lacking the capacity to even pose the right questions to the military leadership.[5] Although the constitution requires that the deployment of defence forces internationally or in support operations internally be approved by parliament, military deployments in Garissa and other parts of the north-eastern region in 2012, where the defence forces were alleged to have committed atrocities, did not have any parliamentary sanction.

Parliament is also expected to exercise oversight over the NIS as a result of the National Intelligence Service Act. The act establishes the Joint Parliamentary Committee on Intelligence and Security, but its oversight roles are restricted to administrative and budgetary matters and the committee is explicitly prohibited from addressing complaints regarding operations by the intelligence service. The act provides for a complaints mechanism, the Intelligence Service Complaints Board, through which individuals can complain about the actions of the members of the NIS. However, this board is not independent of the executive as its members are appointed by the cabinet secretary.

In addition to accountability and oversight, the impartiality and non-partisanship of the security organs is now a constitutional requirement. Article 239(3) prohibits security officers and the national organs from acting 'in a partisan manner' (Article 239(3)(a)), from furthering 'any interest of a political party or cause' (Article 239(3)(b)) and from prejudging 'a political interest or political cause that is legitimate under this Constitution' (Article 239(3)(c)). This prohibition seeks to remedy the history of political misuse of the security agencies in entrenching the political advantage of the government of the day. Even with the promulgation of the new constitution, however, the secretive nature of the operations of the security agencies, coupled with the ethnicisation of the leadership, has left these institutions instinctively inclined to serve the regime in power rather than the public. Dismantling the culture of service to the regime that has been built within the police forces for many years remains a considerable challenge in security reforms. While the Kenya Defence Forces have greater professional autonomy than the police, the same cannot be said of the NIS. Like the police, the NIS is still linked to the political interests of the government of the day (CIPEV 2008; Republic of Kenya 2013a). Moreover, the failure to separate criminal intelligence functions of a domestic nature from intelligence-gathering on external threats provides opportunities for intelligence-gathering and surveillance of political opponents that may be contrary to the constitutional requirements of non-partisanship.

Ethnicisation of security forces, particularly at the leadership levels, has been one of the drivers for the public calls for security sector reforms. From colonial times, ethnicisation of the security forces has been at the core of the deployment of violence and domination of the population. However, over the years, Kenyan security agencies have developed the criterion of district quotas for recruitment purposes. Overall, this has helped to avoid the problem of the numerical domination of the security forces by one or a handful of ethnic groups at the rank-and-file levels. However, Cynthia Enloe has cautioned that 'gross levels of heterogeneity in a country's police force do not reveal very much'. Instead, what is important is whether security planners 'are defining security questions non-ethnically' (Enloe 1978).

The extent to which the Kenyan police response to the 2007–08 post-election violence reflects the definition of security questions being 'non-ethnic' has been the subject of inquiries by both the Waki commission and the International Criminal Court (ICC). The subtle legal arguments of the ICC prosecutor and the defence are not of interest here. What is important is the fact that the police use of live ammunition against supporters of the Orange Democratic Movement (ODM) as well as pre-election police deployments in Nyanza were interpreted in those areas (and by ODM supporters elsewhere) as driven by political and possibly ethnic considerations rather than by security necessity. The extent to which ethnicity shapes the operations of Kenyan police agencies remains unknown, given the opacity of security agencies in Kenya and the entrenched culture of labelling everything associated with security as confidential.

Keeping the leadership of the security forces in the hands of ethnic kin, as has been done by successive governments, has been about ensuring the loyalty of the security forces, including ensuring that these agencies can accept illegal orders issued by the executive. Under Article 238(b) and (c), the constitution now requires that ethnic diversity be taken into consideration in both the activities and composition of the security organs. Since the 2007–08 post-election violence, there has been more attention paid to diversity in appointments to leadership positions within the security forces. The concentration under President Kibaki of the leadership of virtually all the security organs in the hands of the Kikuyu, Meru and Embu – the president's ethnic kinsmen – was identified by the reviews of the 2007–08 post-election violence as one of the grievances that contributed to the climate of ethnic division fuelling that violence. Since the promulgation of the constitution, there have been efforts, principally through parliamentary oversight, to ensure that the Kibaki government redresses the diversity imbalance in the security leadership. Nevertheless, by the end of 2012, as President Kibaki was nearing the end of his term as president, the leadership of the police, Kenya Defence Forces and the NIS largely remained with his Kikuyu, Meru and Embu ethnic kin.

Devolved government, centralised security

The new constitution has created a devolved system of governance with county governments sharing functions with the central government. With regard to security, the constitution has retained a centralised structure for all security organs, including the two police forces – the Kenya Police Force and the administration police. Since colonial times, the provincial administration has provided the link between the state at the national level and the local level. The new constitution provides that the national government must restructure and align the provincial administration with the newly established system of county governments within the next five years.

Although the provincial administration has not been allocated any formal security role under the new constitution, in the past administrators have played a coordinating role on security matters. The administration police in particular has worked at local levels in support of the provincial administration – chiefs, district officers, district commissioners and provincial commissioners. The new constitution has now removed the command of the administration police from the provincial administration and has placed it under the command of the inspector general together with the Kenya Police Force.

At local levels, in villages and in poor urban communities, state security in the past was coordinated through the institutions of the chief and the assistant chiefs. Historically, the institution of the chief, as Mahmood Mamdani noted, stood at the confluence of justice and security (Mamdani 1996). In the years of single-party rule, the institution of the chief was the local enforcer of the state's despotism and repression. Since 2003, however, there has been a movement towards the reform of the institution of the chief in tandem with the broader reforms of the provincial administration. In the ongoing reform and restructuring of the provincial administration and the security infrastructure, it is not yet clear whether the institution of the chief will remain or will be scrapped. Moreover, if the institutions of the provincial administration are not properly aligned with the county governments, there is a risk of tension with the county-level administration.

If the institution of the chief is retained – which is what the government and parliament appeared to suggest as 2012 came to a close – it would require considerable reform to bring it into line with the expectations of accountability, rights and values envisaged by the constitution. Surprisingly, this institution, as well as other local-level security mechanisms, have received little attention in public policy discourses on security and justice reforms in Kenya. Yet without reforming local-level security governance, the national-level reforms will end up securing and democratising only the space for the elites, leaving the majority of the poor population still governed by unaccountable security institutions.

So far, policy debate on security at the county levels has been fixated on security institutions. This way of thinking about security at the county level is, however, not likely to be very productive in terms of making these areas more secure. In fact, in exploring the security roles and functions for the counties, we need to abandon the view of security as a matter of institutions and take security as an outcome of processes and interactions. Institutions such as the police and the provincial administration are just a means to an end and should not be confused with the end, which is a more secure and safe community.

Looking at the constitution, there are several roles explicitly assigned to counties that will lead to security and safety outcomes. This means that by carrying out their roles and functions, counties will in reality be security actors. For instance, county governments will be responsible for controlling drug and alcohol use and the distribution of pornography. The relationship between crime and alcohol and drug abuse has been established in studies all over the world. County governments will also be responsible for issuing trade licences and regulating housing, two functions that can be used effectively to curtail illegal and exploitative businesses and business practices and to enhance the security and safety of residential neighbourhoods and their inhabitants. Another safety function assigned to the county governments is traffic control and the regulation of transport. Transport may not seem to be an obvious security matter, but, in practice, public transport operations – in terms of the location and erection of bus stops, for instance – have a direct impact on public security. Lighting of counties is another obvious intervention that has a clear and direct security and safety implication.

Moreover, county authorities will have a role in the management of education (schools) and health (hospitals and health clinics), and schools and hospitals have crucial security and safety functions. School-based violence is a growing problem in Kenya, as evidenced by recent incidents of students burning down schools, and bullying is a key safety issue for children in schools. With regard to health, there are also important safety and security aspects that county governments can take up: for example, hospitals are the first-line institutions in addressing domestic violence and violence against children.

While policing and the operations of other national security institutions remain a national mandate in the new constitution, the introduction of county governments now provides a hitherto unavailable opportunity for greater inclusivity and participation of communities and their local representatives in decision-making on their own security. Indeed, research in several parts of the world shows that effective security measures – particularly crime prevention approaches – are likely to register better successes if responsibility for them is shared with local authorities and communities.

Key challenges to security reforms

Although the new constitution has provided the framework for the reforms of the security sector in Kenya, effective reforms are far from being a reality. Given its nature, as well as the sensitivity with which the governing elites view the question of security, the security sector may well pose the most intractable challenges to the broader reform agenda.

Whereas the new Kenyan constitution recognises that all state institutions draw their legitimacy from the people, in reality security in Kenya continues to be viewed as the domain and responsibility of the state. Historically, the thinking and planning on security have traditionally privileged the state to the exclusion of other stakeholders. This approach to security has placed more weight on the expertise of state security actors, excluding other knowledge and marginalising the participation of communities in decision-making on their own security.

This thinking has logically led to a view of security as 'something that state agencies do'. This claim of exclusive capacities and expertise has allowed Kenyan security agencies to evade public scrutiny and accountability. It is the reason why the then commissioner of police, Major General Hussein Ali, could defiantly tell the commission of inquiry into the post-election violence that: 'If similar situations occurred today, I would do exactly what I did' (CIPEV 2008: 204).

Although the constitution envisages that agencies such as the police will engage better with the public, state security agencies remain stubbornly wedded to the view that security is the business of the police. Consequently, even though community policing has been adopted as a policy by the Kenyan police, studies and evaluations of past community policing initiatives in Kenya have demonstrated that the police remain reluctant to engage in meaningful partnerships with communities. Instead, they often interpret community policing to mean that community members should act as crime-spotters and informers, while leaving decision-making on security responses to the police (Ruteere and Pommerolle 2003).

While public and policy debate on security reforms in Kenya has largely focused on public security agencies, in reality security in Kenya is produced and governed by a mix of both private and state actors. The numbers of private security actors, as well as the convergence between the activities of public and private security forces, demonstrate the increased prominence of the private sector in security work. In Kenya, there are about 430,000 private security guards compared with 86,000 police officers (Republic of Kenya 2009). These figures represent only the formal security service providers, who fall under the remit of the two main private security associations: the Kenya Security Industry Association and the Protective Services Industry. The actual numbers would be much higher if the many unregistered outfits were factored in. What this means is that a majority of Kenyans spend most of their time in zones where order is regulated and security managed by private security guards rather than by the police.

In many instances, the police have developed symbiotic relationships with private contractors. In some areas of Nairobi, for instance, private security companies provide transport for police officers assigned to patrol duties in their areas of operation. Bruce Baker, who has written prolifically on policing and security in Africa, makes the argument that in the continent the divide between private and public policing has never been well defined, 'since the state police are largely absent in the rural areas and poorer neighbourhoods of towns' (Baker 2004).

An area of concern with regard to private security is the question of accountability. Where private security remains poorly regulated, as in Kenya, accountability options such as those relating to the police are largely unavailable to members of the public. Moreover, civil society groups working on human rights have largely focused their attention on the activities of the police and rarely monitor the activities of private security guards. Yet, in some instances, private security companies now exercise control over public areas such as access roads to residential estates. In some upmarket areas of Nairobi, private security guards even demand identification documents from those using public access roads into these neighbourhoods and can deny access to those who fail to satisfy their assessment.

Remarkably little is known about the security sector in Kenya. There are very few studies on any of the security agencies and very few Kenyan scholars work on this sector. Security reform efforts are therefore confronted by capacity challenges on two fronts: the first is a lack of broad expertise on security outside the state security agencies, and the second is the issue of technical deficits within security agencies such as the police.

Technical deficits at the first level are partly a consequence of the closed nature of the security field in the country. Security work has remained the privileged and exclusive domain of state security actors who have consistently discouraged any outsider interest. The history of the involvement of security agencies in political repression has also meant that security issues have remained cordoned off from outside scrutiny. The consequence of this is that, unlike in countries such as South Africa, the UK or Canada, Kenya lacks an infrastructure of researchers and experts to contribute fresh ideas to the security reform process.

This lack of technical expertise is linked to the second level of deficit: capacity deficits within the different security agencies. The report of the National Task Force on Police Reforms has identified poor training in modern police approaches and the poor embrace and understanding of modern technology as two of the capacity challenges facing the police in Kenya (Republic of Kenya 2009). In the absence of cutting-edge expertise in universities and research centres, it is not surprising that most police training has concentrated on drills rather than the analysis and innovative prevention and management of crime.

Conclusion

Writing about the police in Africa, the security expert Alice Hills has argued that the Kenyan police provides a 'selective service' to the political regime rather than security to all citizens (Hills 2008). The new constitution provides an opportunity to reimagine security and fundamentally restructure security governance in Kenya. Since independence, security has been the justification for violations of human rights in Kenya. Security organs in post-independence Kenya, as in colonial Kenya, have largely been at the service of the government of the day and in particular of the small ruling elite. The post-2010 constitutional order, with its strong focus on human rights, values and principles, provides the basis for rethinking the governing mentalities of security and reconfiguring security agencies.

A security reform agenda in keeping with the human rights vision of the constitution calls for the reconceptualisation of security as the security of the people rather than the security of the ruling elites. The test for evaluating whether reforms have kept faith with the vision and spirit of the constitution is whether the activities and decisions of the security agencies, as well as those of the political leadership, contribute to providing security for the majority of poor and ordinary Kenyans. The powerful and rich have fared well under the old constitutional order and were therefore not the reason for the security sector reforms.

As of the beginning of 2014, the restructuring of the security institutions was still far from complete. Although important institutions such as the IPOA had been established as per the law to provide oversight of police conduct, there has been no subsequent abatement of police killings or other abuses of their power. The vetting aimed at removing those police officers deemed unfit for continued service commenced only at the beginning of 2014 and thus its success and effectiveness are largely a matter of speculation. The hitherto relatively respectable image of the Kenyan military suffered serious damage following the conduct of the military in response to the September 2013 terrorist attacks on the Westgate Mall in Nairobi.[6] In that incident, the military was alleged to have mishandled the operation after taking over from the police, leading to the total destruction of the mall, and there were also accusations of the military looting businesses of valuables and cash. Moreover, the continued involvement of the military in counterterrorist activities in the northern part of the country had left the military accused of serious human rights violations in places such as Garissa as far back as 2012.[7]

Looking at the political context at the beginning of 2014, it is evident that, unlike in the latter days of the presidency of Mwai Kibaki, the government of President Uhuru Kenyatta has no political champions for security reform. Overall, it appears that, while the Kenyan constitution has bequeathed the country the promise of a system of governance in which security actors are expected to promote human rights, the calls for urgent security reforms that had emerged after the 2007–08 post-election violence had lost political support by the beginning of 2014. There is therefore a basis for significant scepticism that the letter of the law as set out in the constitution will result in a security sector that promotes the values of human rights in the absence of an accompanying political vision and leadership.

Notes

1 A number of recent scholarly studies have provided insights into the violence and brutality of the British security forces during the Mau Mau war (see Anderson 2005; Elkins 2005).

2 Tamarkin (1978: 300) has pointed out that following 1964, President Kenyatta set out to infuse some Kikuyu 'blood' into the army and officer corps (see also Katumanga 2010).

3 On some of the brutalities in the north-eastern regions, see Sheikh (2007).

4 Regulations published under the Preservation of Public Security Act, Chapter 57, Laws of Kenya as the North Eastern Province and Contiguous Districts Regulations, 1966 extended the president's power to rule the province by decree to Marsabit, Isiolo, Tana River and Lamu districts (see KHRC 2009).

5 This was in evidence during the investigation into the September 2013 terrorist attack on Westgate by the Joint Committee on Administration and National Security and Defence and Foreign Relations (Republic of Kenya 2013a).

6 Various media reports carried allegations of military misconduct. See, for instance, the BBC News item 'Westgate attack: Kenya CCTV "shows soldiers looting"' (www.bbc.co.uk/news/world-africa-24606152).

7 See Republic of Kenya (2013b) and the BBC News item 'Kenyan soldiers "rampage" after Garissa shooting' (www. bbc.co.uk/news/world-africa-20401136).

References

Anderson, D. (2005) *Histories of the Hanged: Britain's dirty war in Kenya and the end of empire*. London: Weidenfeld and Nicolson.

Baker, B. (2004) 'Protection from crime: what is on offer for Africans?' *Journal of Contemporary African Studies* 22(2): 165–88.

Berman, B. (1999) *Control and Crisis in Colonial Kenya: The dialectic of domination*. Athens, OH: Ohio University Press.

CIPEV (2008) *Report of the Commission of Inquiry into the Post-Election Violence*. Nairobi: Commission of Inquiry into Post-Election Violence (CIPEV).

Clayton, A. and D. Killingray (1989) *Khaki and Blue: Military and police in British colonial Africa*. Athens, OH: Ohio University Press.

Elkins, C. (2005) *Imperial Reckoning: The untold story of Britain's gulag in Kenya*. New York, NY: Henry Holt and Co.

Enloe, C. H. (1978) 'Police and military in Ulster: peacekeeping or peace-subverting forces?' *Journal of Peace Research* 15(3): 243–58.

Hills, A. (2008) 'Policing in Kenya: a selective service'. In M. Hinton and T. Newburn (eds) *Policing Developing Democracies*. London: Routledge, pp. 237–59.

Katumanga, M. (2010) 'Militarized spaces and the post-2007 electoral violence'. In K. Kanyinga and D. Okello (eds) *Tensions and Reversals in Democratic Transitions: The Kenya 2007 general elections*. Nairobi: Society for International Development and Institute for Development Studies, University of Nairobi, pp. 45–73.

KHRC (2009) *Foreigners at Home: The dilemma of citizenship in northern Kenya*. Nairobi: Kenya Human Rights Commission (KHRC).

KNCHR (2008) *The Cry of Blood: Report on extra-judicial killings and disappearances*. Nairobi: Kenya National Commission on Human Rights (KNCHR).

Lugard, Sir F. D. (1922) *The Dual Mandate in the British Tropical Africa*. Edinburgh and London: William Blackwood and Sons.

Mamdani, M. (1996) *Citizen and Subject: Contemporary Africa and the legacy of late colonialism.* Kampala: Fountain Publishers.

Mitullah, W. (2003) *Urban Slums Reports: The case of Nairobi, Kenya.* Nairobi: UN Habitat.

Omenya, A. and G. Lubaale (2012) *Understanding the Tipping Point of Urban Conflict: The case of Nairobi, Kenya.* Working Paper 6. Manchester: Urban Tipping Point (UTP), University of Manchester.

Republic of Kenya (2009) *Report of the National Task Force on Police Reforms.* Nairobi: Government Printers.

— (2013a) *Report of the Joint Committee on Administration and National Security and Defence and Foreign Relations on the Inquiry into the Westgate Terrorist Attack and Other Terror Attacks in Mandera in North-Eastern and Kilifi in the Coastal Region.* Nairobi: Government Printers.

— (2013b) *Report of the Joint Committee*

Investigating the Matter of the Adverse Security Situation, Loss of Property, Loss of Lives of Security Personnel and Civilians in Garissa and Eastleigh Towns, and the Baragoi Environs. Nairobi: Government Printers.

Ruteere, M. and M. E. Pommerolle (2003) 'Democratizing security or decentralizing repression? The ambiguities of community policing in Kenya'. *African Affairs* 102: 587–604.

Sheikh, S. A. (2007) *Blood on the Runway: The Wagalla massacre of 1984.* Nairobi: Northern Publishing House.

Smith, D. (2013) 'Investigating Patrick Shaw, Kenya's most dreaded cop'. *Daily Nation,* 25 March.

Tamarkin, M. (1978) 'The roots of political stability in Kenya'. *African Affairs* 77(308): 297–320.

Throup, D. (1992) 'Crime, politics and the police in colonial Kenya, 1939–63'. In D. M. Anderson and D. Killingray (eds) *Policing and Decolonisation: Politics, nationalism and the police 1917–65.* Manchester: Manchester University Press, pp. 127–57.

About the contributors

Sammy Gakero Gachigua is working towards completion of his PhD in applied linguistics at Lancaster University in the UK, focusing on the tensions between power elites and public interests in Kenyan parliamentary debates using a discourse-historical approach. His research interests include: critical discourse analysis; argumentation theory; parliamentary, political and media discourses; and political cartoon analysis.

Yash Pal Ghai was educated at Oxford and Harvard, and called to the English bar by the Middle Temple. Most of his professional life he has been a law teacher and he was a founder member of the first law school in Eastern Africa. He has taught at the University of East Africa, Uppsala University, Warwick University, and the University of Hong Kong (where he was the first Sir Y. K. Pao Professor of Public Law). He has been a visiting professor at the Yale Law School, Toronto University, Melbourne University, London University, the National University of Singapore, University of Wisconsin and Harvard Law School. His research interests include: constitutionalism and human rights; ethnic conflicts; the sociology of law; and federalism and autonomy. He has published extensively on public law; his books include *Public Law and Political Change in Kenya* (1970, with Patrick McAuslan), *Law in the Political Economy of Public Enterprise* (1977), *The Political Economy of Law: Third world perspectives* (1987, edited jointly with Robin Luckham and Francis Snyder) and *Law, Politics and Government in the Pacific Island States* (1988), among many others. His most recent publications include *The Constitution of Kenya: An instrument for change* (2012), *Ethnicity, Nationhood and Pluralism: Kenyan perspectives* (2013) (both with Jill Cottrell), *Autonomy: Practising self-government* (2013) and *Constitution and Rule of Law in China's Hong Kong: The contribution of the court of final appeal* (2014). He has been on the editorial board of several international journals in law and social sciences. From November 2000 to June 2004 he was chair of the Kenya Constitution Review Commission. In 2011 he co-founded the Katiba Institute in Kenya to promote the values and practices of the 2010 constitution.

Raymond Muhula has worked on governance and public sector reform issues at the World Bank since 2005. Since 2010 he has led the Bank's public sector governance work in post-conflict Liberia, supporting the rebuilding of Liberia's public service (civil service reform, institutional development and capacity-building) and the country's demand for good governance (access to information, anti-corruption and access to justice). He has also managed similar projects in the Gambia and Swaziland, and led the preparation of analytical work on political economy and decentralisation. His most recent publication (with Kelly Krawczyk and Jennie Sweet-Cushman) is 'The road to good governance via the path less accountable? The effectiveness of fiscal accountability in Liberia', published in *International Journal of Public Administration* 36(8) in 2013. He received a PhD in political science from Howard University in the USA.

Wanjala S. Nasong'o holds a BA degree in political science and linguistics and an MA in international relations, both from the University of Nairobi. He obtained his PhD in public and international affairs from Northeastern University, Boston, USA. Professor Nasong'o is currently Associate Professor of International Studies and chair of the Department of International Studies at Rhodes College, Memphis. He is the author and editor of numerous books and more than fifty refereed journal articles, encyclopaedia entries and reviewed book chapters. He has previously taught at Kenyatta University, the University of Tennessee in Knoxville and the University of Nairobi. Professor Nasong'o has served as an expert witness for multiple asylum cases in the US and consults for various organisations around the world.

Stephen Ndegwa is an adviser at the World Bank's Center on Conflict, Security and Development based in Nairobi. In 2010, he was a member of the core team writing the *World Development Report 2011* on conflict, security and development. Since joining the World Bank in 2002 he has worked on governance, political economy, and public sector capacity-building across several regions. Previously, he was a lead specialist for the Africa region at the World Bank and before that worked in the East Asia and Pacific region and in the Poverty Reduction and Economic Management Network. He is the author or editor of several books, including *The Two Faces of Civil Society* (1996), *A Decade of Democracy in Africa* (2001), *The Uncertain Promise of Southern Africa* (2000) and, most recently, he has co-edited with Ellen Lust 'Societal transformation and the challenge of governance in the Middle East', a special issue of the journal *Middle East Law and Governance* (2010), and *Governing Africa's Changing Societies* (2012). His research articles have appeared in several leading journals, including the *American Political Science Review*. Before moving to the World Bank, he was Associate Professor of Government at the College of William and Mary in the US (1994–2002). He holds a PhD in political science from Indiana University (1993).

Mutuma Ruteere serves as director of the Centre for Human Rights and Policy Studies, an independent research centre based in Nairobi. He holds a PhD in political science with a specialisation in human rights. He has taught at universities in Kenya and elsewhere and has published widely on human rights, the issues of criminal violence and policing, terrorism and counterterrorism, civil wars and transitions, and on social justice and poverty. He has advised state agencies, non-governmental organisations, international organisations and private sector organisations on human rights. His current work at the Centre for Human Rights and Policy Studies attempts to link theoretical research with policy-making and innovation, to address human rights and social justice problems. In 2011, he was appointed by the UN Human Rights Council as the Special Rapporteur on contemporary forms of racism, racial discrimination, xenophobia and related intolerance.

E. Njoki Wamai is a Gates Cambridge Scholar at the University of Cambridge undertaking her doctoral studies in politics and international studies. She was previously a Peace, Security and Development Scholar at the Africa Leadership Centre based at King's College London and the University of Nairobi. Her research interests include mediation, transitional justice, the International Criminal Court in Kenya, human rights and women, peace and security.

Paul Tiyambe Zeleza is the Vice-President for Academic Affairs at Quinnipiac University in Connecticut. He has worked in several universities in the USA, Canada, Jamaica and Kenya. He has published many books, over 300 journal articles, book chapters and reviews. His book *A Modern Economic History of Africa* won the Noma Award for Publishing in Africa in 1993.

Index

devolution of government, 79, 87, 125, 130–1, 132, 137–8, 139, 153, 158, 172–4; difficulty of transition to, 137
Diamond, L., 97–8
dictatorships, 107; transition to democracy, 30
Directorate of Security Intelligence, 28, 167
disarticulation of colonial economies, 19
drug use, control of, 174
dual citizenship, 35
Dugdale, Justice, 5

'eating', notion of, 111
economic growth, 32–3, 69; phases of, 27
election campaign news, as hard news genre, 49–51
elections, 33; electronic machinery for (breaks down, 132; supply of, 8); flawed nature of, 2; free and fair, elements of, 8; manual methods of tallying, 8; of 1966, 26, 149; of 1988, 5, 150; of 1992, 1, 31, 83–5, 152; of 1997, 1, 31, 82, 83–5, 101, 104, 153; of 2002, 1, 2, 6, 105, 156; of 2007, 3, 6, 7, 10, 17, 32, 39 (background to, 46–7; mediating of, 66–78; violence associated with, 10, 11, 17, 31, 32, 34, 44–65, 82–3, 87–9, 106–9, 124, 158, 169 (causes of, 68–70; police response to, 172)); of 2013, 7–10, 34, 131, 132, 159; rigging of, 3, 5 *see also* spoilt votes
Electoral Commission of Kenya (ECK), 69, 88, 102
electoral registers, 8
elites: character of, 147–8; compromises of, in 2010 constitution, 144–62; effects of interests of, on constitution, 158–60; theory of, 146; in relation to constitution-making process, 154; pact-making among, 79; trade-offs in constitution-making process, 160
Embu ethnic group, 172
enforceability of constitution, 37
Ethics and Anti-Corruption Commission, 135
ethnic groups and tensions, 18, 22, 24, 23, 31, 69–70, 87 *see also* ethnicisation *and* ethnicity
ethnicisation, 19–20; of administrative boundaries, 68; of leaderships, 4; of security forces, 164, 168, 171–2
ethnicity, 47, 80, 111, 125, 166, 167; in

police operations, 172; in politics, 93; manipulation of, 132; mobilised for political purposes, 33, 119, 139; re-emergence of, 94
European Union (EU), 71
evictions, 136
executions of armed robbers, 167, 168
executive authority, issue of, 158
extraversion of colonial economies, 19

failed state, status of, 17
faith-based groups, 154
'family, the', 146, 148, 149
family values, preservation of, 161
Fanon, Frantz, 20, 146
Finance magazine, 48
First Republic, 17
forced labour, 22
Forum for the Restoration of Democracy (FORD), 151–2
Forum for the Restoration of Democracy in Kenya (FORD-Kenya), 80, 101, 152
Forum for the Restoration of Democracy in Kenya-Asili (FORD-Asili), 101, 152
franchise, of Africans, 122

Gallup organisation, 58
Gama Pinto, Pio, 123
Garissa, human rights violations in, 177
gays and lesbians, perceived threat of, 159
gender issues, 35, 126, 161
General Service Unit, 28, 103
Ghai, Yash Pal, 67, 86, 105, 111, 154; attack on, 155
Ghana, rights in, 37
Gikuyu, Embu and Meru Association (GEMA), 28
Gikuyu ethnic group, 68
Gitari, David, 150
Githongo, John, 110; as anti-corruption tsar, 111
good governance, 31
Government Review Commission, 104–6
Grand Coalition government, 7, 8, 18
Green Belt Movement, 99, 105

Habermas, Jürgen, 44–5
Harbeson, John, 98
hard news genre, 49–51; manipulation of, 51–7, 63
hereditary leadership, 61

Truth, Justice and Reconciliation
    Commission, 7, 136
truth commissions, 7, 84, 136
Tsuma, Chibule wa, 150
Tutu, Desmond, 70

Ufungamano Initiative, 104–6, 154
uhuru, 22, 25, 38, 123
Undugu Society of Kenya, 99
United Nations (UN), 66, 71
UN Charter, Chapter VI, 66
UN Development Programme (UNDP), 74
United Republican Party (URP), 80

violence, decentralisation and
    privatisation of, 18 *see also* elections,
    2007, violence associated with
vulnerable groups, representation of
    interests of, 129, 135

Waki, Philip, 169
Waki commission, 172; report of, 169
Wako, Amos, 47, 67, 86, 108
Wako draft, 87, 106, 108, 158
Wamwere, Koigi wa, 150
Wanjui, Joe, 157
war on terror, 13
Weekly Review, 48
white highlands, 68
windows of opportunity, 81
women: guaranteed parliamentary
    seats for, 79; representation of, in
    governance, 92, 109; rights of, 92, 144
    (inheritance rights, 161; reproductive
    rights, 12)
women's movements, 22, 28, 30
World Bank, 29

Zimbabwe, peace process in, 75